WARNING:
Nonsense Is Destroying America

Vincent Ryan Ruggiero

OLIVER
NELSON

THOMAS NELSON PUBLISHERS
Nashville

To those parents and teachers

who still impart the timeless wisdom

that enriches young lives and

strengthens the nation.

Published in Nashville, Tennessee, by Thomas Nelson, Inc., Publishers, and distributed in Canada by Word Communications, Ltd., Richmond, British Columbia.

The Bible version used in this publication is THE NEW KING JAMES VERSION. Copyright © 1979, 1980, 1982, Thomas Nelson, Inc., Publishers.

Printed in the United States of America.

Library of Congress Cataloging-in-Publication Data

Ruggiero, Vincent Ryan.
    Warning : nonsense is destroying America / Vincent Ryan Ruggiero.
      p.   cm.
    Includes bibliographical references.
    ISBN 0-8407-9678-1
    1. United States—Social conditions—1980–   2. Social values—United States. 3. United States—Intellectual life—20th century.   4. United States—Moral conditions. 5. Education—United States—Philosophy. I. Title. II. Title: Nonsense is destroying America.
HN59.2.R84   1994
301′.0973—dc20
                                       93-41895
                                          CIP

1 2 3 4 5 6 — 99 98 97 96 95 94

CONTENTS

PREFACE

Millions of hours and billions of dollars are being invested in efforts to solve America's social and educational problems. Almost all of these efforts rest upon the same assumption—that parents and teachers are failing to live up to their responsibilities. Where the failure is considered culpable, we find chastisements of parents ("It's ten o'clock—do you know where your child is?") and demands for holding teachers accountable for students' academic performance. Where blame is assigned to circumstances rather than people, the proposed remedies are generally more elaborate and expensive, often involving a new government program, protective legislation, or a strengthening of the criminal justice system. Thus we have initiatives for conquering illiteracy, drug addiction, welfarism, and violent crime; eliminating sexually transmitted diseases, teenage pregnancy, and sexual harassment in the workplace; building civic responsibility and racial and ethnic harmony. Unfortunately, a sense of futility haunts even the best of these programs, a feeling that the problems are beyond remediation.

If parents and teachers are the underlying cause of America's problems, that sense of futility is appropriate. After all, how can young lives be restored if the agencies entrusted with their nurture continue to do harm? And how can uncaring guardians of the young be made to care? On the other hand, if the underlying assumption is mistaken—if parents and teachers are not responsible for our social and educational problems, if instead most of them are caring and conscientious but find their efforts thwarted by a force substantially more powerful than they, and if that force can be transformed into a positive influence that supports home and school and prevents problems from occurring in the future—then we have good reason to be hopeful. By changing that force, we can spare our children physical, emotional, and spiritual pain, and eventually redirect our time, energy, and money from grappling with crises to creating opportunities.

The message of this book is that the assumption *is* mistaken and there *is* reason for hope. Although some parents and teachers are less conscientious than they should be, that condition is not the real problem but only its consequence. The real problem is that popular culture has been infected by *nonsense*—nonsense about truth and reality, nonsense about self, nonsense about thought and feeling. These false views have had a devastating effect on people's lives: they have created attitudes and habits that block the pursuit of excellence, disrupt family life, and lead to self-indulgence and, in some cases, to self-destruction. By undermining morality, religion, and education they have also prevented millions of people from finding meaning, fulfillment, and joy in their lives. All these effects are reversible if we disavow nonsense and reaffirm the wisdom that once guided this country. If we refuse to do so, our best hopes, dreams, and plans for a better country will be doomed to failure. Enterprise zones cannot succeed as long as the idea of enterprise is ridiculed. Total quality management cannot succeed as long as quality is subjectively defined. The federal deficit can never be reduced, special-interest groups restrained, litigiousness controlled, or financial scandals in the business community stemmed as long as self is exalted and morality means "anything goes."

The media, though not the originators of the nonsense that plagues this country, have been its chief disseminators. And as communication technology has expanded, the process of dissemination has become more and more effective. Lest it be thought that I am hinting at some sinister cabal, let me stress that I am not. There was and is *no* conspiracy, *no* secret midnight gathering of media moguls to plot how best to harm an unsuspecting public, *no* knowledge of the incalculable harm being done, *no* malice intended. The situation may, in fact, be exactly the reverse: the men and women who work in the media sincerely believing that the practice of their craft informs, enlightens, elevates, even ennobles the public. Unfortunately, their naiveté and good intentions in no way lessen the harm they have done and continue to do. To paraphrase Pliny the Elder, what they have done to our children for at least two generations, our children are doing to society.

The most celebrated ideas of any age acquire a sacred character, and challenging them is considered heresy. Thus the message of this book will likely tempt some readers to outrage. I urge those readers to resist the temptation and weigh the message carefully. For if it is correct, then it follows that the myriad social and educational reforms now under way will be unproductive without the reform of popular culture. Moreover, if this message is correct, sooner or later circumstances will force us or our descendants to accept it. In the words of Roman philosopher and tragedian Seneca, "the time will come when our successors will wonder how we could have been ignorant of things so obvious." But waiting is a luxury we can ill afford. For as months pass into years America's predicament will grow more serious and less responsive to remedial action. The time to renounce the nonsense that is destroying lives and threatening America's future is now.

Books warn us of the destruction of the ozone layer, the befouling of the earth's lakes, rivers, and seas, the devastation of the rain forests, the eradication of animal species. Warning labels are emblazoned on cigarette boxes, beer and wine bottles, and food packages. But until now the most urgent warning has gone unexpressed: Nonsense Is Destroying America.

ONE

What's Happening to America?

Oprah's guests were teenagers who in their parents' absence had thrown wild parties resulting in thousands of dollars in damages. Furniture had been ripped, fixtures smashed, walls defaced, and personal property stolen. In one case, partygoers urinated in ice cube trays and poured syrup over appliances. A young woman admitted that, after one of her parties demonstrated the potential for such damage, she held another party the very next night. Not surprisingly, the house was nearly destroyed. When her parents returned and, outraged by what confronted them, asked her to identify the guilty individuals, the girl refused to do so out of loyalty to her friends. A young man whose mother works at night said he has wild parties whenever he can, despite his mother's repeated prohibitions. Whenever she learns that he has disobeyed, he explained with a sneer, he just moves to his father's or his grandmother's house until his mother's anger subsides.

When Oprah asked these teenagers the obvious question, why they allowed such things to happen in their own homes, the answer was simply, "Because it's fun." One young woman in the studio audience said she has had *seven* such parties and plans to have more because they were so much fun. At each mention of the word "fun," the studio audience, made up largely of young people, responded with shouts of "Yeah!" and "Woo-ooo!" Later, when a counselor joined the group on stage and denounced the teenagers' behavior as irresponsible, the sneering young man twice interrupted him with "You must never have learned to party when you were young" and "Hey, you only live once," accompanied by sly smiles to the audience.

The whole scene might have been less troubling if the teenagers had given some indication of remorse or at least regret. But instead they seemed defiantly unrepentant, their responses and their body language conveying the attitude "What's all the flap about? It's really no big deal." And many in the audience appeared to share that view. Viewers were left to wonder what makes so many young people disrespectful of their parents' rights and insensitive to their feelings.

The broadcast and print media have provided such an unending succession of similarly depressing stories in recent years that it's appropriate to speculate what effect the constant bombardment of negative reports about marriage and family life, poverty, crime, drugs, and education will ultimately have on us. Will we lose our capacity to feel shock and outrage? Will we be so overwhelmed by feelings of helplessness and futility that we cease trying to solve our country's problems? There is evidence that some are already reacting this way. For them "What can we do?" is no longer a problem-solving query, but a rhetorical acknowledgment of defeat. They speak more and more of containment of problems—teenage curfews, barricaded neighborhoods, more police, larger penitentiaries—and less and less of prevention.

Yet a greater danger than defeatism is *denial*—the argument that America today is little different from America forty or fifty years ago and the events reported in the news are atypical cases or exaggerations calculated to win higher ratings or sell more newspapers. Many people see no contradiction in alternately bemoaning contemporary social problems and denying they exist, the latter perspective adopted whenever a proposed solution poses a real or imagined limitation to their freedom. The most common form of denial is asserting that the same problems have existed in all generations: "Teenagers have always read forbidden books and experimented with sex." "Every generation has its drug of preference." "In the forties Sinatra was considered a bad influence on kids; in the fifties, Elvis; in the sixties and seventies, the Rolling Stones; in the eighties and nineties, heavy metal groups." "Teenagers have always been rebellious." "Every age has its violence." This reasoning implies that the problems we are experiencing are not serious enough to warrant a close analysis of underlying causes, let alone a dramatic response.

GROWING UP THEN VERSUS NOW

How different is growing up today from growing up half a century ago? The way we frame the inquiry is important. If we simply ask "Did poverty, divorce, youthful sexual experimentation, promiscuity, out-of-wedlock pregnancy, teenage rebelliousness, and crimes of violence exist in the 1940s and 1950s?" we may conclude that little has changed. Yet if we ask more probing questions—"Were those problems as widespread then as now? At what ages were they encountered? In what cultural context did they occur?"—we will find that growing up today is very different indeed. Forty or fifty years ago, the great majority of children lived in a stable home with two parents who, though authoritative and often unexpressive of affection, nevertheless loved their children and took their roles as parents seriously. Though the standard of living at that time (particularly in the early 1940s) was generally spartan by today's middle-class standards, most children were reasonably well fed, clothed, and cared for. Most mothers did not work outside the home and so were more available to meet children's needs. (The war years were an exception, with many men doing military service and women working in defense plants.) Children usually respected their parents and tried to please them.

In those years it took some effort to become sexually literate. The most common way was to sneak behind garages and nervously study crudely drawn sex comics. Necking and petting were considered daring and girls were not only expected to resist, but usually did so effectively (to the abiding frustration of ardent boys). Though girls may have yearned to take the initiative in pursuing boys by calling them on the phone and asking them out, few did so because such behavior was considered unladylike. Teens who became sexually active usually did so only after "going steady" for a period of time. The unwavering message of home, school, and church was that it was better to remain chaste until marriage, and most young people believed in the wisdom of that counsel even though their glands shouted a contrary message and they sometimes yielded to temptation.

Violence was present in books and films of the 1940s and 1950s, but it was comparatively tame and bloodless and often confined to a single scene of confrontation, in which the hero would deliver a sound thrashing to the villains and send them away in the custody of an officer of the law. (Incidentally, the hero was easily distinguishable from the villains; psychopaths-as-heros were a later invention.) The body count was considerably higher in war epics such as *The Sands of Iwo Jima* and *Back to Bataan*, but blood is less shocking in black and white than in living color. In any case, the camera spared the audience the sight of bayonets penetrating chests and mortar shells tearing away flesh. Horror films featuring an assortment of mummies, werewolves, and vampires were also a staple of the period, but they frightened more by slowly mounting suspense than by a succession of gruesome acts.

In those days typical youthful offenses in school were chewing gum, throwing spitballs, running and shouting in the halls, and crowding ahead in line. Outside school, children might "sass" a parent, lie, or steal, but more serious offenses were rare. That is not to say there were no bullies, no gang "rumbles" in large cities, no robberies or assaults. But even these crimes were seldom vicious or wanton, and there was a good chance that the offenders would acknowledge that they had done wrong and repent. Incorrigibles were rare enough that most people had little difficulty believing Boys Town founder Father Flanagan's then-famous line, "There's no such thing as a bad boy." Fifty years ago there were fewer high school graduates than today, and a minority of them continued their education in college. Yet those who did graduate could read and write and do everyday arithmetic. Indeed, young people who finished the *eighth grade* in the 1940s and 1950s, as in earlier decades of the century, typically attained a level of proficiency in reading, writing, spelling, penmanship, and mathematics often lacking in today's *college* students.

Today's poverty differs from that of fifty years ago in that it occurs not at a time when the majority of Americans are still experiencing the effects of a major depression, but at a time of relative affluence—more importantly, at a time when affluence is celebrated twenty-four hours a day on television, adding constant visual and auditory insult to the injury of the condition. The National Center for Children in Poverty estimates that one child in four lives in poverty. According to the Department of Health and Human Services, one in eight children under age twelve goes to bed hungry every night and three million children have dangerous levels of lead in their blood. Fetal alcohol exposure is the leading cause of mental retardation in the United States. Illegitimacy, a major cause of poverty, is rampant: One of five births among whites is illegitimate; one of three among Hispanics; two of three among blacks. Illegitimacy costs taxpayers $21 million per year in welfare, and the fact that many of the mothers are young teenagers ensures that poverty and deprivation will increase.

However strict the "spare the rod and spoil the child" parenting of the 1940s and 1950s may have been, child abuse is a greater problem today.[1] The argument that child abuse was not reported years ago is challenged by the upward spiral of statistics in *recent* years. Child-abuse reports increased 31 percent between 1985 and 1990, according to the National Committee for Prevention of Child Abuse. Reports that someone stomped or pummeled an infant to death because he or she cried or soiled a diaper are not uncommon. Ninety-five percent of the 2.5 million incidents reported in 1990 occurred in the home and included neglect, physical and sexual abuse, and emotional mistreatment. A naval officer, for example, was convicted of raping his eight-year-old daughter whenever she brought home a bad report card. A Clearwater, Florida man received two life sentences for molesting a nine-year-old mentally handicapped girl with a sexual device, allegedly with her parents' consent. A New York City man raped his three-year-old niece while a crowd of onlookers watched; only one person shouted at the assailant and gave chase. A 1985 *Los Angeles Times* study concluded that at least 22 percent of Americans have been victims of sexual abuse. (Mike Lew, author of *Victims No Longer*, places the figure at 40 percent.)

Even conscientious, loving parents may unwittingly expose their children to neglect or abuse when they place them in day-care facilities. A 1991 undercover study of U.S. day-care centers revealed that approximately half are not offering the care children need. Conditions are often unsanitary, even filthy, and dangerous. In one facility an unsupervised toddler was observed kicking a five-month-old infant in the head repeatedly. In some states, the report noted, dog kennels are inspected more often than day-care centers.[2] Perhaps the most alarming health statistic is that suicide is the second leading cause of death among today's teenagers. A Gallup poll revealed that 35 percent of American teenagers have contemplated suicide and 60 percent say they know other teenagers who have attempted suicide. Nearly half cited family problems as the cause of their anxiety.[3] The Center for Disease Control reports that the suicide rate for adolescents ages fifteen to nineteen has quadrupled over the past four decades. (Derek Humphry's *Final Exit: The Practicalities of Self-Deliverance and Assisted Suicide for the Dying*, which surged to the top of the *New York Times* bestseller list shortly after its publication, will presumably not ameliorate this situation.)

Today's teenagers are introduced to sex at considerably younger ages than were their grandparents. And they no longer have to sneak behind the barn with a forbidden magazine because sex surrounds them from the time they are old enough to focus their eyes on the television set. Radio shows and TV programs such as "I Love Lucy" or the later "Dick Van Dyke Show" never hinted at premarital or extramarital sex. Today, though many parents teach the same values, the media's message is very different. Soap operas and dramatic shows include tantalizingly graphic sex scenes. Even comedy shows manage to work in abundant sexual references—the 1991 "Murphy Brown" season ended with the single heroine pregnant and the audience uncertain of who the father was and wondering whether the heroine would opt for abortion or single parenthood. When then-Vice President Dan Quayle commented that such program content was a bad example for young people, his charge was treated little differently from his spelling of *potato*. It deserved better. The question of whether television writers and producers do young viewers a disservice by presenting sexual promiscuity and "unsafe" sex in the context of comedy is not a trivial one, particularly at a time when the deadly AIDS virus is threatening everyone on the planet. At about the same time Quayle was being lampooned for raising the issue, the U.S. Center for Disease Control reported that almost one in five high school students has had at least four sex partners and that the teenagers with the most partners are the least likely to use condoms.[4]

Hybrid news/entertainment shows such as "A Current Affair" have a never-ending supply of bizarre sexual scandals and titillating stories about bikini-clad hot dog vendors, topless car washers, and nude wrestlers. At virtually any time of the day, children can zap through the channels and find sexually provocative rock videos, R-rated movies, and interviews with the authors of *The Mayflower Madam* or *How to Cheat on Your Wife and Not Get Caught* or *Confessions of a Rock Groupie*. Some video stores will even rent them X-rated movies. When not graphically displayed, sex is talked about incessantly. Here are some of the shows scheduled on Donahue, Oprah, Geraldo, and Sally Jessy Raphael during a less-than-three-month period (late April to June 1991):

Transsexuals who have romantic relationships with members of their new sex. A mother and her four lesbian daughters. Children of sex addicts. People who fear that the person who tried to kill them will try again. Homosexual teens' coming-out parties. Married truckers who have mistresses on the road. People who cannot forget their childhood sweethearts. Polygamists. The evolution of rock and roll groupies. Three couples who pose nude for public viewing at an art gallery. Single men who prefer to date full-figured women. Fathers and sons who are dating the same women. A woman who allegedly had affairs with two priests. Women who have been sexually involved with their husbands' bosses. Transsexuals who are becoming women and living as lesbians. Bisexuals. Female impersonators. Burlesque.

Raped women forced by circumstances to deal with their rape daily. Women over forty who are exotic dancers. Women over forty who look good in bikinis. "Bikini Open" contestants. Whether or not homosexuals can successfully and completely convert to heterosexuality. Cross dressers.

Montel Williams, a more recent addition to the roster of daytime talk-show hosts, devoted a program to groupies to the stars. Jennifer Lee, author of *Tarnished Angel*, explained that she considers herself an "achiever" rather than a groupie. Williams proceeded to ask her about her sexual exploits, and she responded with details about threesomes with Warren Beatty and a well-known actress and her evaluation of Beatty's genital endowment. Next, Williams brought out several other middle-aged women who testified that their groupie years were among the greatest of their lives. When a woman in the audience questioned the women's morals, Lee interrupted and said, "To confuse sex and moral fiber is David Duke mentality." On the final segment of the show, Williams introduced three young groupies who, predictably, affirmed the emotional and spiritual benefits of their life-style. A young man in the audience offered the view that the groupies looked good to him and if they want to have sex with rock musicians and other celebrities, then "I can't see anything wrong with it." Williams's response was "Good point."[5] When Lee appeared on "The Maury Povich Show" and explained that she chose the title *Tarnished Angel* because she thinks of herself as a good person, an angel, the audience laughed. The host, apparently oblivious to the irony, asked, "Why do you laugh?"[6]

It is hardly surprising that, nurtured on such a diet, even preteenage girls pursue boys shamelessly. The mother of a seven-year-old boy reports that her son is called regularly by female classmates. One sixteen-year-old girl left this message on a boy's family answering machine, apparently unconcerned that his mother might hear it (and she did): "I haven't had sex in a couple of weeks and I really need it."[7]

If the average teenage boy in the 1940s or 1950s had been asked, "If you had the chance to have sex with a girl, would you?" he'd have answered in the affirmative. But if the question were "Does a man have the right to *force* sex on a woman if he has spent money on her?" he'd have said, "No, that would be rape and rape is wrong." Today, when that question was put to seven hundred sixth to ninth graders 25 percent of the boys and 16 percent of the girls answered yes; and in a situation where the couple had dated six months or more, 65 percent of the boys and 47 percent of the girls thought that force was acceptable.[8] In another poll, 84 percent of male college students expressed a belief that "some women look as though they're just asking to be raped."[9]

Violence, too, is available to today's children, not just on Saturday afternoons in a theater but all day every day in their living rooms. And today's high-tech variety is very different from the old black and white make-believe violence: it's ultra-realistic and presented in relentless close-up and living color. Nothing is too gross to appear on camera, and no imagination or advanced level of maturity is required to fill in the gory details. Women are brutally, sadistically raped. Victims' eyes are gouged out, heads exploded, viscera ripped out, bodies set ablaze. Today's heroes are more vicious by far than yesterday's *villains*. Cinematographers began this movement in the name of visual realism and artistic freedom, but in breaking each prior convention and taboo they have created a monster that has proved difficult to control; to maintain audience interest, they must be more and more shocking and revolting. And since film audiences bring the same appetites to television viewing, television producers desirous of high ratings have borrowed the techniques, not only for dramatic shows but for news/entertainment shows as well. For example, when William Kennedy Smith was charged with rape, "A Current Affair" created a vivid dramatization of the alleged attack. Over the course of the next few weeks, as they milked the story of every drop of sensation and dribbled out each day's new revelations, they reran that dramatization over and over again. Since the show airs at 7 P.M. in many markets, millions of children undoubtedly saw it.

Children growing up today see not the few scenes of bloodless violence their grandparents saw each week, but hundreds of bloody scenes. Thomas Radecki, research director for the National Coalition Against Television Violence, estimates that by age eighteen young people have witnessed 200,000 violent acts, including 25,000 murders on television and in the movies. Add to that the violence they encounter in real life. A study of more than eleven thousand eighth and tenth graders in twenty states disclosed that 49 percent of boys and 28 percent of girls were in at least one fight at school in the previous year, 39 percent and 30 percent were threatened with violence in school, and 35 percent and 30 percent were threatened outside.[10]

One predictable result of this constant exposure to violence is that even young children are comfortable with the macabre and tend to think in terms foreign to their grandparents. When a third-grade class in rural upstate New York was given the assignment of writing a creative variation on the classic poem, " 'Twas the Night Before Christmas," one student wrote: " 'Twas the *fright* before Christmas/When all through the house/Not a creature was stirring . . . except Jason/The *children* were hung by the chimney with care. . . ." Moreover, children in their teens and younger are committing *real* acts of violence. A group of sixth-graders in Columbus, Georgia, allegedly plotted to kill their teacher because she tried to make them behave. The group reportedly brought poison, a handgun, and a knife to school.

Children as young as eight or nine years old are committing rape. And assaults with guns and other weapons have become epidemic. In one incident a seventeen-year-old was asked to close a window on the bus. When he refused, and the adults who had made the request closed it themselves, he opened fire on them with a gun. In New Orleans a sixteen-year-old tattooed with white supremacy slogans was accused of killing a fifty-nine-year-old black woman, allegedly because she pulled away from a stop sign too slowly. In an exclusive Pasadena, California, neighborhood two teens shot three young women to death over an argument so trivial they couldn't remember what it was about when police interrogated them.

The most disturbing aspect of juvenile crime today is the attitude of the perpetrators. The young men who savagely raped and beat the jogger in New York City's highly publicized "wilding" case reportedly laughed about what they had done even after they were arrested. In another case, a teen drug enforcer described how he shot an acquaintance whom he thought had stolen drug money: "He begged for his life five times. I shot him in the face at point-blank range and killed him instantly. Blood was everywhere, and some parts of his head were laying [*sic*] in the doorway. I didn't have to kill him. If I'd just pulled the gun, I could have gotten my money. But still I shot him. The man lost his life over nothing." A fifteen-year-old Boston boy, when asked why he and his friends raped, stomped, stabbed, and murdered a woman on Halloween, responded nonchalantly, "There was nothing to do." A twelve-year-old Missouri boy shot another youngster in the face and then bragged about it to his friends. (When, for some reason, he was released by the court, his father asked the police to return the gun so that his son wouldn't develop a fear of guns!) Two young men in Warren, Michigan, offered this chilling explanation of why they stabbed, decapitated, and dismembered a teenage girl: "She was more or less a pest. She wanted to be with everybody all the time."

The 1980s has been dubbed "the decade of educational reform" because it produced a series of alarms and studies, followed by a host of proposals for educational change. Throughout the decade, the National Assessment of Educational Progress (NAEP) periodically tested nine-, thirteen-, and seventeen-year-olds, and with depressing consistency found them deficient in reading, writing, thinking, and math skills. Typical evaluations of their findings are that a majority of seventeen-year-olds have difficulty understanding a bus schedule, analyzing a newspaper or magazine article, writing a coherent essay defending *their own* views (explaining, for example, why they enjoyed a TV show or a movie), and calculating the correct change when paying for a meal. Reformers hoped that the investment in educational change would show dramatic results by the end of the decade. Yet in September 1990 the NAEP reported that their analysis of student performance over a twenty-year period revealed no improvement. Secretary of Education Lauro Cavazos described the finding as a "compendium of disappointment."

Our national high school dropout rate is 25 percent (50 percent in some large cities). Scholastic Aptitude Test (SAT) scores in 1990 were at their lowest point in ten years. For more than a generation now, colleges have had to dilute their courses to make them accessible to ill-prepared students. Marc Tucker, president of the National Center on Education and the Economy, estimates that more than half of our colleges are really high-priced secondary schools. American Federation of Teachers president Albert Shanker suggests that more than half of U.S. students would not qualify for admission to college in Japan or Europe. And yet the college dropout rate ranges between 66 percent and 75 percent and only half of our *high-ability* students receive bachelor's degrees within seven years of high school graduation.

As even this brief comparison makes clear, it is absurd to deny that much has changed in this country over the past half-century or to pretend that the changes are unimportant in children's lives. The questions that beg to be addressed are why these negative changes occurred—that is, why a period of astounding scientific and technological advancement has not produced comparable *social* progress, and why the conscientious efforts of individuals and organizations to solve our country's domestic problems have been so fruitless.

A TIME OF CONTRADICTIONS

Every age has its controversies, issues that divide the best and brightest minds and provoke continuing and not always harmonious debate. Few ages, however, have produced as many *contradictions* as ours. Consider the current contradictions about the family. Everyone seems to agree that the family is the cornerstone of society and that its decline is lamentable. Yet government leaders proceed to pass tax laws that penalize married people, and various groups seek to redefine, for the purpose of housing codes and inheritance laws, what constitutes a family. (If any group of people inhabiting a dwelling constitutes a family, why all the talk about the importance of the family to society?) Families are excoriated for causing a recession by overspending and underinvesting, so government phases out their credit-card interest deductions, while continuing to allow businesses to write off the cost of advertising campaigns that induce spendthrift behavior. Men are told that they must take their responsibilities as fathers seriously and assume a strong leadership role in the family; yet women are urged to be competitive with men at home as at work, to assert themselves and be jealous of their rights; and both men and women are bombarded with enticements to indulge their desires and "take care of number one." Psychologists urge parents to communicate more with their children, while the film and television industries depict parents as old-fashioned nerds whose ideas and values are irrelevant to young people's lives.

Similar contradictions exist about gender. For decades feminists have attacked the idea that men tend to be rational and women emotional as a sexist myth designed to deny women equal access to education and career opportunities. Laws have been revised and government programs established to put an end to the discrimination this myth has caused. To this day, only a foolish man would dare hint in public that the myth had any basis in reality. Yet some feminist authors assert that women and men are very different in their emotional and intellectual makeup. For example, in *Women's Ways of Knowing* Mary Field Belenky and her coauthors argue that the mode of learning emphasized in education is a male mode that is unnatural for women. It is rational, competitive, objective, impersonal, whereas women's is intuitive, collaborative, subjective, and personal. The authors never raise, let alone answer, the question "How did the supposedly male mode of learning survive during the past century or so when women teachers dramatically outnumbered men?" And British geneticist Anne Moir, in *Brain Sex: The Real Difference Between Men and Women,* cites evidence that the supposed myth that women are more emotional than men is supported by genetic research. She adds that men's greater capacity for understanding abstract relationships makes them more suited for disciplines such as math and engineering. Does this mean there was wisdom in the traditional practice of preferring men in those professions and women in nursing and teaching? If the practice was reasonable, shouldn't current prohibitions against it be lifted? On the other hand, is it possible that the differences between men and women are less significant than the similarities, notably their common humanity?

The view of Judaism and Christianity that pervades popular

culture is negative. At best they are seen as quaint; at worst, as archaic perspectives that hinder intellectual maturity and obstruct scientific progress. In recent years disdain has grown to ridicule and open hostility. Yet many of these same critics of traditional religion have welcomed the New Age movement and its resurrection of superstitions that Judeo-Christianity exposed as absurd millenia ago. And the contradictions go even deeper. After dismissing belief in God as unrealistic, popular culture proclaims that everyone is God and should therefore worship himself/herself. It alternates between telling people "You create your own reality, command your own destiny" and "You are a helpless victim of society, vulnerable to innumerable compulsions, so emotionally fragile that you need constant infusions of self-esteem." Popular culture, in other words, sees no inconsistency in asserting that humans are simultaneously *omni*potent and utterly *im*potent! Fashionable people today titter at medieval peasants for believing that dogs and other animals are responsible for their behavior, yet unquestioningly embrace the belief that human beings are not responsible for theirs; they express amazement that anyone could ever have believed that the sun revolves around the earth, and in the next breath assert that the entire universe revolves around the individual human being.

These contradictions about religion are also expressed in a double standard regarding free speech. If priests, ministers, or rabbis make public statements—for example, in a letter to the editor of a newspaper or on a talk show—their views are likely to be dismissed as propaganda or proselytizing, even if they hold an earned doctorate in the subject under discussion. They may also be accused of violating separation of church and state in some unspecified manner. On the other hand, barely literate rock stars who dropped out of elementary school may make sweeping statements on subjects about which they are totally ignorant and be defended for exercising their freedom of speech. Popular culture's hypocrisy in this matter is well established: the schools may not teach religion, government may not smile upon religion, but the media may revile religion and in some cases send taxpayers the bill.

Morality, in the popular view, is a purely subjective matter.

Moral rules are denounced as absolutism, even fascism. Whatever a person decides for himself or herself is, by that fact, morally right for that person; and it is considered intolerant to question anyone else's moral judgment. Thus when Madonna massages herself erotically on HBO in front of millions of people, popular culture not only accepts but lauds her behavior as "bold" and "liberated." (Presumably, had Pee-wee Herman chosen the spotlight instead of a quiet corner of a movie theater, public reaction would have been more favorable.) We might reasonably expect a nonjudgmental philosophy like this to produce a harmonious society in which few people took offense at others' behavior. Yet the actual effect has been quite the reverse. America has more lawyers, in actual numbers and in ratio to total population, than any other country on earth. We are the most litigious country on the planet, probably the most litigious in history. And we have the world's highest imprisonment rate, higher even than the former Soviet Union's and South Africa's.

Given the publishing industry's proclaimed dedication to giving the public what the public wants, we would expect bookstores to be flooded with guides to moral living. After all, polls repeatedly show eight of ten Americans concerned over the decline of morality and desiring a return of traditional ethical values. But few such books are being published. Instead we get books like Dalma Heyn's *The Erotic Silence of the American Wife*, which recounts the stories of married women who have had affairs, feel good about them, and claim their lives have been enriched by the experience. And that is not the only, nor even the oddest publishing omission. Unless one lives in a monastery, it's impossible to get through a day without a dozen or so encounters with narcissism. Individuals suffering from that affliction could certainly profit from books with titles such as *Stifling the Self, Discovering Other People*, and *The One-Minute Emphathizer*. But such books do not exist. Instead, publishers give us advice on getting to know our feelings, putting ourselves first, and loving number one. Forty years ago "Made in Japan" was a joke; today the joke is on us. Shoddy goods and shabby service are a constant reminder that laziness and mediocrity are epidemic, yet articles and books warn us of the dangers of . . . *workaholism and perfectionism*!

Since schools and colleges are not insulated from society, but reflect its ideas and values, it is not surprising that many of these contradictions have found expression in education or that educators have created contradictions of their own. The latest is the embrace of Political Correctness (PC), not by conservative professors, but by the very liberals who in other situations most loudly denounce absolutism, intolerance, and censorship. Ironically, the PC agenda is to stamp out modes of thinking and speaking its leaders have decided are offensive. Their proscriptions cover, among other offenses, "ageism," "heterosexism," "lookism" (references to beauty), and "ableism" (references to disability). More serious, however, than the contradictions of PC are those concerning fact and opinion. In an age whose bywords are "each person creates her own truth" and "everyone is entitled to his viewpoint," logic would dictate that opinion replace fact as the focus of education. Not only has that change *not* occurred, but the emphasis on fact has grown stronger. Fields that long ago rejected objective truth are experiencing not an opinion explosion, but a *knowledge* explosion; and they employ as the measure of learning not a subjective, but an *objective* test composed of *true/false* questions.

How these contradictions arose and how they can be overcome will be addressed in later chapters. For now I want to address a more fundamental question: Why is it that most of these contradictions have escaped the notice of social critics? Each point of view here has many eloquent advocates and opponents, to be sure, and entire forests have been sacrificed to the debate. Astoundingly, however, the contradictions *as contradictions* have gone unremarked. Even many educated people seem unaware of the tension they generate or unconvinced of the value of achieving a balanced, moderate position between extremes. All too many Americans have become, to borrow sociologist Peter Berger's phrase, "experts at excluding the middle."

INTELLECTUAL PARALYSIS

This hospitality toward contradictions is one symptom of a growing intellectual paralysis in America. Another is the widespread acceptance of the democratic fallacy. This offense against logic, the unreasonable extension of "all *men* are created equal" to "all *ideas* are equal," breeds a false sense of tolerance that discourages people from asking probing questions, particularly about the views of scholars.* Consider, for example, James Q. Wilson's theory that violence is inevitable because human beings are violent in their very nature. The basic position is not new, but Wilson has given it a twist that radical feminists would undoubtedly find appealing. He argues that *males*, but not females, are naturally indisposed to civilization. (This view is almost refreshing, since it counters the prevailing romantic idea of the noble savage.) Many questions need to be asked about such a theory. For example, if men in general are indisposed to civilization, why do we find such differences from culture to culture? Why are males in America more violent generally than males in certain other, notably oriental, cultures? How explain the absence of violence among American Amish males? Why has the level of violence in American society risen so sharply in recent decades? Why do heavy metal concerts produce more violent behavior among fans than bluegrass, Boston Pops, or Lawrence Welk concerts? Why are there no riots at operas? The contemporary notion that such questions are somehow inappropriate initially prevents people from asking them and ultimately prevents them from *thinking* of them.

No matter how sophisticated people's intellectual skills may be, if they are unused, they may as well be nonexistent. The habit of accepting other people's ideas or one's own uncritically and without reflection stifles curiosity, imprisons creativity, and blocks insight. As more and more people stop making the effort to address issues thoughtfully, social and scientific progress become more difficult to achieve. Evidence that this is happening is abundant. For example, when the critically acclaimed film *Boyz N the 'Hood* opened around the country, at least twenty incidents of violence involving knives and guns occurred in and outside theaters, leading some theater owners to cancel the

---

*Our respect for other *people* should be unqualified because each human being has an inherent, God-given dignity. *Ideas*, on the other hand, have no inherent value. Because they may be true or false, wise or foolish, only those that prove themselves in light of the evidence deserve acceptance.

film's engagement. John Singleton, the film's director, asked to comment on the situation on "Good Morning America," responded that since films reflect reality, but don't create it, his film did not cause the violence; he also labeled the theater owners' decision to cancel the film "artistic racism." His age (twenty-three) and his understandable dismay at having his film the center of such an unfortunate series of incidents explain his defensiveness. Nevertheless, his lack of interest in why the violence occurred and what it implies about the relationship of film violence and real violence illustrates the vacuity that is becoming more and more common today.

Two vital factors in all problem solving are the habit of looking for relationships among ideas and events, especially cause-and-effect relationships, and the ability to recognize them where they exist. Suppose a family in Maine were troubled over their enormous heating bill and were considering how they might reduce it—for example, by buying fuel oil when prices were low, replacing their furnace with a more efficient model, and turning the thermostat down lower at night. Suppose, too, that they were unaware that several of their windows were an inch or two *open*. No matter how many creative ideas they produced or how diligently they pursued them, their problem would remain unsolved until they noticed those open windows and shut them. It is the same with our social problems: if we neglect to look for or fail to see the causes, we will never be successful in dealing with their effects.

We can't deal with realities we fail to see, of course, and more and more we aren't seeing important realities about the problems that confront us. Consider a recently anointed social problem, compulsive gambling. Loma Linda University psychologist Durand Jacobs and his researchers surveyed 2,700 high school students in New Jersey, Virginia, California, and Connecticut and found that roughly half gambled at least once a year; 13 percent financed gambling with crimes; and 5 percent (as opposed to 1.5 percent of adults) could be classified as pathological bettors. What has been the public reaction to Jacobs's and related research? Expressions of anguished concern, proposals to create gambling hot lines modeled after drug and suicide hot lines, the creation of counseling services and "Just say no"-styled classroom programs for children. Somewhere, no doubt, a biologist is searching for an aberrant gene to blame for this malady, and an anthropologist is working on a tome tracing the gambling urge to a previously undiscovered dark corner of our human nature.

One of the most neglected considerations about gambling, however, is the obvious one: the proliferation of sweepstakes and lotteries. Is it not likely that the daily arrival of million-dollar prize notifications in our mailboxes, combined with seductive ad campaigns for the lottery, have created the problem or at least aggravated it? Isn't it probable that pictures of happy winners frolicking in piles of money on exotic beaches as seductive jingles are chanted ("You can't win it unless you're in it")—campaigns that are *designed* to make gamblers of us all—are largely responsible for the problem? Is it not plausible that if all these inducements to gamble were ended, the problem would shrink to its prior, more modest dimensions? Not only are these questions not being raised, but in a number of states a new state-sponsored gambling scheme—legalized betting on basketball, baseball, and football games—is being advocated as a solution to fiscal problems.

The widespread failure to seek connections among ideas and events suggests that our culture is suffering from an *episodic grasp of reality*, to borrow Reuven Feuerstein's term. Feuerstein, an Israeli educator, has devoted his long and distinguished career to developing approaches to increase human intelligence, particularly the intelligence of retarded people. The chief characteristic of retarded individuals, he has observed, is their tendency to regard each fact or experience as separate and unrelated to all others; in other words, they regard reality as a series of disconnected *episodes*. This poverty of perspective prevents them from seeing relationships, gaining insights, and building new knowledge on old. It also precludes creativity, with its new and unusual combinations of knowledge. With educational curriculums already fragmented, academic specialization increasing, and the broadcast media segmenting programs (including newscasts and talk shows) into smaller and smaller units, it is not hard to understand why even educated people have become content with shallow and simplistic formulas and seldom bother to look for meaningful connections.

The media focus on the phenomenon of sexual harassment and assault offers a good illustration of our episodic grasp of reality. A June 1991 "Donahue" show examined the problem of men's leering and making obscene comments when women walk by on the street. The guests (all women) included a writer for *Penthouse* and the organizer of a group protesting such male offenses. There was a great deal of complaining about how such behavior frightened and dehumanized women and violated their basic rights. Unquestionably, the women's anger and resentment was justified; their demand that they be treated with respect by strangers on the street was perfectly reasonable. But they also professed puzzlement at why men behave that way, why they seem to think that a shapely woman, no matter how demurely dressed, is "asking for it." Apparently the host shared their puzzlement. But no one made what would seem to be the obvious connection: *the way women are depicted in ads, in MTV, and in movies.* No one mentioned the numerous articles and books that celebrate the modern woman's sexual aggressiveness or offer advice on how to pick up members of the opposite sex. (Ironically, two days earlier Sally Jessy Raphael's show had featured women over forty who look good in bikinis and who boasted about turning heads and being approached by young men on the beach.)

Similarly, at the end of a special edition of ABC's "20/20" dealing with rape, Barbara Walters and Hugh Downs agreed that the education of men against rape begins at home and urged parents to teach their sons responsible attitudes about their relationships with women.[11] Neither of the co-hosts nor anyone featured in the program acknowledged the *possibility* that parental neglect is not the main cause of the problem and parental initiatives alone will never provide a solution. Many academicians suffer from identical tunnel vision. In October of 1991 an international "Sexual Assault on Campus Conference" was sponsored by counseling, educational, health, law, and fraternity organizations. Scheduled topics included acquaintance rape, recovery issues, policy needs, task force creation, and campus security. Notably omitted from the list was the role of popular culture in shaping the values and attitudes of rapists.

EXAMINING OUR ASSUMPTIONS

Every age, C. S. Lewis reminded us, has its characteristic illusions, and they "are likeliest to lurk in those widespread assumptions which are so ingrained in the age that no one dares to attack or feels it necessary to defend them."[12] In order to gain insight into the causes of our social problems, we must examine our society's fundamental assumptions. A good place to begin is with the ongoing discussion about education. Virtually every educational reformer, as well as every government official, social critic, and journalist who has commented on the academic deficiencies of American youth, assumes the cause to be parental neglect and/or teachers' incompetency. Most of the highly publicized proposals for educational reform rest on this assumption, including the movement to extend the school year from 180 days to 240, the Hirsch Cultural Literacy plan, school-based management, and the Holmes Report. To be sure, not all these proposals explicitly place the blame on parents and teachers; nevertheless, by focusing only on home and/or classroom solutions, they reveal the assumption that responsibility rests exclusively with home and school.

Most business leaders seem to share this view. Former Chrysler CEO Lee Iacocca voiced it in these stern words to a recent Association for Supervision and Curriculum Development (ASCD) convention: "Your product needs a lot of work, and in the end, it's your job . . . Your customers don't want to hear about your raw materials problem—they care about results. That's your responsibility and you can't duck it. Graduating a student who can't read is like selling a car without an engine under the hood . . . It's massive consumer fraud."[13]

That there are neglectful parents and incompetent or irresponsible teachers, and arguably more today than at any time in this century, is undeniable.* But these people are not the only ones having difficulty with young people. The most conscien-

*Any meaningful inquiry into this phenomenon will address the question that most analysts ignore: Exactly *why* are there more irresponsible parents and teachers today than forty or fifty years ago? Is the answer a physical factor, such as eating too much junk food or drinking fluoridated water? Is it, instead, that today's parents and teachers have different attitudes? If so, where did they get them?

tious parents are finding the job of imparting their values a formidable one; and the very best teachers, armed with the most exciting material, are finding more and more students bored and apathetic. Illiteracy is constantly discussed in the press; but the more serious problem of *aliteracy*, the utter disdain for reading among students who can read, has gone largely unreported. Critics make much of the lengthening list of matters about which students are ignorant: history, geography, grammar, and so on. But few critics notice what students are *knowledgeable about*. In one study of District of Columbia children, students aged seven to twelve were asked to name as many presidents and as many alcoholic beverages as they could. On average they knew 4.8 presidents and 5.2 kinds of booze.[14] Presumably few parents or teachers instruct children in the lexicon of liquor, so who or what is providing that training? And what makes it so much more effective than the lessons of home and school? Such questions as these would be a worthy focus of national discussion.

Over the past half-century a dramatic shift has occurred in America. The education of the young, once carried out by home, school, and church, has gradually been taken over by the communications and entertainment media—newspapers, magazines, books, music, movies, radio, television—and the agency that permeates all of these, advertising. Technological advances in mass communication have made popular culture (that is, the ideas, attitudes, and values expressed in the media) the dominant force in this society. Its influence is more powerful than the combined influence of home, school, and church. By age eighteen the average person has spent 11,000 hours in the classroom and 22,000 hours in front of the TV set. He or she has completed fewer than 10,000 homework assignments, yet has seen almost *three-quarters of a million* commercials and print advertisements. Moreover, TV has a vast array of attention-holding devices not available to parents and teachers, including background music, laugh and applause tracks, sensory appeals, scene shifts, and changes of camera angle.

It is not only reasonable to conclude that popular culture has a greater influence on children's lives than the traditional culture espoused by parents and teachers: it is logically inescapable.

"One of the fundamental propositions of the sociology of knowledge," observes sociologist Peter L. Berger, "is that the plausibility. . . of views of reality depends upon the social support these receive. Put more simply, we obtain our notions about the world originally from other human beings, and these notions continue to be plausible to us in a very large measure because others continue to affirm them." Though it is possible to resist the social consensus, Berger argues, there is strong pressure to embrace it, even if it challenges what we have been brought up to believe. When a particular view receives constant "affirmation, confirmation, reiteration," we tend to cling to it; when it is scorned, attacked, ridiculed, we tend to reject or abandon it.[15]

In this technological age popular culture has greater potential for good or evil than any other social force in history. It could virtually guarantee the success of parents' and teachers' efforts by providing reinforcement for the habits, attitudes, and values they try to impart. Yet tragically, it has generally tended to undermine those efforts in a variety of ways. Parents and teachers tell children that truth is discovered by study and reflection and that informed opinions are preferable to uninformed. Meanwhile, Shirley MacLaine and other New Age gurus say that truth is created by the individual to suit his or her fancy; opinion polls, which make no distinction between knowledgeable and ignorant people, imply that all opinions are equal; and talk shows, cluttered with entertainers talking glibly about whatever subject they wish, proclaim that the views of celebrities are more valuable than those of scholars.

Parents and teachers say that self-improvement is attained by close observation, self-criticism, and constructive change, and they encourage young people to value substance above artifice. Self-improvement books, meanwhile, advise accepting and asserting oneself, even inflicting oneself on others, and tennis star/Canon spokesman André Agassi looks out from his dark glasses, peers into our living rooms, and intones, "Image is everything." (Does anyone doubt that Canon had an audience of young people in mind when they hired Agassi and chose this advertising slogan?)

While parents and teachers quietly try to persuade young

people that intellectual activities are satisfying and to encourage them to become creative, critical, reflective thinkers, popular culture—with nonstop action films filled with car chases and explosions, the artificial excitement of game shows, flashing Nintendo displays, and MTV's pyrotechnical cacaphony—conditions young people to reject any activity that does not dazzle the senses. Moreover, commercials manipulate viewers with advertisements that play on their needs and desires and induce them to suspend critical judgment and accept biased testimony as fact. In some cases commercials directly attack the lessons of home and school. A blatant example of such an attack is a recent series of commercials for Budweiser Dry beer. Here is a sample of the format:

> The Mona Lisa has no eyebrows. Why?
>
> The Venus de Milo has no arms. Why?
>
> Chickens have no lips. Why?
>
> *Why ask why? Try Bud Dry!*

The humorous context of the ad may mitigate the negative effect on adult viewers, but hardly on children. What makes this ad especially pernicious is that "Why?" is the most philosophical of questions, the essence of wonder and creativity, and the viewer is encouraged to replace being curious with drinking alcohol! (Undoubtedly Anheuser-Busch executives saw no inconsistency between sponsoring this ad and lamenting the schools' failure to develop students' thinking skills.)

Parents and teachers say that students should live by a moral standard more demanding than personal preference and should accept the challenge of dedicating their lives to something noble, whereas many movies and TV dramas promote doing whatever feels good at the moment or whatever satisfies one's desires. Moreover, the publishing and TV industries regularly reward felons such as Sidney Biddle Barrows with lucrative contracts and talk-show appearances and thus glamorize their offenses; and television personalities from party animal Spuds McKenzie to Robin Leach (of "Lifestyles of the Rich and Famous") preach that the purpose of life is possessing things and having fun.

While parents and teachers urge students to become active participants in learning and in life, television programming promotes a spectator mentality and a desire to be entertained. Moreover, it effectively blocks development of the single most important element in school and in the workplace, a mature attention span. (The greatest obstacle to learning, as any teacher will testify, is students' inability to concentrate for more than a few minutes at a time.) Over the last few years I have conducted some revealing research concerning the number of attention shifts forced on television viewers during television programs. Counting as a shift in attention each movement from one plot line to another, or to a flashback or flashforward, or to a newsbreak or commercial, or from one commercial to another, I found as many as seventy-eight shifts per hour, excluding the shifts *within* commercials.

During my original study it was my impression that shifts within commercials were even more numerous, so I next conducted a similar study on commercials themselves. (Over the past thirty years the Federal Communications Commission has allowed the average length of a commercial to be reduced from sixty seconds to thirty seconds and, most recently, to fifteen seconds. Thus there are, typically, four commercials scheduled for each commercial break.) This study disclosed that the number of attention shifts ranged from six to fifty-four per commercial, the average being seventeen shifts. Ironically, an IBM commercial detailing the company's efforts to help solve the nation's education problem contained *over thirty-five shifts.*

Combining the studies, I found that in a typical television hour containing eleven minutes of commercials,[16] viewers' attention is forced to shift over eight hundred times, or *almost fourteen times per minute!* Is it really any wonder that students are unable to concentrate on their homework or that they twist and squirm and cast nervous glances at the clock whenever class discussion of an idea extends beyond a few minutes?

SEDUCED BY NONSENSE

How can it be that so many intelligent, educated social analysts and critics are so tolerant of contradictions, so blind to relationships between ideas and events, so oblivious of the massive influence of popular culture? How explain the business community's first spending more than $115 billion annually to sponsor programs and advertising messages that impede education, next spending $35 billion annually in corporate classrooms to teach the skills they have obstructed, and then planning to donate $200 billion more* to improve the effectiveness of the educational system they have thwarted? How grasp the logic of a society's producing books, magazines, records, movies, and television shows that promote disrespect for parents and teachers and then castigating parents and teachers for their lack of success in reaching young people?

I submit the answer is that America has been seduced by nonsense—that is, by a number of fundamental ideas that run contrary to human experience, thoughtfully considered. The communications and entertainment media are the means by which this seduction has occurred, but they are not, generally speaking, the creators of the nonsense. Whatever ideas they disseminate already exist. (In this sense, their defenders are quite correct in claiming that the media merely hold a mirror to society.) What is not yet fully appreciated, however, is that the media's unparalleled efficiency and technological sophistication intensify the impact of ideas. This is particularly true of cinema and television. When ideas are made visual, dramatized, and enhanced by music, they are more readily assimilated and more persuasive. And when the characters in dramatic shows, the talk-show guests, and the reporters of the news are known, respected, and admired, the line between representation and endorsement is blurred. Shallow and fallacious ideas have always had the potential to do mischief, as sound ideas have had the potential to do good. Contemporary media facilitate that mischief.

The first step in overcoming the seductive power of nonsense is to examine the cherished doctrines of our age, the ideas we have been conditioned to regard mindlessly, recite dutifully, and applaud when we hear recited. No easy task, this requires a degree of irreverence toward intellectual fashion and thus takes

*This was the amount projected in the Bush administration's "America 2000" educational reform program.

courage. The following questions, each of which will be examined in detail in subsequent chapters, are among the most profitable to raise.

Popular writers, particularly those of New Age disposition, are fond of saying that each person creates his or her own reality and that truth is whatever we want it to be. What are the practical implications of the idea? If doctors believe they create their own truth, will their diagnoses improve? Will juries deal with evidence more carefully, serve justice more effectively? Will this idea prompt us to prepare our income tax returns differently? Will it improve the quality of scientific research, history, education, and government? Will it make the instant replay in sports obsolete and force changes in the parimutuel system at the racetrack? Will it sharpen or erase the distinctions between knowledge and ignorance, wisdom and foolishness, excellence and mediocrity, sense and nonsense? If we come to believe each person's idea is the best of all possible ideas for him or her, will our curiosity be stimulated or suppressed? Will we be more or less inclined to value reading and learning?

No doctrine has achieved certitude in any age more quickly than has the doctrine of self-esteem in this age. Its principal tenet is that we must hold ourselves in high esteem before we can achieve anything in life. Accordingly, lack of self-esteem is considered the cause of every social evil from academic deficiency to criminality. But what line of thought prompted this reversal of our parents' and grandparents' view that feeling good about ourselves is the *result*, rather than the *cause*, of achievement? Since most of our grandparents came from authoritarian families in which duty and respect were emphasized and criticism was more common than praise, how is their success to be explained? Did the immigrants at the turn of the century have self-esteem? Did the children who worked in sweatshops fourteen hours a day, seven days a week? Did the survivors of concentration camps? Is it possible that too much self-esteem is more harmful than too little? (The myth of Narcissus comes to mind.) Is the self-esteem doctrine more reasonable than Christ's admonition, "And whoever exalts himself will be humbled, and he who humbles himself will be exalted" (Matt. 23:12)? Does unconditional self-acceptance motivate people to self-improvement or promote complacency? Does liking ourselves make us likable?

Feelings, popular culture advises, are more trustworthy than thoughts. Emotion is considered more natural and more reflective of our individuality. Is this actually the case? Does careful thinking make one more vulnerable to conformity? Is the heart more intelligent than the head? Will trusting feelings help a prejudiced person become fair-minded, a suspicious person trust others, a wife beater overcome his violence, envious people count their blessings? Will it prompt us to forgive people who have offended us and seek forgiveness from those we have offended? If everyone put emotion above thought, would marriages be stronger, careers more productive, neighborhoods safer? Are criminals and compulsive individuals more proficient in thinking than in feeling? If we are more likely to be victimized by our minds than by our hearts, why do most advertisements appeal to the emotions? (Is it because advertisers want us to make wise choices?)

The defenders of popular culture assure us that what we see on television, hear on tapes, and read in books cannot do us any harm. But if this is true, if words and images have no power to harm us, how can they be said to *help* us? Are we then wasting money on public service ads, such as those urging women to have mammograms done, partygoers to prevent drunk friends from driving, students to stay in school, and everyone to protect the environment? If ads have no power to affect behavior, does it make any sense for advertisers to pay billions of dollars to celebrities to endorse their products and billions more for the creation and presentation of commercials and print advertisements?

For several decades popular culture has advanced two not quite consistent ideas about morality. One is that morality is entirely subjective—in other words, that each person decides what is morally right and that decision is "right for that person," together with the often-stated corollary that it is wrong to challenge another person's morality. But isn't it possible to make a mistake in moral judgment, just as we err in other kinds of judgment? May not an action that appears or "feels" good for us actually be harmful? Are our moral judgments ever affected by self-deception and rationalization? Is it unreasonable to judge rape morally wrong in all cases, no matter how sincerely the rapist believes "she was asking for it"? In light of the increasing evidence that some people feel no remorse for the most heinous crimes and thus either lack a conscience or at least have been successful in stifling it, is it reasonable to trust one's conscience implicitly? If each person decides what is moral for him or her, is it fair for society to enact laws proscribing certain behaviors?

The second popular idea about morality is that each *culture* decides for itself what is right and wrong and no one has any business criticizing the moral standards of another culture. What does this imply about the Western Allies' judgments of Nazis in the Nuremburg trials? About world opinion concerning the Russian gulags? About the United Nations Declaration of Human Rights? Was Mohandas Gandhi wrong in opposing British imperialism in India? (The British were in charge, after all, and they had made the rules he protested.) Was Martin Luther King wrong in challenging the dominant culture's system of segregation? Are there, perhaps, some moral principles that transcend culture?

Why are many talk show hosts uncomfortable, suspicious, even openly hostile toward Judaism and Christianity, yet uncritical of astrology, numerology, channeling, and other occult beliefs? Why do the same hosts who smile benignly at the suggestion that each individual is God become skeptics when someone suggests that *God* is God? Are Christians as intolerant, prissy, and irrational as they are made out to be in the media, or is this image a stereotype? Are religious convictions incompatible with democratic ideals? Is secular humanism a product of the overactive imaginations of conservative Christians, or does it really exist? Are the traditional questions of good and evil, salvation and damnation anachronistic or relevant to our time?

What has caused education to abandon the pursuit of goodness, truth, and beauty? Why have creative thinking and critical thinking been neglected in schools and colleges alike, not for a decade or two but throughout this century? What exactly is meant by the term *standards* as used in popular discussions of educational reform? (Do those who use it have any clear meaning in mind?) Why do immigrants, for whom English is a foreign language, often speak better English than many native-born

American high school graduates? Why is sex education so woefully ineffective, even when it is most widely and freely given? Was Alex Comfort, the author of the best-selling *The Joy of Sex*, speaking prophetically when he wrote a couple of decades ago, "We may eventually come to realize that chastity is no more a virtue than malnutrition." Or instead, has repetition made this idea a self-fulfilling prophecy? If, as many people claim, ignorance of sexual matters is the cause of teenage pregnancy, why wasn't this problem epidemic in our parents' and grandparents' day, when both home and school left them uninformed?

Is it possible that the incivility and rudeness so common today is essentially imitation of movie and television characters? Does wearing a Bart Simpson "Underachiever and proud of it, man" T-shirt affect a child's attitude toward scholastic achievement and excellence? Is the low estate of logic and language attributable to the media's celebrity-worship? Do the people whom columnist George Will terms "professional wallower[s] in the bountiful publicity that accrues to the weird" debase public discourse by filling the airwaves and viewers' minds with uninformed opinions? The 1960s term *generation gap* has by now settled comfortably into the language. It denotes a philosophical conflict between teenagers and parents that popularizers hint is not only unavoidable but also a natural step toward independence. But if generational conflict is healthy, then shouldn't the rebellion of modern American teenagers against their parents' values be cause for celebration? And shouldn't non-Western cultures, with their tradition of generational harmony and respect for elders, be concerned about the harm they are doing to *their* youth? On the other hand, is it possible that the generation gap theory is merely a figment of its popularizers' imaginations, that the principal cause of youthful rebellion has been the *expectation* of that rebellion?

It is well known that impulsiveness, instant gratification, and self-indulgence are central themes of advertising and are celebrated in many films, television shows, magazine articles, and books. Is it possible that constant exposure to these themes affects people's attitudes and values and thereby shapes their behavior? Might not the tendency to act without thinking, so artfully stimulated by advertisers, spill over into other areas of life? Is it, perhaps, a causative factor in hate crimes, shoplifting (which costs an estimated $5 billion annually), and the present epidemic of sexually transmitted disease? Does the desire for instant gratification underlie drug and alcohol abuse? Might not this desire explain why today five fifteen-year-old girls in ten have had sexual intercourse, compared to one in ten in 1960? Since excellence can only be achieved by *deferring* gratification, is it unreasonable to link the decline of excellence in American society to popular culture's emphasis on instant gratification? Similarly, might not popular culture's unrelenting promotion of self-indulgence—"Let yourself go, enjoy yourself, you can have it all, you deserve pleasure, live your fantasies"—be largely responsible for social problems involving violations of other people's rights (for example, rape, spouse abuse, child molesting, and assaults on the environment)?

In recent years, addiction has become the explanation of choice for any condition of unknown cause. When people are sexually promiscuous, overeat, make themselves vomit, commit incest, gamble away the rent, or abuse alcohol, tobacco, or drugs, it is fashionable to say that they are acting under some compulsion and to encourage them to undergo years of expensive psychological counseling. If a sizable number of people are so diagnosed, a crisis is pronounced, telephone hot lines are established, and the schools are directed to initiate special courses to educate students about the problem. (At least three states—Iowa, Minnesota, and Massachusetts—now have education programs aimed at gambling "addiction.") The failure of such efforts generally prompts pleas for greater public and private financial commitment. And the depressing cycle proceeds: larger effort, more failure, more pleas, and so on. Is it possible that much of what we now call addiction is really the conditioning of popular culture and would shrink to modest proportions if the media promoted different attitudes and values?

Asking these questions is often regarded as attacking the integrity and the motives of the men and women who comprise the communications and entertainment media. This equation is reinforced when speakers at political conventions make disparaging references to "cultural elites" and suggest that media people, like the speaker's political opponents, are intentionally corrupting people's minds. Any such notion is not only uncharitable but fallacious. Although anyone is capable of acting without regard for the welfare of others, the idea that millions of people in a number of related industries are doing so in concert strains belief. It is more reasonable to believe that when people's actions harm others, it is usually in spite of their good intentions rather than because of their bad intentions. In all likelihood, the vast majority of people who promote or support popular culture believe sincerely that those values are at least harmless, perhaps even laudable. The analysis presented in succeeding chapters is offered on the premise that it is possible to challenge even the most cherished ideas without disparaging the people who hold them. If America has been seduced by nonsense, and if the social and educational problems we are experiencing are the consequence of that seduction, then the success of social and education reform will depend on our acknowledging that fact and doing something to change it.

TWO

Customized Reality

"YOU are the only thing that is real," writes New Age author Jack Underhill. "Everything else is your imagination . . . There are no victims in this life or any other. No mistakes. No wrong paths. No winners. No losers. Accept that and then take responsibility for making your life what you want it to be."[1] This message, increasingly common today, is an expression of relativism, the belief that there is no objective reality, that each of us creates his or her own reality, and that what we say is true is, by that very fact, "true for us."* Thus a critic calls *Roshomon*, a Japanese film that explores widely differing perceptions on a real (imagined?) rape, "the classic statement of the relativism, of the unknowability, of truth"; a Harvard researcher conducts research into how people "structure their reality"; Yoko Ono, in a poetic variation on the theme, proclaims that "a dream we dream alone is only a dream, but the dream we dream together is reality"; an actor describes Oliver Stone's nonfactual film *JFK* as "emotional truth"; many teachers begin their courses by

---

*Relativism should not be confused with the idea that people's actions reflect their beliefs—for example, that if you think I cheated you, you will treat me as if I did, even if I did not. Relativism says if we believe it, *it is so*.

informing students that "there are no right answers in this course" (and then proceed to administer true/false tests); respected educational psychologists such as William Perry treat relativism as a normal stage (a higher one, at that) of human intellectual development; and an accomplished scholar and author writes, "We're not missionaries; we're educators. We teach not to give students our truths but to make it possible for them to discover their own."[2]

Relativism also underlies the currently fashionable theory of literary criticism, deconstructionism. Deriving from the work of French writer Jacques Derrida, deconstructionism holds that there is no hierarchy in literature—in other words, that the quality of a work cannot be determined objectively but depends entirely on each reader's individual point of view. A work means whatever one thinks it means, and if ten people find ten different meanings, it means all of them. The question of how people with differing views can move beyond serial monologue to meaningful dialogue is judiciously ignored, as is the question of on what basis a professor grades a student's essay, which after all is a rudimentary form of literature. It would seem unfair to hold students responsible for honoring the conventions of grammar, usage, and punctuation or the principles of clarity and coherence if all those are matters of personal preference and taste.

An old philosophical idea, relativism has been given wider currency in this century by the equation of contemporary physics with everyday life.[3] Some eminent physicists, including Niels Bohr and Werner Heisenberg, have encouraged that equation. (Einstein, on the other hand, rejected it.) The idea survives in scholarly circles for a reason the layperson—indeed, *any* person who values common sense—may find difficult to understand: because many scholars treat their disciplines and their professional lives as special oases from reality. They find pleasure in highly abstract ideas and are unconcerned about whether these are affirmed or contradicted by daily experience.

This cavalier attitude notwithstanding, no theory should be excused from the test of reasonableness, which as Fulton Sheen noted, is easy to apply. "One fact," he explained, "is often the refutation of a whole philosophy. Berkeley, the English Empirical Idealist, refuted his own philosophy by dodging a runaway horse.

Diogenes answered Zeno's philosophical arguments about the impossibility of movement by walking. Henry More answered Descartes' philosophical argument of the reciprocity of movement— that it is indifferent to say that we move to our destination or our destination moves toward us—by asking Descartes the reason of fatigue after running toward his destination. Schopenhauer nullified his philosophy of cosmic suicide by dying a natural death. Mr. Chesterton upsets the extreme determinist philosopher by asking him why he says 'thank you' for the mustard."[4]

RELATIVISM EXAMINED

The central claims of relativism are that we create our own truth and therefore truth often changes, that perception equals reality, that whatever an individual believes is by that fact true for him or her. Let's examine these ideas closely and see how well they apply to everyday intellectual challenges. Scientists were absolutely certain that the coelacanth had been extinct for millions of years. But when a bathysphere descended deep into the waters of the Pacific Ocean and the crew looked out, they saw a coelacanth, some say with the hint of a smile on its ancient face. Does it make more sense to say, as relativism implies, that the crew created the truth by *looking the fish into existence*, or that they discovered the truth that the coelacanth still exists? For centuries it was believed that the human body cannot survive more than four or five minutes under water. After that length of time the brain was believed to suffer irreversible damage due to the lack of oxygen. Then in 1977 an eighteen-year-old Michigan student was trapped underwater for *thirty-eight minutes* after his car plunged into a frozen pond. Though he was pronounced dead when removed from the pond, he recovered completely and was again pursuing his college studies within two weeks. The researcher who studied this case and many others, Dr. Martin J. Nemiroff, theorizes that the coldness of the water decreases the person's need for oxygen and that an "automatic diving reflex" similar to that in whales and porpoises permits more oxygen to be channeled to the brain in emergency situations.[5] Is it more reasonable to agree with the relativists that the truth about the capacity of the human body to survive submersion changed, or merely to say that the earlier view was false?

Knowledge is constantly expanding. In 1780 there were six known planets; in 1781, seven; in 1846, eight. Today there are nine, but some astronomers suspect the existence of a tenth. The atom that was considered impossible to split is now known to be divisible. The same cigarette smoking once considered beneficial to our health has been proved harmful. And the art world was shocked some years ago to learn that the famous Rembrandt painting *The Man with the Golden Helmet* is not genuine. To speak of creating truths in such cases implies that someone constructed a planet where there was none before, that the nature of atoms is now different than it once was, that the effects of smoking on the body changed, that someone stepped back in time and changed the authorship of the painting.

How presumptuous to believe that reality is altered by our ignorance or our convenient interpretations of it. Psychologists have long wondered why Freud abandoned his theory that hysteria in women was caused by sexual abuse in childhood and embraced the view that women's claims of abuse were sexual fantasies. Jeffrey Moussalieff Masson believes the change is related to Freud's efforts to protect the reputation of a friend, ear/nose/throat specialist Wilhelm Fliess. Freud had referred a client, Emma Eckstein, to Fliess, who operated on her nose to cure her of the habit of masturbating, but accidentally left in the incision a half-meter of surgical gauze, which later caused massive bleeding. In defense of his friend, Freud argued that the cause of Eckstein's bleeding had been *longing for her psychoanalyst*.[6] Did this interpretation escape absurdity because an eminent person advanced it? Hardly.

Some years ago Donald Naftulin, a University of Southern California psychiatrist, ran a novel experiment to test the perceptiveness of mental health educators. He hired a professional actor, gave him a false name, Dr. Myron Fox, and a false *curriculum vitae*, and coached him in delivering a calculatedly nonsensical speech titled "Mathematical Game Theory as Applied to Physical Education." The actor was told to be charismatic, yet to use doubletalk and meaningless reference. The lecture was shown, variously, to psychiatrists, psychologists, social work educators, and administrators, fifty-five in all. Each was asked to complete a questionnaire. All had more favorable than unfavorable responses, often adding comments such as "Excellent presentation," "Enjoyed listening," "Good analysis," "Knowledgeable." One respondent claimed to remember having read Dr. Fox's work.[7] A relativistic interpretation robs this incident of its inherent ironic humor: the relativist must say that people heard something, they took it to be true, and so it was true, period. Yet it is precisely because we do not create truth, because even the most theoretically perceptive of us can be deceived or deceive ourselves, that the incident has meaning.

If applied consistently, relativism compels us to affirm the validity of people's statements without exception. If a man believes his wife is being unfaithful, then she is; if a student believes her roommate stole her sweater, she did. The Flat Earth Society is, of necessity, justified in its foundational premise. The neo-Nazi who says Hitler's concentration camps are a figment of Zionist imagination is correct, as of course is the survivor of the Holocaust who says, "I can testify that they existed because I was there." Saddam Hussein, as he proclaimed, really didn't invade Kuwait but merely responded to a request to "stabilize" the political situation there; on the other hand, as the United Nations declared, he *did* invade. According to relativism, when the anorexic looks at her skeletal image in the mirror and says "I'm obese," not only is she expressing an opinion to which she has a right, but we are obliged to regard her opinion as correct and to denounce as intolerant any attempt to dissuade her. Likewise, we commit an offense when we try to prevent someone from jumping from a tall building because his girlfriend jilted him and "life is no longer worth living." If he says it is not worth living, then he is unassailably right.

A true relativistic spirit would require us to be as tolerant of other cultures and other ages as we are of our own, and without qualifications or exceptions. Thus we should affirm the belief of the Yanomama Indians who inhabit the Amazonian rain forest that evil charms carry death through the air and that gremlins haunt the treetops looking for souls. We are also required to agree with the ancients that human sacrifice pleases the sun god and ensures a good harvest. If relativism is correct, all human beings enjoy, as the New Agers suggest, a mastery bordering on omnipotence. Denying the existence of cancer or AIDS provides immunity to its devastation. Turning off the television set and wishing away the savings and loan crisis and our trillion-dollar national debt achieves those ends (thereby giving new meaning to the term "voodoo economics"). And we can elimi-nate the suffering of the world's children—40,000 dying each day from starvation, war, and disease; 100 million engaged in hard labor; 80 million homeless—by simply imagining a more pleasant reality.

THE CONSEQUENCES OF RELATIVISM

If such absurdity were isolated in the realm of abstract ideas, relativism would be harmless nonsense. Instead, it has per-vaded modern thought and undermined the commonsense view of the world that took centuries to develop and on which America's achievements in every field depend. Science begins in wonder, proceeds to hypothesis, investigation or experimentation, and rigorous examination of data to prove or disprove the hypothe-sis. Epidemiologists, for example, those medical detectives who protect us from the ravages of rampant disease, thrive on inquisitiveness. They ask, among other questions, Who are the victims? What do they have in common? How do they differ from others? When exactly did they fall ill? What were they doing just before that? With whom did they associate? What were their occupations? Where did they buy their food? Research scientists are equally curious as they delve into the mysteries of the genetic code, searching for the insight that will cure cancer, Alzheimer's disease, or some other scourge. What drives them is the search for the right, the true, the only acceptable answer. Meanwhile, relativism proclaims that there is no such answer, that one view is as good as another, and wonder is without legitimate purpose or benefit. It is hardly surprising that fewer and fewer students are willing to dedicate their lives to arduous activities, such as scientific research, that seem utterly pointless.

The humanities are no better served by relativism than are the sciences. Sensitivity to the subtle cause-and-effect relation-ships that occur among people and between historical periods is a prerequisite to historical understanding; by making such relationships purely subjective and free from error, relativism denies the need for such sensitivity and for careful assessment of events.* Further, it reduces to mere fussiness the scholarly ideals of accurate reporting, separating fact from opinion, supporting assertions with evidence, and quoting precisely and citing one's sources.

This view is undoubtedly responsible for the increasing incidence of plagiarism even among the nation's social and political leaders, of dishonesty in research, and of résumé fraud. It is also responsible for the subjectivizing of journalism: if reality doesn't exist independently of people's perception and if every perception is valid, what is the point of reporting the news objectively and confining interpretation and commentary to the editorial page, and what is so wrong about altering direct quotations or endorsing products in a news story? Thus a major newspaper runs a news story on a newly formed condom club business (which mails "seasonally themed" condoms, such as glow-in-the-dark for Halloween) and *includes the company's mailing address.*[8] Similar reasoning encourages popular biographers such as Kitty Kelley to include questionably documented material in their books and the authors of film and television "docudramas" to blend reality and imagination. Oliver Stone's film *JFK* is a noteworthy example of the trend. Stone does not claim that his thesis is true but that it "speaks an inner truth." This perspective leaves no room for falsity.

The focus of logic is the quality of arguments. An argument is considered sound if both its premises are true and the reasoning from premises to conclusion is valid. It is unsound if either premise is false or if the conclusion does not follow (*non sequitur*) from the premises. Central to traditional logic is the principle of contradiction, which states that *something may not be both true and false at the same time and under the same circumstances.* (Challenge: What about the case of a person changing her name? Response: The times are different—at one time she had

*Educational Research Analysts, an education watchdog group, found almost 5,200 errors of fact in four new history texts by leading publishers. The publishers were reportedly baffled at how so many errors could have escaped notice.[9] Given the dominance of relativism, the greater wonder is that there were not more errors.

one name; then later, another. Challenge: What about $H2O$ being either liquid, solid, or gas? Response: The circumstance of temperature varies.)

The 1991 Senate hearings on the nomination of Clarence Thomas to the U.S. Supreme Court provide an apt example of the role of the principle of contradiction in serious issues. For one long weekend the Senate and the entire country wrestled with the issue of Thomas's credibility and that of his accuser, Professor Anita Hill. Relativism would suggest that there were two truths involved, her truth that he sexually harassed her and his that he didn't. But neither the Senate nor the public accepted such a view; they wanted to know not "her truth" nor "his truth," but *the* truth. The Committee's pointed and occasionally offensive questioning of the two, the long hours of testimony by people who knew them, the wide and sometimes wild speculating about possible motives, fantasizing, and so on—all of these efforts were directed toward a single purpose: deciding which person's story was true. The effort was necessary (if ultimately futile) because the two accounts were diametrically opposed and could not both be true at the same time in the same way. The American public adopted various positions on the controversy, but to my knowledge no one publicly expressed the belief that Thomas's version and Hill's version of what happened were *both accurate.* The reason no one took this view is that it is unthinkable, a logical absurdity.*

By accepting opposing arguments as equally valid, relativism denies the principle of contradiction and thus trivializes logic and weakens every domain in which logic plays a prominent role, notably our legal system. The rule of law is based on the idea that there is an objective truth, and it is unaffected by our knowledge of it or the liberties we decide to take with it. If truth were relative, consistency would demand the abandonment of our legal system. The whole point of accumulating evidence, indicting a suspect, swearing in a jury, and holding a trial is to

*Cases such as this provide compelling evidence for philosopher Mortimer Adler's view that the fundamentals of logic, like the rules of mathematics to which they are related, are not different from culture to culture but the same across cultures. It is incorrect to speak of Western logic or Oriental logic, he concludes, because logic is universal.[10]

determine the truth of the matter. Those who testify are admonished to tell not what it pleases them to think, but "the whole truth and nothing but the truth." The rules of evidence are designed to ensure that the truth emerges. If truth were relative, there could be neither victim nor perpetrator, merely individuals with different "truths"; rehabilitation would be unnecessary and punishment unfair.

In addition to influencing logic, relativism has influenced another basis of discourse, lexicography. For the past several decades, since the publication of the *Third New International Dictionary*, the philosophy of dictionary-making has changed from *prescriptive*, presenting the correct meanings of words as determined by the usage of linguistically sensitive people, to *descriptive*, presenting the meanings in common usage regardless of the users' linguistic sensitivity. A single example will suggest the effect this change has had on language: the word *fact* is now defined as "1: Something known with certainty. 2. *Something asserted as certain.* 3. Something that has been objectively verified . . . [emphasis added]."[11] The second, italicized definition affirms the notion that anything anyone asserts, however uninformed, however ludicrous, is a fact. *Not an opinion, a theory, a viewpoint, or a position, but a fact.* Thus before the time of Copernicus and Galileo, when sages asserted that the sun revolved around the earth, they were expressing a fact. By implication a rapist who says "she was asking for it" is also stating a fact—because merely saying something is so *makes* it so! The warning of ancient Greek historian Thucydides is instructive here: "A nation falls apart not when men take up arms against each other, but when key words do not mean the same thing to a majority of citizens."

Relativism's impact on logic and language explains why the level of discourse today, both public and professional, leaves so much to be desired. "Inquiring Reporter" columns, like the public opinion polls they mimic, are based on the relativistic notion that everyone's opinion is equally valid. At the time of the Iran-contra furor, one such interviewer asked a logger, a house cleaner, an executive, a carpenter, a secretary, and a dentist, "Did President Reagan know about the earlier arms sales to Iran and use of the money to finance Nicaraguan contras?"

More recently, another asked a porter, two teachers, a truck driver, a film editor, a security guard, and a secretary, "How serious is racial tension in New York?" More than likely, many of these people are not sufficiently informed about the issue to give a meaningful answer, but the interviewers are unconcerned. One is expected to answer the question: since everyone creates his or her own truth, the plea of ignorance is unacceptable. Modern psychiatry has become similarly entangled in the web of relativism. As Thomas Szasz notes, the faking of illness is now classified as an illness, specifically as a "factitious disorder." He cites the example of people who have never been in battle but who claimed to have Posttraumatic Stress Disorder being treated for a real disease. (This reasoning he compares to saying that a Picasso and a copy of a Picasso are both Picassos or that a person who pretends to be a doctor is in fact a doctor offering "factitious therapy.")[12]

An ironic effect of relativism is the anger so much in evidence in the discussion of important issues. As long as those who disagree can meet on the common ground implied by objective reality, fruitful discussion is possible. Persuasion can occur precisely because each person has an implicit commitment to something apart from and greater than his or her opinion: to the truth. But relativism removes that common ground. Each side becomes hardened in its view, and discourse degenerates into a clash of intransigents. Much of the discussion of multiculturalism fits this description. Radical feminist literature does also; consider Anne Wilson Schaef's preemptive challenge to "the white male myth of reality," significantly titled *Women's Reality*. Or consider the refusal of New York University law school students to deal with the case on the custody rights of a lesbian mother (assigned by the Law School's Moot Court): writing arguments against the mother's side, wrote one student, would be "hurtful to a group of people and thus harmful to us all."

Sadly, relativistic legal reasoning is not an affliction of students only. It is evident even in the writings of eminent jurists. Supreme Court nominee Robert H. Bork, an authority on constitutional law, observes that "like most people, judges tend to accept the assumptions of the culture that surrounds them, often without fully understanding the foundations of those assumptions or their implications." This uncritical acceptance of the reigning cultural themes, he believes, underlies "the fact that the Supreme Court has approved reverse discrimination on the basis of sex and race under a statute that clearly forbids it, found a right to abortion in the Constitution without explaining even once how that right could be derived from any constitutional materials, and came within one vote of finding a constitutional right to engage in homosexual conduct."[13]

Clearly evident in relativistic reasoning is the attitude that opinion needn't be grounded in reality; it need only express the way one wishes to think, or the way the culture at that moment deems it fashionable to think. "My argument is valid," the relativist says, "because it is my argument (my reality)." Such indifference to reality outside oneself ultimately erodes respect for other people who are, after all, realities outside oneself. The effect may not occur immediately. Relativists may affirm the rights of other people today and again tomorrow, but only because, coincidentally, they choose to affirm them, not because they believe those rights have a force independent of their affirmation. If next week they decide to deny them, they will do so regardless of tradition or reason or evidence. This indifference to reality is a more serious problem than is generally acknowledged, as Elie Wiesel noted in his Nobel Prize acceptance speech. "If there is one word that describes all the woes and threats that exist today," he explained, "it's indifference . . . Indifference, to me, is the epitome of evil. The opposite of love is not hate, it's indifference. The opposite of art is not ugliness, it's indifference. The opposite of faith is not heresy, it's indifference. The opposite of life is not death, it's indifference. Because of indifference, one dies before one actually dies."[14]

Many social critics have noted and lamented the decline of listening, but few have attempted to explain why this decline should have occurred in this so-called age of communication. The answer, I submit, is that relativism has persuaded many people that, other than for the sake of appearances, there is no good reason to listen to other people because "their truth is not my truth and my truth is sufficient unto itself." And when people talk, they are often talking for themselves with no concern about meeting the demands of logic or reasoned debate. Even scholars are adopting this debased form. In *The Book of J*, for example, literary critic Harold Bloom argues that the earliest known tests of the Hebrew Bible were not religious writings but a work of literature and that they were written by a woman. One would expect such an argument to be accompanied by evidence that readers could evaluate. However, as Bloom is quick to point out, the work is not historical scholarship at all, but a "sublime fiction." As Professor Jacob Neusner, an authority on the history of Judaism, rightly observes, discourse on Bloom's argument is impossible: ["One] can't argue with someone's intuition."[15] Precisely.

Relativism's effect on education, though subtle, has been noteworthy. By proclaiming that the truth lies inside each individual rather than in textbooks and the vast record of human inquiry, it makes grammar and syntax arbitrary, history irrelevant, geography inconsequential, math* and science unnecessary. We really should not be surprised that students who have grown up under this influence don't care about learning. *Why should they strive to master the truths of the various academic disciplines when popular culture assures them they have the power to shape all truth to their own specifications?*

Arguably the most harmful effect of relativism is that it misleads people about the way to live. It gives false hope to those who buy penny stocks over the phone, respond to chain letters with money, bet on long shots at the racetrack, and build their hope for the future on the dream of winning the lottery. It provides an excuse for every self-serving politician, every alcoholic, every harasser of women, every lazy, irresponsible lout. If psychologist Chris Thurman is correct in saying that "Most of our unhappiness and emotional struggles are caused by the lies we tell ourselves . . . and until we identify our lies and replace them with the truth, emotional well-being is impossible,"[16] then relativism must be counted a formidable impediment to happiness, for it promotes denial, projection, wishful thinking, and

---

*It may be that much of the disinterest in mathematics is due to the fact that even elementary study of it exposes the emptiness of relativism: no matter how strong one's belief that he creates reality, two plus two cannot be made to equal five.

other forms of self-deception. Moreover, it frustrates what may well be the most important human drive, *the drive for meaning*. This drive, according to Austrian psychologist Viktor Frankl, is more fundamental than Freud's sex drive or Adler's drive for power. Long after the concentration camp experience had stilled those urges, Frankl (himself an inmate) found, the drive for meaning burned bright, enabling many to survive unspeakable treatment.[17] The search for meaning in our lives entails sorting out and classifying experience, and this process is possible only if we distinguish between good and evil, truth and falsehood, profundity and superficiality, logic and illogic, reality and illusion, excellence and mediocrity, knowledge and ignorance, wisdom and foolishness. But relativism obliterates distinctions: "One person's good," it argues, "is another's evil; your truth may be my falsehood. Everything is a matter of perspective."

A REASONABLE VIEW OF REALITY

To equate reality and truth with our individual perception, even if we grant others a similar equation, is the height of arrogance. If we all create our own truth, then everyone is always right, no one is ever wrong, and dialogue is meaningless. Albert Schweitzer's "reverence for life" is no better than a serial killer's bloodlust; Mother Teresa is no more admirable than Charles Manson; caring for children is no more laudable than abusing them. Carried to its logical conclusion, relativism would halt the printing presses, end all inquiry, and shut down the schools and the courts of law.

To deal with the challenges life poses for us, we need a view of reality that gives us more helpful guidance. The first requirement of that view is that it be compatible with everyday experience. Reality precedes human theories about it. If existing theories (such as relativism) conflict with everyday experience, good sense demands that we reject the theories, not deny reality. The second requirement is that it encourage reflection and careful judgment. All higher-order thinking involves evaluation and judgment, which imply weighing and sorting ideas, separating the unworthy from the worthy and the more worthy from the less. Problem solving seeks the most effective solution; issue analysis, the most reasonable viewpoint; decision making, the wisest course of action. Because relativism holds that all ideas are equally valid, it discourages judgment. What, after all, is the point of monitoring our mental processes if any thought we think is true because we think it? Why be vigilant if there is nothing to be vigilant about?

Our view of reality should also give us the confidence necessary to address difficult questions. The enthusiasm with which we approach challenges is directly proportionate to our conviction that there are truths to discover and that anything less than truth is unsatisfactory. Does God exist? Is there a black hole at the center of the star cluster known as M15? What is causing the puzzling, uniformly disturbed bursts of gamma radiation detected by NASA's observatory—dark matter, exotic objects on the fringe of the solar system, cosmic strings, neutron stars, or something else? Is class size a significant factor in learning? Has child abuse increased over the last half-century? Does a permissive upbringing tend to produce caring, other-directed individuals? Are Drs. Herman Sno and Don Linszen right in believing that the experience known as *deja vu* is really a false memory triggered by a present experience that has something in common with a past one? What caused the mass extinction of dinosaurs millions of years ago? Which, if any, of the thirty-odd vaccines that have been developed to treat AIDS will reverse the deadly disease? What harm, if any, does the use of growth hormones in cattle do to humans? Many cosmologists have pronounced the long-accepted Big Bang theory flawed—what theory will ultimately be proved correct? What harm, if any, does mercury amalgam vapor, once widely used in dental fillings, actually do to people? The men and women who devote their lives to answering these questions and millions of similarly difficult questions in every area of inquiry are sustained by their belief that there are truths to know and discovering them is worth the effort.

Finally, our view of reality and truth should reflect what we know of our human nature. Everyday experience illustrates our fallibility. All too often we perceive selectively, form opinions carelessly, forget important information, oversimplify complex matters, and draw hasty conclusions. We need to be reminded that no matter how educated or gifted we are, there is still much we don't know, and this understanding must prevent us from taking things for granted, must keep us curious and ever questioning: "Has my analysis penetrated deep enough?" "Is there a more reasonable belief?" "Is there a more effective approach?" Life is full of paradoxes, ironies, surprises—they make life interesting. Who could have guessed, for example, that Billy Tipton, the famous jazz musician, was in reality a woman? The deception had begun when Tipton was a teenager and was detected only by "his" wife, who kept the secret even from their three adopted sons. Millions who knew "him" personally or through "his" work had no doubt "he" was a man. Only when "he" died in 1989 and an autopsy was performed was the deception discovered. Those who seek the truth outside their own minds are able to be surprised by life, unaccepting of inconsistency and contradiction, and eager to grow in wisdom.

It is crucial that we dispel the confusion and misunderstanding relativism has created about truth. Philosopher Charles S. Peirce's definition is admirably precise: "The opinion which is fated to be ultimately agreed to by all who investigate is what we mean by the truth, and the object represented in this opinion is the real."[18] More simply, truth is *correspondence with reality*. Whatever agrees with reality is true; whatever disagrees is false. Many modern philosophers refuse to accept this definition.* Nevertheless, it continues to enjoy the unqualified endorsement of common sense. As George Santayana rightly observed, "You cannot prove realism to a complete skeptic or idealist, but you can show an honest man that he is not a complete skeptic or idealist, but a realist at heart. So long as he is alive his sincere philosophy must fulfill the assumptions of his life and not destroy them."[20]

---

*Immanuel Kant set the course for this rejection by denying not the existence of reality independent of the mind, but the knowability of that reality. Martin Heidegger, while not initially denying correspondence between truth and reality, focused his attention on the *basis* of correspondence, which he argued was the open realm in which reality and assertion meet and truth is created. Heidegger's error, according to William Barrett, lay in thinking his idea was not compatible with correspondence theory. In fact, says Barrett, "Heidegger's theory should be added to the tradition and not seek to replace it." [19]

Much of the confusion and error of relativism is caused by careless use of language—specifically, the equation of the terms *truth* and *belief*. It is quite correct to say that people's perceptions differ and that what they perceive to be so, they will believe to be so. But it is also correct to say that biases and preconceptions can distort perception. I recently saw a greeting card that expressed this idea nicely: "Sometimes we see things not as they are but as we are." This is why, as Professor Elizabeth Loftus explains in her fascinating book *Eyewitness Testimony*, what people swear that they saw is often very different from what occurred. Accordingly, it is incorrect to say that what people believe is necessarily true. Wherever relativists speak of "my truth" or "his or her truth," it would be more appropriate to use the term *belief*.* Like the words *hypothesis, assertion, theory,* and *contention*, the word *belief* refers to point of view, the correctness of which is not to be assumed, but remains to be demonstrated. This linguistic change would in no way compromise the much-vaunted "right" to hold an opinion, but it would perhaps serve as a reminder that although everyone is entitled to an opinion, responsible people rest their case on evidence rather than on mere entitlement.

That we do not create truth, but discover it (often with considerable difficulty) is affirmed by thoughtful men and women in every field. "The most essential value in history," according to Diane Ravitch, is "the search for truth."[22] Philosopher Israel Scheffler affirms that reality is "independent of human wish and will," adding that "interpretation must . . . be interpretation of something, and that something must itself be independent of interpretation if the interpretive process is not to collapse into arbitrariness."[23] "A subjective experience, or a feeling of conviction," Karl Popper argues, "can never justify a scientific statement," and he continues:

---

*The same holds true for scholarly discussions about changing viewpoints in light of new evidence. For example, the statement "As academics we have recognizable ways of *changing* the truth: We do research, we find evidence, we test hypotheses against test cases . . . The process can maintain its integrity only if it allows *new truths* to emerge,"[21] is more accurately expressed ". . . ways of *discovering* the truth . . . allows *the truth* to emerge."

Thus I may be utterly convinced of the truth of a statement; certain of the evidence of my perceptions; overwhelmed by the intensity of my experience: every doubt may seem to me absurd. But does this afford the slightest reason for science to accept my statement? . . . The answer is, "No"; and any other answer would be incompatible with the idea of scientific objectivity. . . From the epistemological point of view, it is quite irrelevant whether my feeling of conviction was strong or weak; whether it came from a strong or even irresistible impression of indubitable certainty (or "self-evidence"), or merely from a doubtful surmise. None of this has any bearing on the question of how scientific statements can be justified.[24]

In a related manner, Nobel Laureate physicist Richard P. Feynman writes, "The first principle [of scientific integrity] is that you must not fool yourself—and you are the easiest person to fool. So you have to be very careful about that. After you've not fooled yourself, it's easy not to fool other scientists."[25]

The view of truth presented here poses no danger of the absolutism or dogmatism that relativists are forever warning us of. Nor does it in any way deny life's complexities. Because things are not always what they seem, circumstances often do alter cases, and our fallibility and the imprecision of our tools can prevent us from discovering particular truths for hundreds, even thousands of years, we should be slow to claim certainty and willing to discard any belief, no matter how cherished, when there is sufficient evidence to do so. But these important qualifications in no way dispute the idea that there is a reality outside the human mind and that the search for that reality leads to knowledge and wisdom.

THREE

The Idolized
Self

The year was 1987, the occasion the opening banquet of the National Council of the States on In-Service Education, an organization concerned with the continuing education of the nation's teachers. The keynoter, a well-known motivational speaker, asserted that 85 percent of success is self-confidence, and that it doesn't matter whom you know* or what you know, but what you think of yourself. Additional proclamations included that the biggest problem in education is students' low self-esteem; "Success is living your life the way you choose"; and "If you believe you're right, you're right; if you believe you're wrong, you're wrong." The audience of educators vigorously applauded this speaker. No one stormed out during her talk. No one rose to ask, "If what we know doesn't count at all, where does that leave education and what's the point of this conference?" or "Does living as one chooses mean a sense of responsibility is passé?" or "Aren't the penitentiaries filled with people who believed they were right when they were wrong?" Interesting and appropriate questions, but it's no surprise they went begging. Self-esteem has become the leading theory of intellec-

*She actually said "who you know," perhaps to illustrate her subjectivist philosophy.

tual development and academic achievement. Teachers are advised that they must accept children as they are, praise and encourage them, and shield their self-image from damage. In practical terms, this is achieved by avoiding criticism of children's behavior and setting standards that prevent failure and guarantee success (translation, not demanding much of them). Stroking psyches replaces stretching minds.

So powerful has the self-esteem movement grown that it now has it own annual conference. Hundreds of books, musical programs, training materials, and entire curricula are available. Special school assemblies are held and students encouraged to stand and give testimonials about how wonderful they are. (Such spectacles are supposed to increase achievement.) A number of states are finding money for self-esteem programs in schools, while funds for laboratory supplies and teachers' aides are in short supply. One such program, Power of Positive Students, boasts the participation of five thousand schools. And the influence of self-esteem proponents goes far beyond the schoolhouse. A number of states have established self-esteem task forces, Rhode Island Senator Claiborne Pell announced his intention to introduce legislation for a National Commission on Self-Esteem, and many people regard building self-esteem as a social vaccine against dysfunctional behavior, a way of making people more productive, a basis for solving all social problems.

I was walking in a mall recently and overheard a teenage boy brush past a middle-aged woman and remark, "Get out of my way. . . ." (There followed an obscene reference to her anatomy.) A week or so later I boarded a plane and put my garment bag in the overhead bin across from my aisle seat. Soon another passenger came in, pulled my bag out of the overhead bin, *threw it on the floor,* put his bag in its place, and became furious when I demanded that he return my bag to the bin. According to the self-esteem theory both these individuals—and indeed all rude, irresponsible, even criminal people—are suffering from a poor sense of self-worth and need to have their confidence restored. It is curious that an age so downright skeptical about everything else, including morality and religion, could embrace this psychological theory as an article of faith, exempt from the normal process of inquiry to which we subject other ideas. For that reason alone it is prudent to examine self-esteem's lineage and implications.

THE ROOTS OF SELF-ESTEEM THEORY

Self-esteem theory is an outgrowth of humanistic psychology. This psychology, a reaction against the reductionism of Freudian and behavioral psychology ("humans are nothing but a collection of urges or stimulus-response bonds"), affirms the special dignity and worth of the human person. For this reason it is commonly viewed as compatible with or even a secular extension of the Judeo-Christian perspective. In fact, however, it is very different. Judeo-Christianity claims that human beings have an immortal soul created in the image and likeness of God and a nature flawed by original sin; humanistic psychology is based on the Rousseauvian idea that man is inherently good but is corrupted by society. Eric Berne put it, "We are born princes and the civilizing process makes us frogs."

Humanistic psychology has unceremoniously displaced the concept of soul with the concept of self. Like the former, the latter is considered a mystical inner reality, but with a significant difference—it is not subordinate to God. The soul finds fulfillment in its Creator, the self in itself. It is precisely this difference that has made humanistic psychology vulnerable to extreme interpretations and applications. In 1925, more than a quarter of a century before humanistic philosophy was established, Bishop Fulton Sheen published his masterful analysis of modern philosophy, *God and Intelligence in Modern Philosophy*, warning against "the divinization of human intelligence . . . [and] human nature."[1] Ignoring that warning, or perhaps oblivious of it, pioneering humanistic psychologists Carl Rogers and Abraham Maslow flirted with equating the human and the divine. Rogers did so by asserting that the only important question for a psychologically healthy person is "Am I living in a way which is deeply satisfying to me, and which truly expresses me?" and in claiming that "when an activity *feels* as though it is valuable or worth doing, it *is* worth doing."[2] Abraham Maslow did so by placing self-esteem and self-actualization at the pinnacle of his well-known hierarchy of human needs.*

With the advent of New Age thinking, this flirtation became a marriage and humanity was divinized. Shirley MacLaine claims to be guided by Ramtha, a 35,000-year-old master from Atlantis who informs her that "God is within." MacLaine spreads the holy word in her writing, her "Connecting with the Higher Self" seminars, and her television appearances, telling her audiences it is blasphemy to worship anything but themselves.[3] New Ager J. Z. Knight appears on television and explains how she appeals to "the Lord God within me."[4] Swami Muktananda advises his flock: "God dwells within you as you; worship your Self."[5] Science fiction writer Ray Bradbury writes, "[T]he living God is not out there. He is here . . . [Human beings] must stand as God. Not *represent* Him, not *pretend* to be Him, not deny Him, but simply, nobly, frighteningly, *be* Him . . . We are God giving Himself a reason for being."[6] And best-selling author and psychiatrist M. Scott Peck writes as follows:

> If you want to know the closest place to look for grace, it is within yourself. If you desire wisdom greater than your own, you can find it inside you . . . To put it plainly our unconscious is God. God is within us . . . Since the unconscious is God all along, we may further define the goal of spiritual growth to be the attainment of godhood by the conscious self. It is for the individual to become totally, wholly God . . . We are born that we might become, as a conscious individual, a new life form of God.[7]

As an exercise in irony, consider all the people through the ages who were locked away in asylums or executed for claiming that they were God. Had they not been born too soon, they might have enjoyed a more pleasant fate as gurus of selfism.

Even religious leaders have gotten caught up in the selfism craze, undoubtedly because they fail to recognize its inherent rejection of traditional religion. The most notable example is the

---

*It bears repeating that I am speaking here not of the intentions of Rogers and Maslow, but of the practical implications and consequences of their ideas, which may have been very different from what they had in mind. Nor am I denying the value of their other contributions.

prolific and influential author and preacher, Robert Schuller, whose enthusiastic, uncritical endorsement of self-esteem is unparalleled in religious or secular experience. According to Schuller: "A person is in hell when he has lost his self esteem"; "The will to 'self-love' is the deepest of all human desires"; "The core of original sin . . . is an innate inability to adequately value ourselves"; and " . . . The core of sin is a lack of self-esteem."[8] (The application of this new theology is not always consistent: a Catholic scholar blames masturbation on a lack of self-esteem, while a Presbyterian committee recommends masturbation as a *cure* for lack of self-esteem.[9]) Such endorsements explain why so many self-help books focus on self-exaltation and self-congratulation rather than self-examination and self-criticism. They also explain why useful terms such as *egocentrism* (excessive self-absorption, the fault of Narcissus)* and *ethnocentrism* (excessive group-centeredness) have vanished, why the term *personality differences* has replaced *character*, why so much is said about rights and so little about responsibilities, and why lack of concern over other people is fast becoming the norm in America.

THE ERROR OF SELFISM

Assertions about the exalted nature of the self are not supported by everyday experience. When psychologist Will Schutz, speaking for Everyperson, chants, "I am everywhere, I am omniscient, I am God,"[10] reality mockingly replies, "Then how come you can't find your glasses half the time, remember people's names, balance your checkbook, or program your VCR? Why, in your holy name, are you worried about gaining weight and losing your job and afraid to walk alone outside your neighborhood at night? And why are you so easily deceived without being aware of the fact?" Just how easily are people deceived? When experimenters in the 1950s put catsup in a milk bottle and milk in a catsup bottle, people called them red milk and white catsup, respectively. Similarly, many people believe that larger chunks

*Theologian Thomas Howard believes the best interpretation of the concept of original sin is that it was an act of egocentrism.[11] This view diametrically opposes theological selfism.

of coffee produce richer-tasting coffee. And when Corningware changed the name of a baking dish from "Gourmet" to "French White" and the picture on the box from shrimp to a pot roast, sales doubled.[12] If we forgetful, gullible, anxious, bumbling creatures are God, we are all in bigger trouble than we might imagine. The idea that God is dead and we all must face existential dread, as Camus and others said, may have been erroneous, but at least it was not as transparently foolish as the divinization of Everyperson.

New Age author Nathaniel Branden says, "It's impossible to have too much self-esteem" and reminds us that self-esteem concerns not what others think of us, but what we think of ourselves.[13] On a recent talk-show, when discussion turned to a topic of special fascination to celebrities, their view of self, actress Joan Collins explained that she had learned to like herself and opined that this lesson is important for everyone.[14] A Los Angeles sales trainer advises his clients:

> Whenever you hear yourself thinking a negative, immediately translate it into a positive. That's how it goes away and that's the only way... Say you get conscious that [*sic*] you tell yourself "I'm a procrastinator." The instant you realize that, block the negative and replace it with: "I'm decisive." Or "impatient" becomes "I am patient." "Too talkative" becomes "I'm a listener"... Flood your brain with statements like "I'm graceful"; "I'm smart"; "I'm a people-person." Once you start focusing on the positives, the negative side has to go away. It can't survive if you don't feed it. Pretty soon, your brain will begin expecting positives and once that happens, there's no limit to what you'll get done.[15]

To appreciate the asinity of this program for instant competency, consider whether you would get into a plane with someone whose only flight training was an interminable chanting of "I am a talented pilot" or whether you would submit to an operation by a medical layman who persuaded himself that he was a surgeon.

The implication in these cases, as in all expressions of selfism, is that *everyone is already talented or likable and need only accept the fact*. What a foolish notion. As if people's self-estimates were always too low, as if they never lied to themselves and rationalized so as to justify unjustifiable behavior! Consider the case of the Florida widow and her stepdaughters who were so adamant about their conflicting claims to the ashes of the deceased that a circuit court judge (not named Solomon) had no alternative but to divide the poor fellow into equal piles. Or the father who viciously punched his four-year-old in the head and ground her face into the floor because she spilled a few french fries in a restaurant. Or the Hicksville, New York, school bus driver who pleaded guilty to raping and sodomizing sixteen kindergarten youngsters.

It is a strange logic indeed that demands we stifle our revulsion, empathize with those who do vile things, and urge them to like themselves more. The gurus of selfism have an obligation to explain precisely how a transfusion of self-esteem will help such people reform, how their believing "I am a good person, a wonderful person; I am God" will lead to the acknowledgment of their crimes and the resolution to offend no more. Common sense suggests it will lead, instead, to a feeling of empowerment, justification, and transcendence of law and morality. Is it merely an ironic coincidence that since self-esteem has reigned, crime has increased? Is it coincidence that such bizarre and wanton offenses as random drive-by shootings, satanic cult torture, cannibalism, and serial killing have become almost commonplace? I think not.

Selfists postulate a perfect inner self that somehow remains insulated from all outside influence. "You are unique in all the world, an individual," they advise; "look inside yourself, see your true self, *be* that self, and resist those who would have you be different." (With such counsel abroad, little wonder that parents have such difficulty socializing their children.) Behaviorism may have contributed more error than insight about the human condition, but it deserves credit for demonstrating the reality of human conditioning—we are impressionable even *in utero* and we continue to be so throughout our lives. That is why abused children tend to become child abusers, unloved people unloving, neglected individuals neglectful. Evidence of human imitativeness is inescapable. For decades basketball players wore their shorts as tight as possible; they'd have rather given up the sport than wear baggy shorts. Today they all wear shorts three sizes too large and sagging below the knees. Why? Because of one man, the same one who singleheadedly popularized the bald look, Michael Jordan. Why does every other teenage girl, and more than a few women, look as if she's put her underwear on over her clothes? Because one woman, Madonna, embraced that bizarre mode of dress. Few boys or girls, men or women, would acknowledge being influenced by these or any other fashions, including language fashions. Yet when one prominent sportscaster (Howard Cosell?) incorrectly used the comparative *more* in place of the superlative *most*, other sportswriters and even scholars imitated the error. Today we're as likely to hear a college professor say "She is one of the *more* perceptive individuals on the committee" as we are to hear "He is one of the *more* versatile players in the game." Similarly, when a member of the White House staff used the word *gravitas*, columnists around the country immediately injected it into their writing and counted themselves original.

So it goes with everyday experience. What we hear and see enters our minds, mingles with what is already there, and creates the illusion that it all originated with us. That illusion is among the greatest obstacles to authentic individuality. Only when we acknowledge our vulnerability to outside influences are we able to be curious about our beliefs and values, weigh conflicting ideas, and make wise choices. But such an admission requires intellectual humility, that awareness of imperfection that is anathema to selfism.

Some of the most damning evidence against selfism comes from research done on self-esteem. Neuroscience researcher David Shannahoff-Khalsa challenges the alleged benefits of enhanced self-esteem, citing studies of international math performance. In one such study, American students boasted that they would score the highest on an examination, and South Koreans believed they would score the lowest. The reverse occurred.[16] A Purdue University study comparing the problem-solving performances of a high self-esteem group and a low group concluded that "the higher the self-esteem, the poorer the performance."[17] Moreover, a National Institute of Mental Health study found no significant relationship between low self-esteem and juvenile delinquency.[18] And Yochelon and Samenow's research with over two hundred criminals revealed that every single one "thought of himself as a basically good person . . . even when planning a crime."[19]

No reasonable person would deny that we need a measure of confidence in our basic capacity before we can ever accomplish anything, whether it be mastering a subject in school, solving a problem at work, or succeeding in a relationship. Such faith is a prerequisite to effort, so when we sell ourselves short, we invariably reach too low and end up doing, having, and being less than we might. The error of selfism is that it has taken this useful insight and inflated it into an absolute value, indeed an idol.* Unqualified acceptance of self is as extreme and unreasonable as unqualified rejection of self. Each of us is, in a sense, two selves, an ideal self and an actual self. The ideal self exists in our hopes and dreams and plans for the future. With the passing of time it may change or be forgotten, but the smallest of events—the sight of a child kissing her mother, an old photograph or song—can bring it vividly to mind. Perhaps the best men and women among us manage to merge that ideal self with the actual, but they are the exceptions. The rest of us must live with the knowledge that we have not achieved our goal. This knowledge may sadden us, but it is never negative as long as we aspire to become that ideal self.

The essential error of selfism is that it transforms "I can be" into "I already am."** It emphasizes accepting what we are rather than becoming what we might or should be; therefore, it discards the entire network of values that *becoming* implies.

*Historian Arnold Toynbee explained that "idolatry may be defined as an intellectually and morally purblind worship of the part instead of the whole, of the creature instead of the Creator, of time instead of eternity. . . In practical life this moral aberration may take the comprehensive form of an idolization of the idolater's own personality, or own society. . ."[20]

** There is a more modest form of selfism that asserts, "I have unlimited potential to become anything I wish." This has a measure of validity in the moral sphere: each of us can be truthful, faithful, fair in our dealings with others, and caring. But it is invalid when applied to careers. Not everyone has the grace to become a ballet dancer, the speed to become a sprinter, the manual dexterity to become a brain surgeon—at least not in the context of competency or excellence. Instead of telling children, "You can be anything you want," we ought to tell them, "Try to excel in as many activities as you can so that you can find those for which you have unusual potential."

Thomas Harris's well-known expression "I'm OK—You're OK," which he claims describes the healthy person's emotional outlook, is a typical example of this error. The truly healthy outlook is not uncritical acceptance of self (or of other people). Rather, it is positive curiosity and openness to the truth, however unpleasant that might be, and is best expressed as "Like others, I have the potential to be OK, but that doesn't mean I have actualized that potential in every situation." Only this formulation reflects the wisdom of Socrates' admonitions "know thyself" and "the unexamined life is not worth living."

Acknowledging the distinction between "I can be" and "I am" enables us to ask the question that is fundamental to genuine self-improvement: "Exactly *when* should we feel good about ourselves?" And the answer is simple: We should feel good about ourselves when our conduct warrants that feeling. When we behave wretchedly toward others (or toward ourselves, as in the case of substance abuse), we should feel wretched. Thus, saying *mea culpa* when the facts warrant it is emotionally healthy. Similarly, self-loathing can be a positive reaction, provided the behavior in question was really loathsome and the reaction leads not to despair, but to a commitment to do better in the future. Is it possible to be too scrupulous or too lax in our self-assessments? Of course, but there is little danger of either of those extremes as long as we are guided by reasonableness and honesty and we maintain the baseline, empowering view, "I can," which for the religious believer takes the form, "I can with God's grace." What is necessary to function effectively in life is not feeling good about ourselves but understanding our possibilities for change.

This view is more realistic than selfism. It acknowledges the most obvious fact about humanity, a fact prerequisite to the practice of charity toward others: that we are not all we could be. It also acknowledges the possibility of improvement. Compared to "Take heart, you can be better than you now are," selfism's "Rejoice! You are wonderful" is an empty anthem. Moreover, as psychologist/attorney Barbara Lerner points out, selfist advocacy of "feel good now" self-esteem, rather than "earned" self-esteem is pessimistic and demeaning. It regards people as emotionally fragile, unable to cope with frustration and failure, and unfit for everyday life.[21]

THE LEGACY OF SELFISM

"When the habitual behavior of a man or an institution is false, the next step is complete demoralization," writes José Ortega y Gasset. The false view of self promoted by humanistic psychology and the false view of truth promulgated by relativism have aggravated serious social problems and undermined the habits and attitudes required to solve those problems. Consider, for example, the debilitating confusion caused by selfism's simultaneous suggestion that everyone is God and can do whatever he or she wishes, yet everyone is a victim of one kind or another in desperate need of a massive injection of self-esteem. This was perfectly illustrated on a talk-show dealing with date rape. A confessed date rapist said, "I am not a bad person," and the audience loudly booed the statement. Then later, a woman in the audience said to the same man, "Don't you have enough self-esteem to avoid such behavior?"[22]

Over the last couple of decades the lexicon of *self*-words has been purged of all terms selfists regard as negative. Banished are *self-centered* (as a pejorative), *self-criticism, self-denial, self-discipline, self-control, self-effacement, self-mastery, self-reproach,* and *self-sacrifice.* Even *self-knowledge* and *self-respect* are in disrepute, the former because it implies that we don't already know ourselves perfectly, and the latter because it implies certain qualifying conditions. Remaining are *self-confidence, self-contentment, self-expression, self-assertion, self-indulgence, self-realization, self-approval, self-actualization,* even *self-worship.* According to selfist theory, the resulting view of ourselves and our relationships with one another should be salutary: more and more people should experience happiness and satisfaction in life. But the reverse seems to be occurring. Many people don't bother to thank the stranger who holds the door, tip the waiter who serves them efficiently and cheerfully, or acknowledge the kindnesses of friends and co-workers. They curse their parents for giving them an imperfect childhood, their teachers for not providing a flawless education, their country for having been historically less than utopian. Obsessed with their rights, they go through life with an attitude of entitlement; they are so fixated on the superior treatment others owe them that they cannot experience the appreciation and gratitude indispensable to inner peace and contentment. Expecting too much, they are never satisfied.

In a thoughtful article entitled "Our Fixation on Rights," University of Oregon law professor David Schuman calls the present concern in this country over individual rights "dysfunctional and deranged." Rejecting both the liberal idea that such rights are too few or too weak and the conservative idea that they are too numerous and too strong, he argues that the "fixation" on rights breeds "separation, exclusion, and alienation" and magnifies the tendency to see other people as "potential oppressors and threats."* What America urgently needs, in Schuman's view, is a new perspective on rights, one which places them in the context of community and the "shared quest for a common definition of the good life."[23]

When people believe that they must have unconditional self-esteem, and that negative thoughts about themselves destroy their mental health, they are certainly not inspired to evaluate their thoughts and actions, acknowledge their mistakes, or change their minds. Rather, they are prompted to defend themselves against all doubts, *even those that arise in their own minds.* Defending what they say and do becomes a sacred mission; changing their minds and compromising with others seems a form of emotional suicide. Thus *feeling* offended by others will constitute *proof* that others have offended them, and they will make no allowance for their own misunderstanding, hypersensitivity, or overreaction. The idea that *they* have committed an offense and are merely projecting their guilt on others (a possibility always worth considering) will be unthinkable to them. That this is a fairly common response to everyday living no doubt accounts for the growing number of people in various kinds of psychotherapy and for the relatively low success rate of all therapy. It's not easy to help people overcome their personal problems when they are convinced that they have none and that

---

*One measure of that tendency is the fact that rage now enjoys its own academic conference. Entitled "Rage Across the Disciplines," it was held at California State University in San Marcos in June 1993. The call for papers encouraged papers and performances on "AIDS or gay rage, women's rage, the rage of ethnic minorities or working class rage."

other people are to blame for their difficulties. Nor are people who are absorbed in themselves or consumed by self-pity likely to avail themselves of such traditional solutions as visiting a hospital cancer ward or turning their thoughts to abused children or the homeless, and thereby seeing their problems and grievances from a different perspective.

Selfism promises freedom but produces only a different confinement that is ultimately more oppressive for being utterly familiar and inescapable. In a prison of brick and mortar, one can turn inward, but where does one turn from the prison of inwardness? The celebration of diversity and multiculturalism seems to offer a way out, but inevitably disappoints. As long as popular culture proclaims that everyone creates his or her own reality (relativism) and emotional health requires unconditional acceptance of self (selfism), diversity and multiculturalism will mean, at best, separatism, and at worst, factionalism. The animosity and resentment evident in gender feminism,* white and black racism, and other forms of political correctness can only be cured by disavowing stereotypes, by resisting misconceptions and rash judgments, and by realizing that every human being shares the same human nature—that we are all brothers and sisters, children of God. When we are tempted to think otherwise, we should remember the wisdom of Shylock, the Merchant of Venice, offered to the culture that alienated him: "Hath not a Jew eyes? hath not a Jew hands, organs, dimensions, senses, affections, passions?" and "If you prick us, do we not bleed? if you tickle us, do we not laugh? if you poison us, do we not die? and if you wrong us, shall we not revenge?" While there is nothing inherently wrong with diversity, it is *unity* that is lacking today, and selfism is undermining its restoration.

Selfism, like relativism, has contributed to the decline of excellence in America by elevating the song "I Did It My Way" to a philosophy of life. (Wonderful tune, disastrous philosophy.) For every person for whom "doing it my way" has proved wise, there are a hundred or so for whom it has been foolish and harmful, including heavy smokers and drinkers, gamblers, lazy

---

*I use the term *gender feminism* to mean extreme feminism that holds, among other views, that all men are chauvinist villains and that women who love them and seek harmony with them are traitors to their gender.

workers, procrastinators, liars and cheaters, assorted trouble-makers, and neglectful children, spouses, and parents. Excellence means doing things the best way, and that is not always the easiest or most comfortable way. Under the best of circumstances, people tend to be stubborn about acknowledging their limitations. But selfism intensifies the tendency. "Self-love," La Rochefoucauld noted, "is the greatest of all flatterers." By filling us with pride, it deprives us of the humility needed to learn from others and so imprisons us in our limitations. "Whoever exalts himself will be humbled" (Matt. 23:12) has a secular as well as a theological dimension. Feeling unqualifiedly good about ourselves invites the illusion that self-improvement is unnecessary, that our habits and attitudes are already admirable. The self-validating rejoinder we so often hear people express when they are criticized, "That's the way I am," carries an additional, unstated implication—*"and it's wonderful!"* Were it not for several decades of conditioning by selfism, the silliness of that implication would be evident to us, as it was to satirist Ambrose Bierce when he wrote his *Devil's Dictionary*, first published in 1911. A brief sampling of his definitions will reveal what he thought about this human inclination to self-flattery:

Absurdity—a statement of belief manifestly inconsistent with one's own opinion.

Bigot—one who is obstinately and zealously attached to an opinion that you do not entertain.

Egotist—a person of low taste, more interested in himself than in me.

I—the first letter of the alphabet, the first word of the language, the first thought of the mind, the first object of affection.

Man—an animal so lost in rapturous contemplation of what he thinks he is as to overlook what he indubitably ought to be.

Self-evident—evident to one's self and to nobody else.

Self-esteem—an erroneous appraisement.

Yet another legacy of selfism is the rejection of the Golden Rule in human relations. At first consideration, it might seem that the idea that everyone is God would promote harmony and mutual respect. But it doesn't work that way—the human propensity to put self before others doesn't vanish just because a foolish age chooses to deny it. Selfism gives the commandment to worship God a self-serving reading—"I am the Lord *my* God; I shalt not have strange gods before me"—thus encouraging unconcern, if not contempt, for others. As Peggy Rosenthal rightly observes, the emphasis on fulfilling self tends to be unhealthy to those nearby: "Clinging to the developmental ladder for support, focusing my attention upward to the goal of self-fulfillment, I don't notice that my colleague next to me is overworked, or that my elderly neighbor needs a ride to the doctor, or that my children, playing on the steps, have been crushed beneath my feet as I triumphantly raise myself to the next rung."[24]

Christianity has always taught the necessity of dying to self and becoming humble servants of God. The saints and holy people held up as models of emulation put self last rather than first. *Selflessness* was considered healthy, *selfishness* unhealthy. But selfism reverses these classifications. Those who dedicate their lives to helping others are regarded as emotionally ill. For example, a talk-show host used the phrase "disease to please" to refer to women who are eager to please their husbands. Not surprisingly, this happened on a show featuring singer/actress Cher, whom the host and the audience praised for living as she wishes.[25]

Of course, it is possible to focus on serving other people to the point of neglecting one's own needs, but one doesn't need more than rudimentary powers of observation to see that the *opposite* problem is plaguing America. The most alarming increase is in the number of self-absorbed individuals and organizations who demand their rights but ignore the rights of others, who in the pursuit of their own narrow interests would foul the air, contaminate water systems, destroy rain forests, wipe out animal populations, ruin the economy, and threaten the future of the nation. Out of the thousands of examples that might be cited, consider just one: the National Rifle Association's outrageous campaign on behalf of assault weapons. With violent criminals and psychopaths using such weapons, the police in mortal danger, and the general public increasingly apprehensive, we might think the NRA would concede, "These are unusual times and we will gladly accept this minor compromise of our right to bear arms in order to increase public safety." But instead they remain intransigent and, from all indications, uncaring.

The increase in the number of psychopaths among us may be the most frightening legacy of selfism. Although no definitive connection has been established between psychopathology and a preoccupation with the self, the characteristics of the psychopath—supreme egocentrism, incapacity to feel empathy or love, and lack of shame, guilt, or remorse—are strikingly similar to the characteristics of extremely self-centered people. The constant repetition of selfist slogans, while probably not causing psychopathology, surely provides a fertile climate for its activation.

A BALANCED VIEW OF SELF

Any view that would lay claim to the title "humanistic" should, as a minimal requirement, reflect everyday experience and help people live more meaningful lives. Humanistic psychology does neither. Though the goal its authors sought was worthy—displacing the prevailing reductionist psychology—in the end they merely exchanged one extreme for another. In other words, they were right in protesting the notion that man is merely an animal, but tragically mistaken in implying that man is divine. Now we desperately need a corrective to the corrective, a balanced, realistic view of human nature that is simultaneously devoid of false promises and full of hope. Before addressing that view, it may be helpful to examine critically Abraham Maslow's famous theory of human needs, which continues to occupy a central place in the literature of selfism.

Maslow expressed his theory in the form of a pyramid, each level representing a particular set of needs. From base to peak, the needs are: (1) physiological (food, shelter, and clothing), (2) belongingness and love, (3) self-esteem, (4) aesthetic and cognitive (intellectual), and (5) self-actualization.* The fulfillment of

*Over the years Maslow revised the needs in his pyramid, but this is the version that has been most popularized and, presumably, most influential on popular culture.

needs, in Maslow's view, is a hierarchical process—in other words, physiological needs must be met before belongingness/ love needs, and so on up the pyramid. Thus all the other needs must be met before the highest one, self-actualization, can be fulfilled. Note in particular the place of self-esteem, below aesthetic and cognitive needs and self-actualization. The logical conclusion to be reached from Maslow's theory is that education and the realization of a person's highest potentialities are *impossible unless the person first has self-esteem.* This is precisely the conclusion the proponents of self-esteem have reached. (Their definition of self-esteem, it should be noted, is more extreme than Maslow's.)

Despite its widespread acceptance, Maslow's theory of human needs has not gone unchallenged. For example, a Dutch scholar has concluded that Maslow's hierarchy doesn't always hold true in other countries. He points out that in Belgium, Greece, and Japan job security is often a greater need than self-actualization, and that in Denmark, Norway, and Sweden the need for affiliation and acceptance by others is stronger than self-actualization.[26] In addition to the question of cultural bias, other questions may be raised about Maslow's theory. One interesting question is what relationship might exist among human needs other than a hierarchical relationship. One answer is that the needs might be *concurrent,* each urging its fulfillment but not in any rank order. In this case, the need for food, clothing, and shelter would be present along with the need for belongingness and love and self-esteem, but no one would be prerequisite to the others. A variation on this would regard *only the need for food, clothing, and shelter* as prerequisite (a view that Aristotle, for example, seemed to support). In either case, self-esteem would be acknowledged as a genuine need, but not one that had to be met before education or the fulfillment of potential could be achieved. If either of these views were adopted, teachers would be freed from the burden of serving as psychological counselors, a responsibility that few have had training for, and permitted to devote all their energies to guiding students' learning.

Another question about Maslow's theory is this: assuming the relationship among needs is hierarchical, but the actual hierarchy is different than that expressed in Maslow's pyramid, what might the hierarchy be? There are a number of possibilities, but the most interesting, in terms of social implications, is placing self-esteem in the final position: at the top of the pyramid, after and perhaps flowing from the fulfillment of aesthetic/cognitive needs and self-actualization. This would reinforce rather than challenge the lesson most people over age forty learned at home and in school: that hard work in school and in life in general is rewarded by a sense of accomplishment and self-respect. A very different lesson indeed from selfism's "If you don't feel good about yourself, you can't succeed," this view would encourage parents and teachers to set high moral and academic standards and offer children challenging experiences without fear of destroying their self-image and devastating their lives.

A third, more important question is: Does Maslow's list omit any important needs? And the answer is yes, it does. In an earlier chapter I briefly mentioned Austrian psychiatrist Viktor Frankl's theory that the most important drive in human beings is the drive for meaning. This theory, based upon his distinguished professional practice and upon his experiences in Hitler's concentration camps, is an effective antidote to selfism.* Frankl rejects mechanistic "libido hydraulics" and argues that "the primordial anthropological fact [is] that being human is being always directed, and pointing to something or someone other than oneself: to a meaning to fulfill or another human being to encounter, a cause to serve or a person to love." The most human of needs, Frankl asserts, is not self-actualization but self-*transcendence*: A person becomes fully human "by forgetting himself and giving himself, overlooking himself and focusing outward." Making self-actualization (or happiness) the direct object of our pursuit, in Frankl's view, is ultimately self-defeating; such fulfillment can occur only as "the unintended effect of self-transcendence."[27]

The proper perspective on life, Frankl believes, is not what it

---

*Actually Frankl's work predates the humanistic psychology of Rogers, Maslow, and others, but did not become well known in the United States until the early 1960s and never penetrated popular culture as humanistic psychology did, undoubtedly because it emphasizes our responsibility for what we are and what we do.

can give us but what it expects from us; life is daily, even hourly, questioning us, challenging us to accept "the responsibility to find the right answer to its problems and to fulfill the tasks which it constantly sets for [each of us]."[28] Finding meaning involves "perceiving a possibility embedded in reality" and searching for challenging tasks "whose completion might add meaning to [one's] existence." But such perceiving and searching is frustrated by the focus on self. "As long as modern literature confines itself to, and contents itself with, self-expresson—not to say self-exhibition—reflects its authors' sense of futility and absurdity. What is more important, it also creates absurdity. This is understandable in light of the fact that meaning must be discovered, it cannot be invented. Sense cannot be created, but what may well be created is nonsense."[29]

Unlike humanistic psychology, Frankl's psychology acknowledges the paradoxes of life: the fact that wholesome self-love acknowledges human limitations rather than ignoring them, rejects base and unworthy tendencies rather than celebrating them, and draws its sustenance from humility rather than pride. This psychology wisely regards self-actualization not as an end in itself, but as *a means to self-transcendence*. The self it postulates is not a perfect reality within us to be accepted, worshiped, and inflicted upon the world; it is something not yet existing, something better we are challenged to become. Thus Frankl replaces humanistic psychology's promise of becoming what one can never become—omniscient, omnipotent, infallible— with the freedom to be what one ought to be, more fully human; and so it can produce exactly the responsible, caring, sensitive people a society needs to be healthy.

The contrast between selfism and Frankl's perspective is striking. By telling us how wonderful and deserving we are and how much the world owes us, selfism practices a cruel deception. It first leads us to expect people *and life itself* to give us preferential treatment. Then when disappointment comes, as it inevitably does, it leaves us feeling outraged, victimized, and looking for someone to blame (or sue). Frankl's view restores the adventure that selfism has drained from modern life. It reminds us that though we are not accountable for the circumstances into which we were born, we are accountable for our response to those circumstances, and that nothing or no one controls our response. Defective genes may handicap us; poverty, abuse, and neglect may present formidable obstacles to our success; and the temptation to corrosive self-pity may be powerful. Yet we need not succumb. In its focus on transcending self, Frankl's view is uniquely compatible with the biblical view of human nature. Both prompt us to see difficulties positively, as opportunities to be seized and profited from, and physical or spiritual pain as an occasion for practicing nobility and thereby becoming more fully human.

FOUR

The Exaltation of Feelings

A research consultant to *Fortune* 500 companies tells his clients, "The route to success is to do what moves your heart." The prestigious American Management Association advertises a collection of tapes as follows: *"Assertiveness for Career and Personal Success* will show you how to use proven assertiveness skills to improve your personal life. Through a series of exercises, self-evaluations, personal inventories, and self-awareness sessions, you'll learn to respond to all sorts of situations according to your own desires, interests, and feelings." A company called Mind Communication offers a series of subliminal tapes. One for intuitive decision making urges, "Learn to trust your infallible intuition." Sample messages include, "My choices are good and my judgement [*sic*] is sound." "My life is better every day because I make good decisions quickly by feelings." "I trust my own first impressions." "Intuitive decisions I make prove to be good." The implication is that convincing ourselves that we have a certain quality magically gives us that quality.

Everywhere we turn we are told, "Trust your feelings; follow your intuitions." Always effusive and warm, this feelings talk is nevertheless hopelessly vague. What exactly do proponents of following feelings mean by the term? Wishes? Perceptions?

Impressions? Hunches? Intuitions? Desires? Dreams? Emotional states? All of the above? One thing is certain: They definitely do not mean analysis, reflection, reasoning, evaluating, or critical thinking. Following feelings implies acting on some basis other than thought, doing what gives pleasure and satisfies our most insistent urges.

Tension between thought and feeling is not new; it has existed from the time of the ancient Greeks. The birth of this nation, for example, occurred during the Enlightenment, the so-called Age of Reason, when thought reigned and feeling was in disrepute. The principal philosophical tension was between what historian Page Smith terms the "Secular Democratic Consciousness" of Jefferson and the "Classical Christian Consciousness" of John Adams—the former placing faith in reason and science, the latter in the wisest thought and experience of the past.[1] During that very period, however, the Romantic movement was gathering force and in the nineteenth century displaced the Age of Reason. Though commonly thought of as only a literary movement, Romanticism is preeminently philosophical. It asserts that in the primitive uncivilized state, human beings are naturally good and blessed with imagination, creativity, and genius. Romantics view education and other forms of socialization as stifling and corrupting influences. Romanticism is properly considered a revolutionary movement because it sought no compromise with reason but rejected it categorically. Philosopher David Hume wrote, "Reason is and ought only to be the slave of the passions." Jean Jacques Rousseau argued that "What I *feel* is right is right, what I *feel* is wrong is wrong [emphasis added]." Author George Sand honored "emotion rather than reason; the heart opposed to the head."

The last century and a half has witnessed a series of changes in dominance. Social Darwinism, with its emphasis on scientific reasoning and its theory of evolutionary progress, temporarily restored faith in reason and science. Then Freudianism, with its fascination for the unconscious mind and its suspicion of reason, tipped the balance in favor of Romanticism. "At the present time," writes philosopher William Barrett, "our popular culture tends to be swamped by images of the psychopathology of human reason. As the lingo of psychoanalysis and psychotherapy have [*sic*] spread and become [debased,] reason tends to be looked at as a faculty of distortion and concealment—the instrument by which we build elaborate structures by which to hide from the truth of our emotions."[2] In addition, as psychiatrist Thomas Szasz has pointed out, Freud's doctrine of the "psychopathology of everyday life" obliterated the distinction between sanity and insanity. Freud's motivation in advancing these ideas, Szasz claims, was to establish himself not as a psychiatrist, but as "a religious (or quasi-religious) leader."[3]

Social Darwinism, Freudianism, and Behaviorism have all been inhospitable or downright hostile to religion. By comparison, humanistic psychology, which challenged those movements and acknowledged a metaphysical reality beyond natural selection, unconscious drives, and stimulus-response bonds, seemed singularly compatible with religious faith. This explains why many religious leaders rushed to embrace it. Alas, humanistic psychology has proved to be a new form of the old Romanticism, its relativism and selfism more blatant than ever and inimical both to religion and to philosophy. So pervasive is this New Romanticism that it finds collaborators even among those professionally committed to rationality. Richard Restak, physician and popular interpreter of brain research, asks, "Do we make our own choices? Plot our destinies? Are we truly conscious?" His answer is no, "there is not a center in the human brain involved in the exercise of will any more than there is a center in the brain of the swan responsible for the beauty and complexity of its flight."[4] Consider the logical implications of this idea: if we don't make our own choices, if we aren't really conscious, then it's ridiculous to be concerned about learning to think critically, solve problems, and make decisions. If analysis and judgment are illusory, only emotion remains. Thus the scientific study of thought, rather than countering this age's exaltation of feelings, effectively surrenders to it.

The irony runs deeper. The leading psychotherapy in this country is cognitive therapy, the first principle of which is that emotional disturbance is caused by irrational patterns of thinking and cured by mastering rational patterns. At first consideration this emphasis on the thought process seems to balance the inordinate emphasis on feelings. But the striking fact about much of the literature on cognitive therapy is its *similarity* to the popular celebration of feelings! The thought patterns that are held to be irrational are typically self-deprecating—for example, "I'm a total failure, I know I can't ever succeed in my career," "I never do anything right," "I'm always late," "I'm worthless, unlovable," and so on. The focus of cognitive therapy is almost exclusively on how one's irrational thoughts obstruct his or her self-actualization. Self-criticism is considered anathema, and the client is advised to avoid using the words *should, ought,* and *must.* (*Should* statements are actually considered cognitive distortions.[5]) The proper—indeed, the only rational—response to self-criticism is thought to be self-defense.[6]

What is missing in cognitive therapy is a comprehensive, balanced perspective on *cognition* itself. To be sure, some people criticize themselves too much and should be more accepting of themselves; but others criticize themselves too *little* and should be *less* accepting of their behavior. Some set themselves an impossible standard of perfection; but others demand too little of themselves.* Some use the words *should, ought,* and *must* masochistically, but others avoid using the words where they are most appropriate and necessary, as in "I ought to treat others as I would have them treat me" and "I should try to be the best spouse and parent I can be." Cognitive psychologists often fail to make the important distinction between legitimate self-defense and the self-defensiveness that undermines mental health.

Albert Ellis, prolific author and creator of Rational-Emotive Therapy, confesses that he is "haunted" by the reality that almost all people tend to "continually indulge in short-range rather than long-range hedonism, that they are obsessed with the pleasures of the moment rather than of the future, and that this is the main (though hardly the only) source of their resistance to achieving and maintaining mental health." Among the factors that he says perpetuate emotional disturbance are ignorance, stupidity, unperceptiveness, rigidity, pollyanaism, indif-

---

*Anyone looking for an interesting doctoral dissertation topic might consider exploring why psychotherapists get a preponderance of clients who demand too much of themselves, whereas teachers get so many students who demand little or nothing of themselves.

ference, and defensive mechanisms such as rationalization, denial, compensation, projection, avoidance, and repression. With admirable forthrightness, Ellis acknowledges that despite the commendable efforts he and other cognitive therapists have made for decades, most people in therapy resist the cure; indeed, they have a "prodigious tendency" to remain disturbed.[7] Why has cognitive therapy failed to fulfill its promise? Principally, I submit, because it is rooted in the same humanistic psychology that created selfism. Because it assumes that self-actualization is the highest human need, and therefore rejects the higher need of self-transcendence, it continues to prescribe self-affirming, self-absorptive activity for its clients and dissuades them from the very critical (and self-critical) perspective that would free them from slavery to whim and caprice.

FEELINGS ARE UNRELIABLE

Although the terms *feeling* and *thought* are often used interchangeably, they are not synonymous. Feelings are emotional phenomena; they ebb and surge capriciously, requiring no command or direction from us.* Thinking, on the other hand, is a conscious mental activity over which we exercise some control—an activity that helps us formulate or solve a problem, make a decision, or fulfill a desire to understand. We may have our minds full of ideas without thinking; we may even express those ideas eloquently and not necessarily be thinking.** We are thinking only when we are *searching for answers, reaching for meaning.*

The prevailing notion that feeling is preferable to thinking is mistaken. To begin with, feelings are notoriously unreliable. At times they can inspire us to wise decisions and noble deeds; at others, to stupid or reprehensible ones. As children we felt aggrieved by teachers who made us work hard, but now we realize they served us better than those who gave high grades

*It's possible to *make* ourselves happy or angry on purpose, but we more often experience feelings without any conscious attempt to do so.

**This most commonly happens when we recall and/or recite something we read or heard.

for substandard effort. Those of us who had strict parents undoubtedly felt persecuted, until maturity enabled us to understand the relationship between discipline and love. Feelings may prompt people to forgive or to seek revenge, to honor or dishonor commitments, to act altruistically or selfishly. Moreover, feelings are often capricious and tend to resist reasonable boundaries. When we sleep well and rise cheerfully, we may be inclined to pat the dog on the head, joke with our spouse, wave other motorists on ahead of us, and smile at our co-workers; but when our mood is different, watch out world.

Today many people regard the strength of an emotion as an index to its quality. They trust feelings of rage more than mere annoyance, revulsion more than distaste, ecstasy more than simple pleasure. But there is no correlation between strength and quality. As often as not, the relationship is inverse: the most powerful inclinations are for the actions guaranteed to harm others and ourselves—for example, infidelity, stealing, lying on our resumés, or abusing drugs. Mindlessly following feelings thus puts people at the mercy of their own worst tendencies. It leaves them vulnerable to manipulation by others. Unlike thinking individuals, people who are guided by feelings are prone to yield to sales pitches and buy things they don't need, surrender their hard-earned money to scam artists, join extremist movements and religious cults, and deliver their votes to politicians who wrap themselves in the flag and appeal to emotions. Worse, following feelings can be a form of slavery, as John Dewey recognized. "Impulses and desires that are not ordered by intelligence," he argued, "are under the control of accidental circumstances. It may be a loss rather than a gain to escape from the control of another person only to find one's conduct dictated by immediate whim and caprice; that is, at the mercy of impulses into whose formation intelligent judgment has not entered. A person whose conduct is controlled in this way has at most only the illusion of freedom. Actually, he is directed by forces over which he has no command."[8]

How important is it to evaluate our feelings? Consider the following examples of feelings that are very much in evidence today. The parenthetical expression in each case represents conclusions resulting from thoughtful evaluation of the feeling.

Anger that foreigners don't speak English in public places. *(People feel more comfortable speaking their native language, especially if they haven't yet mastered English.)*

Resentment at black workers because of affirmative action. *(Black workers didn't create affirmative action programs; in most cases, white officials did; and whether such programs are advisable or not, they are responses to a real evil, discrimination, that must be eliminated.)*

Outrage at women because they want equal rights. *(Women have historically been denied basic rights, and their demand for equality is not only understandable but justified.)*

Hostility toward Mexicans and Haitians for sneaking into the U.S. *(The conditions they are trying to escape are deplorable; their vision of the United States as a land of opportunity where effort is rewarded is a tribute to this country.)*

Suspicion of those who use food stamps. *(Many people are not to blame for their poverty; though the food stamp program can be misused, it is a godsend to deserving people.)*

Enthusiastic approval of business leaders who call for trade embargoes so that American jobs can be saved. *(Many business leaders, and not just those in the automotive industry, routinely send their products to Third World countries for assembly. It is inconsistent, and perhaps hypocritical, of them to fault others for the same actions they take.)*

In each of these cases, as in hundreds of everyday situations, feelings are often unrestrained and thus lead to overgeneralizing, stereotyping, and oversimplifying. Nor are feelings very helpful in meeting the complex challenges that arise in every important area of life, including law, medicine, government, education, science, business, and community and personal affairs. What caused that airplane to crash? What's wrong with the economy? What approach to national health care is best? Should extremist groups such as the Ku Klux Klan be allowed to hold rallies on public property? Should women's athletic teams receive the same funding as men's teams? Under what circumstances, if any, should researchers be permitted to use living animals in their experiments? Should the government give parents vouchers to enable them to send their children to private schools at public expense? Does prayer belong in the public schools? The only responsible approach to such challenges is careful thought—raising questions, pursuing promising lines of inquiry and investigation, interpreting evidence, identifying alternative judgments, and choosing the most reasonable one.

With advertising omnipresent, highly sophisticated, and designed to serve advertisers more than consumers, the public need strategies to protect their interests. A *Consumer Reports* (CR) study, for example, describes pharmaceutical companies' manipulation of the news to sell their products. Typical devices used are the use of celebrities and other attractive, articulate spokespeople who appear to be unbiased but are actually on the companies' payrolls, and thinly disguised promotional videos given to television stations to be used as news releases. CR offers its readers several guidelines to avoid being victimized by these deceptions, including being skeptical of wonder cures, questioning the expertise of the person offering the testimonial, and evaluating the data offered in support of the claim.[9] This approach is the polar opposite of "following our feelings." The appeals are designed to trade on our feelings of admiration for the celebrity, respect for the (supposed) medical authority, and desire for simple answers to our medical problems. Although the majority of the producers of goods and services surely don't intentionally make false claims, advertising agencies may persuade them to use advertisements that encourage consumers to act mindlessly, on impulse. Our only protection is mental alertness and control of our feelings.

Nowhere is the inadequacy of feelings as a guide to behavior more evident than in the case of child abuse. Experts tell us that the physical, psychological, and sexual abuse of children is epidemic in this country and that perpetrators generally lack awareness of the pain their victims experience and the maturity to control their urges. Will following feelings lead an abuser to awareness or maturity? Hardly. Without reflection and reasoning, the pleasurable feelings of dominance and sexual excitement that drive abusers are not likely to yield to sublimation or empathy. Nor is immaturity overcome by an increase of feeling. Immature people generally feel mature—the inappropriateness of that feeling to their situation defines their problem. To make matters worse, the prevailing relativism and selfism in popular culture provide justification for the child abuser's behavior rather than censure. If everyone creates his or her own reality, the abuser's belief that his behavior doesn't harm children is validated. And society's urging of unconditional self-acceptance prevents him from experiencing the self-loathing that is prerequisite to his reform.

Looking back on the years of physical and psychological abuse her children suffered at her hands, recalling the horrible rage that prompted her to hurl a curtain rod at her son, puncturing his eye and brain and killing him, a mother lamented, "I wish I had known the reason that I lost my temper with my children was that my expectations were unrealistic, not that their behavior was unacceptable."[10] How might she have gained that insight and averted the tragedy? Certainly not by assuming her feelings were right and yielding to them, but rather by evaluating them, wondering where they originated (she herself had been abused), where they might lead, and how they might affect her children and herself.

When we are attempting to counsel other people, common sense requires us to move beyond their feelings (and ours) and *reason with them*. If an HIV-infected person wanted to exact revenge by infecting others, we'd surely argue that infecting innocent people would not only be unfair but would represent descending to the level of the person who victimized him. And we surely would advise rapists, nags, alcoholics, compulsive gamblers, procrastinators, and would-be suicides to examine their feelings critically rather than to follow them unquestioningly. (A group of inmates in a Rahway, New Jersey, prison, having learned by painful experience the value of thinking before acting, have developed a program that encourages teenagers to think carefully and weigh the potential effect on their lives before engaging in criminal activity.) Surely if we would offer others such sensible counsel, we should accept nothing less in our own careers and personal lives. Placing thought above feeling helps us distinguish between illusion and reality and ensures that our decisions will be wiser, our actions more responsible, and our lives happier.

THE CONSEQUENCES OF
NEGLECTING THOUGHT

Whereas thought can add light to our perspective, feeling can add only heat. In order to be responsible, committed, contributing individuals, we need both; but the triumph of Romanticism has destroyed the balance. As a result, the values associated with thought—moderation, restraint, fair-mindedness, and a regard for distinctions and logic—have been discarded and millions of people remain in the grip of glandularism, imprisoned by impulses and first impressions. Worse, relativism and selfism delude them to regard this sorry state as a form of higher consciousness. The effects of this condition are all too evident in the various varieties of Political Correctness. At a recent international conference I conducted a workshop for college professors on the teaching of ethics from a critical thinking perspective. I began by explaining the ethical principle of respect for persons: that every person, regardless of race, creed, ethnic origin, age, or circumstance is deserving of respect and should never be treated merely as a possession or an instrument or an obstacle to the achievement of our ends. (Later I demonstrated how analysis of ethical issues can help students understand ethical ideals and obligations and measure the consequences of actions.)

A woman in the audience said she wasn't sure that this principle met the test of gender neutrality.

"In what way doesn't it meet such a test?" I asked.

"I'm not sure."

"Well, can you point to some scenario in which it might fail, or suggest some basis for our deciding?"

"Not really—I just have a feeling it might not."

Hiding my disappointment at her refusal to proceed beyond her initial feeling, I expressed my belief that the civil rights movement and the women's rights movement are expressions of the principle of respect for persons: they protest social practices that deny blacks and women such respect. By the nodding I observed in the audience, I knew that most of the men and women there agreed. Yet the woman said again, "I still don't know. It doesn't feel right to me somehow." Caution, of course, can be appropriate: we ought not give assent to any idea unless we are satisfied that it is worthy. And feelings, impressions, and intuitions serve us well when they inspire caution. But that woman was refusing to make the necessary progression from caution to careful analysis and judgment. This refusal, a natural consequence of choosing feeling over thought, effectively blocks understanding, insight, and wisdom.

When I finished that workshop, I joined a group of conferees for the banquet luncheon. Eight people were seated at my table and a lively discussion was under way when I arrived; it seemed to be the continuation of a discussion that had begun in an earlier conference session that I had not attended. As the exchange of ideas proceeded, one woman said that all academic disciplines are not only male dominated, but male *corrupted*. I asked, "If every field is corrupted by men, what do you say of the women who undoubtedly received their training from men? Have they been corrupted too?" Without hesitation, she answered, "Yes."

"Does that mean those women shouldn't be trusted to conduct the reform of their disciplines?" I continued.

"Yes, exactly that."

"Then who will? If not the men in the disciplines because they are men, and not the women because they were trained by men, then who? *Untrained* women? Would you have math, science, engineering, the humanities, and so on reformed by people who are uneducated in those areas?"

The response was silence. Not, it seemed, the silence that attends chastening, that says "I'm afraid my feelings have caused me to overstate my case," but rather the angry silence of intransigence. Outrage at the historic mistreatment of women and stifling of their talents is appropriate, but it should stop short of absurdly blaming every man and denouncing every male achievement. Consistent application of that view would require that women shun plane, train, or auto travel on the chance that a man invented the wheel, reject antiseptic operating rooms because of their association with Joseph Lister, denounce the Salk vaccine, and refuse to own a refrigerator, use a telephone, or purchase frozen foods. Happily, life is not as neat as the extremists assume. There is nothing to prevent a man from being an ardent feminist or a woman from championing male chauvinism. History has provided numerous examples of both.

To cite gender feminism as an example of the exaltation of feeling over thought is not to disparage feminism in general. It is to say that the cause of feminism deserves better. It deserves the kind of thoughtful advocacy offered by psychologist Carol Tavris. In *The Mismeasure of Woman*, she applies the same keen analysis used in her excellent earlier study, *Anger: The Misunderstood Emotion*. Tavris asks whether there are more important questions than "Do men and women differ, and if so, who's better?" and wonders why so many writers are interested in differences and why differences are regarded as deficiencies.[11] In examining the relevant research, she finds that it does not support the radical feminists' contention that there are numerous and profound differences between men and women, that women are more "connected, attached, loving, and peaceful, that they speak in a different voice, have different ways of knowing, or different moral values."[12] She notes that recent research suggests men and women do not differ appreciably in their moral reasoning, that "the behavior that we link to gender depends more on what an individual is doing and needs to do than on his or her biological sex," that "when studies measure physiological signs of empathy... or behavioral signs of empathy... gender differences vanish."[13]

Men and women, she concludes, are not polar opposites. Most of us have a blend of so-called masculine and feminine qualities and would do well to enrich that blend.[14] Instead of each side worrying about the awful "them," the opposite sex, we should both consider "What shall we do about *us*, so that our relationships, our work, our children, and our planet will flourish?"[15] Feeling may have led Tavris to undertake the research for this laudable book, and it may have sustained her in the arduous task of writing it. But it could never have produced the insights she reached. Only careful, reflective, critical thought could do that.

Given the popular belief that there are no standards of excellence applicable to ideas and that strong feeling is equivalent to validation, it comes as no surprise that mindless speech and action is increasingly evident today. The newsletter of a lobbying group supporting the right to bear arms, for example, offered these reasons for buying an assault weapon: "to assist the police in an emergency... to pay the federal tax on guns, which goes to aid wildlife... to appreciate the evolution of firearm technology... to own one of the most mechanically safe firearms... to appreciate the mechanical genius of firearm designers... to reject anti-gun media bias...to own a firearm that is difficult to conceal... to own a firearm that might be banned." The author added that the test for whether a person needs an assault weapon is *whether he says he needs one*.[16]

Presumably many people are making marital and parenting decisions, giving or withholding support for political candidates or governmental programs, and making judgments in their careers on the basis of vague impressions, intuitions, or self-serving rationalizations rather than on careful thought. We should not be surprised that so many of these choices are unwise. Take, for example, automobile industry executives' refusal to spend fifty or seventy-five dollars extra per vehicle and install safety windshields (with a layer of plastic on the inside) to prevent glass from shattering inward, front-seat reinforcements to prevent seats from breaking and occupants from sliding into the backseat and sustaining neck injuries, and roof reinforcements to protect occupants in rollovers.

Similar examples are the federal government's sale of cheap water to farmers so they can grow crops for the government to purchase and destroy or the Hudson Beach, Florida, undercover detectives' raid on a septuagenarians' pinochle game played on picnic tables in the park for a stake of *twenty cents a hand*. (Bear in mind that the state of Florida sponsors one of the biggest gambling operations in the nation, a lottery whose payoffs can exceed $100 million. Moreover, Florida, like other states, has enough serious crimes for police to keep busy night and day.)

Virtually every one of the social problems plaguing this country is aggravated by the mindless following of feelings. That is the most reasonable explanation of both the vicious beating of Rodney King and the violence and destruction of the Los Angeles riots. In the latter case the mobs not only assaulted innocent people—they looted and destroyed *their own neighborhoods*. Speaking two months before the Los Angeles riots, professor

Shelby Steele traced the evolution of "the politics of difference." The black power movement, he asserted, "encouraged a permanent state of rage and victimhood" that replaced the idea of civil rights with that of entitlement. Black demands for entitlement were followed by the demands of Hispanics, Asians, Eskimos, American Indians, homosexuals, the disabled, "and other self-defined minorities." The "grievance identity" that fuels these demands, Steele argued, has a single dimension: "anger against oppression."[17] According to anthropologist Richard J. Perry, multiculturalists tend to approach the discussion of controversial issues viscerally and intuitively rather than thoughtfully, therefore ignoring the insights of anthropology—specifically that other people are not profoundly different but "three dimensional beings of the same human substance as ourselves."[18]

This explains, too, why sexual harassment and rape remain serious problems among people of every social stratum and every level of education despite the unprecedented number and quality of consciousness-raising campaigns. Studies of high school and college males reveal that few use condoms, even though the vast majority understand that condoms prevent the spread of AIDS; those studies also reveal that young men with multiple sex partners are even less likely to use condoms than others.[19] The urge to act impulsively is apparently stronger than fear of the greatest plague in modern times.

It strains credulity to believe that any sort of thoughtful consideration or analysis precedes experimenting with drugs, becoming anorexic or bulemic, dropping out of school, or attempting suicide. Only the most impulsive person would attempt bank robbery, a crime that invites response at every level from the local sheriff's office to the FBI and boasts a success rate of about 15 percent; yet bank robbery is increasing in some parts of the country, notably southern California. The city of Newark, New Jersey, has been grappling with a new problem. Teenagers are stealing cars and returning to their neighborhoods to show off in front of their friends. They spin in circles, race around, and even crash into squad cars. They have no fear of police or concern about punishment for their crimes. So brazen have they become that in one case a teen stole a car and drove it to his trial for stealing a car.[20] The problem has resulted in criticism of the legal system, and that may well be appropriate; but it would be shortsighted to overlook the role played by popular culture's elevation of feeling over thought.

The legal system is also blamed for the increase in the number of single women and children living in poverty. No-fault divorce laws, the argument goes, did not safeguard the rights of women and children as their authors intended, so more and more divorced men are avoiding their financial obligations. This reasoning is illogical. Though ill-conceived laws may facilitate irresponsible behavior, they don't cause it. Attitudes and beliefs do. Men who withhold support payments and instead spend the money on their own pleasures are simply practicing what popular culture preaches: "Whatever you feel like doing is all right to do, so follow your feelings."

Another consequence of the exaltation of feelings over thought is the current epidemic of hooliganism and other antisocial behavior. When impulse reigns, if young (or old) people feel like spitting on the floor, throwing bottles and other refuse out of car windows, shouting obscenities at other people, torturing a kitten, or spraying bullets into a crowd of people, they don't pause, reflect, and consider stifling the urge. They simply obey the slogan on their T-shirts and "Just do it!" The word *attitude* was formerly flexible—good, bad, or neutral depending on the context. Now it is exclusively bad, and that is considered good. "Having an attitude," as in being an offensive slob, is no longer shameful but something to be proud of. Bumper stickers advise the world of the drivers' penchant for obscenities. Ever ready to cash in on a trend, even one that destroys civility, many companies create new lines of products to celebrate negativism and rudeness, from Bart Simpson T-shirts ("Underachiever and proud of it") to The Final Word, a "pre-programmed state of the art electronic voice synthesizer" made in China for a New York firm. At the push of a button, this product enables us to "tell them all off . . . You'll be happier in the end." Messages include a variety of obscenities. The latest contribution to the genre is Kenner's collection of rude toys named after body wastes.

Yet another effect of the displacement of thought by feelings is the exaggerated sense of victimization many people experience. Sadly, many psychotherapists still specialize in having clients dredge up childhood resentments against their parents and confront the parents with them. Instead of leading to forgiveness of others and accepting responsibility for one's life, this approach tends to heighten the client's sense of outrage. Identifying childhood feelings can be beneficial, but only if we remain open to the possibility that the feelings were inappropriate—for example, that we misunderstood the circumstances at that time, or that the feelings were constructed to lessen our sense of guilt over an offense we committed. If ever there were a prescription for discord, it is the idea that other people (parents, teachers, etc.) are to blame for all our problems.* Social harmony depends on a sense of proportion and a willingness to listen to others, to reconsider one's position, and, wherever principle allows, to compromise. Since powerful feelings tend to be immoderate, when they are untempered by reason they promote scapegoating, oversimplification, and intransigence—precisely the reactions that teachers, marital counselors, and judges are seeing in their clientele and that fill the news.

A group of militant female artists, for example, accused the Metropolitan Museum of Art of sexism because 95 percent of the paintings on display represent the work of male artists, while 85 percent of the nude statues are of females. (The charge would be reasonable if the exhibits were of contemporary art, but the Museum can hardly be held responsible for the history of art.) Similarly, Operation PUSH argues that blacks should have a larger share of jobs in sneaker manufacturing companies because blacks buy a disproportionate share of the sneakers. (Aside from the fact that it is illogical, this thinking, if extended to other industries, would undoubtedly result in a sizable *loss of jobs* for black workers.)

These examples are different forms of the same psychological phenomenon, ethnocentrism. Thirty years ago, most psychologists agreed that ethnocentrism, like *ego*centrism, is an unhealthy perspective on life. They recognized that a "mine is different" outlook can easily become "mine is better" and the corollary "yours is inferior," and that the consequence is social

*If parents are always at fault, then logic compels us to conclude that no one is ever at fault, for everyone has parents he or she can blame, back through the mists of time to Adam and Eve, who are also innocent because "the devil made them do it."

disharmony.* As psychologist and authority on prejudice Gordon Allport explains:

> By taking a negative view of great groups of mankind, we somehow make life simpler. For example, if I reject all foreigners as a category, I don't have to bother with them—except to keep them out of my country. If I can ticket, then, all Negroes as comprising an inferior and objectionable race, I conveniently dispose of a tenth of my fellow citizens. If I can put the Catholics into another category and reject them, my life is still further simplified. I then pare again and slice off the Jews . . . and so it goes.[21]

Political Correctness (PC) is the ethnocentrism of the 1990s. It is proving more disruptive than earlier forms because it is fueled by the conviction that feeling is superior to thought, as well as by the relativistic idea that everyone creates his or her own reality and the selfist preoccupation with self. Passion is seldom responsive to evidence and reason; passion convinced of its superiority is immovable. That is why dialogue with the politically correct is so unfruitful. Generally dogmatic, humorless, and unwilling to listen to views divergent from their own, they typically use one of two protocols. If their antagonist is not of their group, they say he or she lacks the credentials to speak to the issue. (To the politically correct, only Jews can speak to Jews, only blacks to blacks, only women to women, only young people to young people.) If the person is within their group, they label him or her a traitor or "sexist," "fundamentalist," or "reactionary." The prevalence of Political Correctness explains the breakdown of communication between races, ethnic groups, and genders, as well as the growing demand for separateness in academic programs.

The most frightening effect of popular culture's urging that people follow their feelings is violence. Today muggings, physical assaults, and rapes occur not only at night on urban streets

---

*Anthropologists long ago discovered that in the languages of some of the most violent primitive tribes, the word for "human being" is the same as the tribe's name. That seemingly insignificant linguistic fact had enormous social importance. It allowed nonmembers of the tribe to be regarded as *not human* and beheaded, eaten, or otherwise victimized.

but also in broad daylight in shopping malls. Little children are abducted and raped on their way to school. Predator gangs attack randomly, sparing no one, not even octogenarians or pregnant women. As I write, the local news is carrying the story of two teenage boys who fired a shotgun at another motorist, killing him instantly, because they felt he gave them a disapproving look as he passed. "House invaders" break into people's homes and terrorize the occupants. Because there is no pattern or motive to these crimes, police are virtually powerless to respond.

The U.S. Center for Disease Control estimates that one in five high school students carries a weapon, often a more powerful weapon than is available to the police. Moreover, as one authority put it, "the streets are invading the classroom." So great is the danger and the actual incidence of student assaults on teachers and other students that many schools ban evening sports events or hold them in empty gyms. At least one teachers' union offers a special program for coping with classroom violence. America leads the world in juvenile violence: author Merry White notes that the number of juvenile arrests made *daily* in a single borough of New York City (Manhattan) equals that made *annually* in Japan's second largest city, Osaka.[22]

THOUGHT AND FEELING:
A BALANCED VIEW

The rationalist and the romanticist views of feelings are both mistaken. Feelings are neither inherently bad nor inherently good. They can inspire us to conquer apathy and procrastination, transcend self, turn conclusions into convictions, and generate the passion needed to sustain us through long, arduous, thankless tasks. Or they can nurture apathy and procrastination, foster narcissism, and imprison us in unworthy habits and trivial, meaningless, ultimately self-defeating pursuits. Because their counsel may be wise or foolish, noble or base, we cannot afford to follow them unquestioningly but must evaluate them and determine their worth. Allowing thought to monitor feeling does not imply that thought is infallible; nor does it depreciate feelings. It merely puts our two great human capacities in the relationship that provides us sound, reliable guidance.

Though it is widely believed that our culture has lavished attention on thought but ignored feelings, in reality thought has also been neglected. Most parents and teachers have told young people *what* to think but not taught them *how* to think. There is no malice in their method; they simply do what was done unto them, in many cases believing that thinking ability is inherited and cannot be taught. Research, however, has proven that thinking is not a mysterious phenomenon but is composed of specific dispositions, habits, and skills that virtually anyone can master.[23] (In thinking as in any other activity, of course, proficiency will vary.) The dispositions include curiosity about our mental processes, the desire to reason well and to base judgments on evidence rather than prejudices, willingness to subject our own ideas to scrutiny and to entertain opposing views, passion for truth, and tolerance of complexity and ambiguity. Among the most important habits are looking for connections among ideas, deferring judgment, imaginativeness, fair-mindedness, asking probing questions, and reflectiveness. The skills include identifying unstated assumptions, making distinctions, detecting errors in reasoning, and drawing sound conclusions from evidence.

Research has also demonstrated the error of the notion that rationality and logic are controlled by one side of the brain and intuition and creativity the other, and that the two are incompatible. The popular idea that some people are left-brained and others are right-brained is the most common expression of this error, and this idea underlies the argument that women think differently from men and that some races or ethnic groups lack certain thinking capacities. In a review of the literature on brain studies Jerre Levy of the University of Chicago refutes this idea, noting that "both hemispheres not only play critical roles in the purposes of language, but also in organizing the perceptual and cognitive processes that are prerequisite to understanding"; that "[no studies show] that one side is more 'creative' than the other"; and that "both hemispheres are involved in thinking, logic and reasoning, each from its own perspective and in its particular domains of activity." Moreover, Levy explains that the structure of the brain, with the corpus callosum connecting the two hemispheres, implies a profound integration that is evidenced in all areas of human thought.[24] And that integration, it should be added, is no less profound for one gender, race, or ethnic group than for another.

This idea can help break down the artificial barriers to understanding that relativism, selfism, and the exaltation of feelings have created. Women's anger over millenia of subjugation is justifiable, as is blacks' and Hispanics' anger at discrimination. But those feelings will be productive only if they are controlled by reason and focused on finding solutions rather than celebrating resentment. Feminists who work to end discrimination and gain equality for women are solving problems; those who hate all men, argue that consentual coitus is rape, and demean their sisters who value marriage and family life are merely celebrating resentment. Blacks who press for fairness in education, employment, and housing are solving problems; those who preach distrust of whites and historically white institutions are celebrating resentment.* If the literary canon has unfairly excluded works by women and racial or ethnic minorities, feeling will understandably urge discarding white male authors, even those of the rank of Shakespeare, Chaucer, Melville, and Twain; but reason suggests that literary history be reviewed and the canon be revised on the basis of true merit. If historians have wrongfully omitted reference to African civilizations and Afro-American achievements, feeling will understandably propose setting up new courses and writing new books that acknowledge black contributions and ignore white ones; but reason supports revising courses and textbooks to include writers of excellence regardless of race, religion, or ethnic background.

The first step in achieving balance between feeling and thought

---

*Football Hall of Famer Jim Brown's rehabilitation program, Amer-I-Can, is based on a similar insight. Brown advises his clients that they must overcome the victim mentality and stop hating policemen and those from other races and social classes. "Conditions have affected your mind," he tells them, "and your mind is keeping you down. So you have to start rising above the conditions and learn how to deal with them step by step." Dealing with conditions means learning "how to seek a job, how to deal with their family, how to communicate, how to control their emotions, how to solve problems."[25]

is to consider the possibility that many of our feelings are really conditioned responses. It is generally recognized that the way we react to a person or event today often mirrors the way we reacted on some earlier occasion; yet it is seldom recognized that many of our feelings do not originate with us, but merely echo other people's feelings and thoughts. Just as we borrow from our earlier experience, so too we borrow from our parents, teachers, and friends. The spine-tingling love of country we experience when the national anthem is played may have its origin in the emotion our parents displayed in similar circumstances and the way we heard them talk about that emotion. Unfortunately, unworthy feelings and thoughts, such as those associated with prejudice, can be similarly derived. In this time of mass communication, when from infancy we are ceaselessly bombarded by emotion-laden images—many of them specifically designed to manipulate our minds—as well as briefer and briefer sound "bites" of other people's opinions, the number of these influences is arguably legion.

The next step is to evaluate both our feelings and our thoughts. That means suspending emotional attachment and stimulating our curiosity. More specifically, it means practicing restraint, probing why we feel or think as we do, and considering whether other feelings or thoughts may be more appropriate. In this way we ensure that we will not be victimized by nonsense that has silently taken up residence in our own minds. Whether this process confirms our initial feelings and thoughts or leads us to embrace other ones, we will have gained insight, the confidence to express our views with conviction, and the enthusiasm to translate ideas into action. Equally important, we will have disposed ourselves to learn from others and cooperate with them in solving social problems. Until such a balanced view of feelings and thoughts is widely accepted among scholars, nurtured in home and school, and celebrated in the entertainment and communications media, social harmony is likely to remain unrealized and progress stifled.

FIVE

Media and Popular Culture

The T-shirt depicts a human brain wearing fashionable sunglasses with a neckstrap dangling from each bow. Surrounding the brain are eight printed words: *history, math, English, biology, chemistry, physics, art, and sex.* All words except *sex* are lined out in red; above each is scribbled "Party." The legend reads, "The mind is a wonderful thing to waste." As easy as it is to find people lined up to protest things today, it would be difficult to find a group protesting such T-shirts and carrying signs reading "This message hinders teachers' efforts" or "The lessons of home and school need support, not ridicule." And if by chance such a protest occurred, it would quickly be countered by groups denouncing censorship and proclaiming the inalienable rights of T-shirt manufacturers, defining the wearing of such shirts as constitutionally guaranteed free speech, and perhaps even inviting the artist who designed the shirt to apply for an NEA grant.

Even a relativistic age like ours has its dogmas, and among the most sacred is the belief that ideas can't harm anyone. This belief is inconsistent with contemporary understanding of cause/effect relationships in other matters. Economists recognize that events in one sector of the economy or of the world market impact on all others. Scientists recognize the effects of hydro-fluorocarbons on the atmosphere, of defoliation of rain forests on weather, of volcanic eruptions in one part of world on temperatures in others. But people's minds are considered impervious to harm. Thus Texas movie critic Joe Bob Briggs scoffs at the film rating system: "All movie ratings are based on the idea that a film can actually damage the mind of a person, as though he'll watch too much and go off the deep end and start strangling cats or something. But go to any theater and watch the most mindless horror film—let's say one of the Friday the 13th movies—with the intended audience of 14-to-19-year-olds, and you'll find that they never get confused. Jason is on the screen. They're sitting in a chair. Screen, chair. Jason, real life. They never get mixed up and think they are Jason or that Jason is going to come down off the screen. They know that it's only a movie."[1]

When the Surgeon General called for a restriction on beer advertisements, the usually discerning columnist James J. Kilpatrick thundered, "There is no evidence—repeat, no evidence—that beer commercials inexorably lead children down the primrose path to a drunkard's grave," and went on to reason that beer commercials are not deceptive because the young men and women who appear in them "appear to be having a good time."[2] Even the highly respected Robert Brustein, artistic director of the American Repertory Theater and director of Harvard's Loeb Drama Center, argues that ideas can't harm us. "I don't believe," he explains, "that outside of pathological people, violent movies or plays cause violence in society; they simply reflect it. The violence is there already."[3] So pervasive is this dogma that millions of otherwise sensitive and intelligent people are dissuaded from speculating about a possible relationship between what happens in the media and what happens in the street. The opening scene of the sexually preoccupied show Sisters, for example, was originally planned to be the women sitting in the sauna discussing their orgasms. Only when a skittish sponsor threatened to withdraw half a million dollars in ads was the topic of discussion modified. Still the executive producer's view was "Look, we all talk about sex and we all deal with it. So why not put it on the air in as frank a manner as possible?" And so they do.

The dogma that ideas can't harm people carries a crucial implication that is often, perhaps conveniently, overlooked: ideas can't *help* people either. Interestingly, in our society it has always been an article of faith that ideas *can* help people. This belief underlies all therapy and all education. It was evident in the concern of Bill Cosby that his TV show support such traditional parental values as the worth of reading, the demand that homework be given high priority, and the importance of a sense of responsibility. It is also why self-improvement books, diet books, and nutrition books are published, and why Oprah Winfrey airs so many shows that bring people together to discuss social issues, such as spouse and child abuse and drunk driving. Why would any writer write, especially a writer of fiction, except to move the reader in some way? As T. S. Eliot, one of the most famous poets and literary critics of this century, explained in his well-known essay "Religion and Literature": "The author of a work of imagination is trying to affect us wholly, as human beings, whether he knows it or not; and we are affected by it, as human beings, whether we intend to be or not."

Every public service advertisement, like every sex education class, drug awareness program, and suicide hot line, proclaims that expressing the right ideas can make a difference. When actors and other celebrities speak out for the environment, education, responsible sexuality, and other social causes, they do so on the conviction that their contributions can be a force for change. When film director Spike Lee created an advertisement depicting a playground with lots of vivid colors on the court and surrounding buildings, then introduced some black and white players who refused to play together, and finally admonished them "The mo' color, the mo' better," he was surely hoping to persuade people that racial harmony is preferable to racial hatred. When basketball star Magic Johnson startled the country by announcing that he is HIV positive, there was not only an immediate outpouring of sympathy and goodwill but near-universal confidence that his personal experience and his advocacy of responsible attitudes toward sex would do great good. Fred Allemann of the Cascade (WA) AIDS Project, for example, stated that Johnson "probably saved thousands of lives in that one act."

The conviction that ideas have power and that the right expression can change lives is based on experience as well as hope. Simple expressions—"I am sorry," "I love you," "You inspire me"—have healing power. Even songs that celebrate these expressions can be inspiring. (Who among us is not touched by the lovely song, "You Are the Wind Beneath My Wings"?) The twenty thousand members of the "Andy Griffith Show Rerun Watchers Club" consider the show a model for many people in parenting and community life and testify to the way it has enriched their own lives. A Torrington, Connecticut, boy who lost a leg in an automobile accident is still playing basketball because he saw a television commercial about a double-amputee who had conquered his handicap. A single Ann Landers column persuaded more than a million people to write President Nixon, urging him to sign the National Cancer Act in 1971, ultimately securing $100 million for cancer research; and another of her columns motivated hundreds of hotels and restaurants to distribute their leftover food to the poor. And the magnificent Civil War series that premiered on public television in 1990 informed, inspired, and humbled those who watched it. Consider a single detail from that series: Sullivan Ballou's letter to his wife, Sarah, written barely a week before his death at the first battle of Bull Run. In it Ballou expressed love of country and his wife, willingness to die for his beliefs, sorrow for his offenses, and profound sadness at the prospect of never returning. At times his words rose to poetry, as in the line "when the last breath escapes me on the battlefield, it will whisper your name." Producers received hundreds of appreciative letters from viewers saying the series enriched their lives.

If daily experience dramatically supports our conviction that ideas can help people, it also supports, just as dramatically, the corollary—ideas can harm people. Hitler's vile propaganda influenced millions of Germans to tolerate and even embrace his insanity. Ku Klux Klan hate literature inflamed prejudice and resulted in violence against blacks, Jews, and Catholics. More recently, on a thankfully more modest scale, the landmark movie *Thelma and Louise*, which glamorized the heroics of two female antisexist criminal commandos, affected the thinking of many members of the National Organization of Women (NOW).

The movie was the subject of considerable discussion at the 1991 annual NOW convention in New York City, many speakers referring to it approvingly, T-shirts and buttons celebrating its message, and NOW Vice President Patricia Ireland announcing that the organization "for the first time in its 25-year history, officially calls for civil disobedience."[4]

Many people who deny that the media influence people pretend that the public's decisions are all made freely and independently. They apparently believe that the $4 billion spent annually on cosmetics and the $30 billion spent on beauty salons have no connection to the beauty standard nurtured by the media, that every other man and boy on the street would wear the most popular shirts, sneakers, and pants even if those items were not heavily advertised. The implication is that the world has no followers, only leaders. Yet when these same media defenders are asked why antisocial and criminal behavior is on the rise, they refer vaguely to "peer pressure." Even if we overlook the contradiction (followers yield to peer pressure, leaders do not), we are left with the question, whence comes this pressure? Does it spring forth from the void without earthly influence? Surely at some point in time there was a first peer that initiated the pressure. What influenced him or her?

Advertisers have no such illusions about the power of positive or negative image in buying habits. When a TV news program included footage of a high school sex education teacher fitting a condom to a banana a few years ago, the banana industry went, well, bananas. Its spokespeople objected loudly and no doubt hoped for the substitution of a zucchini in future classroom demonstrations. They didn't have to commission a ten-year study to determine whether the teacher's choice of props had any impact on their business; they knew that the negative image would translate to a drop in sales. Nor do we need a research study to affirm the reality that ideas can do good or harm, depending on whether they reflect truth or error.

Those who deny this reality absolve the most powerful force that ever influenced the human mind and heart—the media*

*Media is defined here in the broadest sense, including newspapers, magazines, books, cinema, radio, television, popular music, and the advertising intertwined with most of these.

—from all responsibility for their actions. In reality the media are the primary disseminators of popular culture—that is, of the dominant themes and perspectives on life of the time. In our time those themes are selfism, relativism, and the exaltation of feelings. Ignoring the media's process in the promotion and maintenance of popular culture has expedited the unraveling of America's social fabric. Several decades ago, Viktor Frankl linked the rise of violence, drug addiction, and suicide to literature that debunks human values and preaches futility and despair.* He admonished writers to reflect on their responsibility: "If the writer is not capable of *immunizing the reader against despair,* he should at least refrain from *inoculating him with despair*"[5] [emphasis in the original].

Popular discussion of America's educational and social problems generally rests on the assumption that since children learn from parents and teachers, academic or social deficiencies must be attributed to poor parenting or teaching. That assumption oversimplifies the learning process. Among the best documented and most widely accepted principles of behavior are that children learn by modeling, imitating what they see and hear from the moment of birth; that practice creates habits, and the practice need not be actual but may be imagined or fantasized; and that rewarded behavior tends to be repeated, even if the rewards are vicarious, such as seeing fictional characters prosper.[6] The fundamental points so often missed today are that children imitate not only parents and teachers, but all the real people and fictional characters they see, and that in this age of mass communication the aura of celebrity enjoyed by media models gives their example a formidable advantage over that of parents and teachers.

Influences can be subtle as well as obvious. The fact that people don't immediately mimic what they have read or seen doesn't prove that a book or film has not affected them. They can be strongly influenced even if they don't run out and perform the same sex acts in the same manner as depicted in the book, or slash someone in precisely the same pattern with the same

---

*Today, even more than when Frankl wrote these words, the most influential form of literature is television.

brand of cutlery as depicted on the screen. It is possible to be deeply affected at the level of attitude and perspective and not at the level of overt action; to be persuaded for example, that promiscuity is acceptable or the world is frightening and malevolent, or to be inclined to regard violence casually. What is reported in the news and covered in quasi-news shows such as "A Current Affair" and "Hard Copy" carries a measure of validation. An act as revolting as cannibalism, if mentioned often enough, even in a context of public horror and outrage, seems a little more normal than it did previously. It is likewise possible for what is seen and heard and read to dispose people to actions to which they had been indisposed before reading the book or viewing the film. These possibilities warrant greater curiosity about the attitudes and values implied in the media and fair-minded evaluation of the evidence.

SEX IN MEDIA

Exactly what messages are the media sending about sex? Part of the answer can be found in the performances of the reigning queen of popular culture, the ironically named Madonna. Even her name has been used to mock the mother of Christ, and Columbia House Record Company advertising compounds the irreverence, announcing "Madonna: The Immaculate Collection (Greatest Hits)." Her Blonde Ambition Tour, broadcast in a variety of time slots on HBO, begins with her trademark self-massaging and proceeds to a series of simulated sexual encounters. Filthy language alternates with suggestive dancing. The use of religious imagery in her highly publicized "Like a Prayer" number makes it a morality play for perversity.

If Madonna's act is on the cutting edge of outrageousness, other media "acts" are not lagging very far behind. MTV is filled with videos such as George Michael's *I Want Your Sex*, the music sensual and the camera close-ups featuring a supine, lingerie-clad woman wrapped in black satin sheets and moving provocatively as the camera rhythmically scans her body. Prominent in the lyrics are references to the naturalness and delightfulness of sex, and toward the end a hand writes "EXPLORE" on a woman's thigh. Michael Medved, film reviewer and co-host of *Sneak Previews*, sees the problem as endemic in the industry. "The popular music business," he writes, "...has become a global enterprise of staggering proportions that generates billions of dollars every year through the simple-minded glorification of animal lust. Nothing could stand at a further remove from the selflessness and discipline that are essential to successful family life than the masturbatory fantasies that saturate MTV 24 hours a day."[7]

Professor Sut Jhally of the University of Massachusetts at Amherst conducted a detailed analysis of MTV's depiction of women in rock videos and documented his findings in the videotape *Dreamworlds: Desire/Sex/Power in Rock Video*.[8] Jhally demonstrates that the images of women in rock videos are drawn from adolescent male fantasies and carefully choreographed to convey the impression that women are nymphomaniacs with an insatiable desire for sexual contact with any available man. Whether depicted as virgin temptresses, jungle Amazons, or dominatrixes, the women in rock videos are typically exposing themselves, dancing provocatively, and engaging in sexual activity. And the camera spends a disproportionate amount of time lingering on breasts, buttocks, and crotches. Only rarely does a rock video woman reject a man's advances; and even then, when the man becomes aggressive, she surrenders eagerly, passionately, thereby establishing that "No" really means "Take me by force." Jhally suggests that this depiction of women legitimizes voyeurism, lust, and rape, and teaches men to regard women not as individual human beings, but as "body parts to be watched and used."

Then, too, there are the nightly family-hour stories of string-bikini-clad hot dog vendors, topless car washers, people who videotaped their own or other people's lovemaking, prostitutes claiming that nymphomania made them do it; and innumerable articles about sex in men's and women's magazines. A fairly typical example is a *Cosmopolitan* article, "The Sexual Fantasies of a Married Woman," which begins with a boldface quote: "Have you ever imagined fierce love with a stranger, a group grope, perhaps a lusty spanking? Such secret scenarios are normal, even good for you . . . so let's stop with the guilt and indulge!"[9] The media regularly promote irresponsible attitudes toward life by giving celebrities a platform to offer such ideas as Kim Basinger's remark to Maury Povich, "Take every experience and live it to the fullest," and Joyce DeWitt's proclamation to Phil Donahue, "Conscience was invented by priests to keep people under their control." Talk shows glamorize promiscuity: Wilt Chamberlain is prodded to discuss his claim of having had twenty thousand sexual "encounters." The nationally syndicated television show *Studs* premiered in 1991. As its name suggests, promiscuity is the show's focus: two men go on arranged dates with the same three women, and then all meet in the studio to determine which guy is the "winner."

Amazingly, experts are wondering why rape, teenage pregnancy, and sexually transmitted disease are rampant. For example, when a study by the Alan Guttmacher Institute revealed that the sexual activity of teenage girls had risen sharply throughout the 1980s, Jacqueline Forrest, Institute Vice President for Research, expressed surprise: "We had thought that increases in sexual activity might have reached a plateau in the early 1980s, but what we're seeing is a significant increase throughout the decade. *That was unexpected* [emphasis added]."[10] No doubt similar bafflement prompted the National Institute of Child Health and Human Development to apply for $18 million of federal money for a five-year study of teenage sex (and other) habits, hoping to gain insight into their cause.

The fact that we are perplexed about the cause of these problems is a far greater scandal than the existence of the problems. In the present social climate, common sense should prompt us to *expect* sexual problems to worsen, not to be surprised when they do. Even if young people don't (or can't) read the printed word, they can see and hear, and therefore cannot escape the media's incessant proclaiming, ever more boldly and blatantly, that uninhibited sexual expression is normal and healthy. The conclusion that this message leads directly to early sexual experimentation and promiscuity, and indirectly to teen pregnancy and the contracting of sexually transmitted diseases, is logically inescapable. Equally inescapable is the conclusion that the depiction of women as craving sex and fantasizing about being taken by men, even against their will, is a strong influence in young men's attitudes toward women, and therefore a significant factor in the psychology of rape.

One media response to such charges is to claim that the public wants such programming. For example, sex therapist and frequent talk-show guest Judith Kuriansky says that we Americans are "kids in our [sexual] mentality" compared to people in other countries. She believes that sex in the media is no big deal and that we can expect to see more of it in years to come because viewers will demand it.[11] If her prediction about entertainment proves accurate, one thing is certain—it will not be because of public demand but the entertainment industry's pandering to sensationalism. A more typical media response to criticism of their treatment of sex is that sex is part of life and realism demands that it be expressed, not hidden. This response is disingenuous. We are asked to accept as realistic an interminable parade of elaborately choreographed, marvelously inventive sex scenes of extended duration while talk-show therapists assure us that, for the average American, sex occurs once or twice a week in a wumpity-wump encounter. (Incidentally, if the TV and film industries discourage the modern equivalents of *Boys' Town, It's a Wonderful Life,* and *Going My Way* because they are unrealistic, on what basis do they accept incredible science fiction and Ninja warrior scripts?)

In any case, the central issue is not the portrayal of sex but the manner, context, and frequency of that portrayal. The media's treatment of sex is puerile; it is characterized by uncritical acceptance of the Freudian premise that the sex drive is the dominant drive in human beings. This premise—never a scientific finding as Freud pretended, but only his personal fantasy— has been dramatically refuted. The suffering that Viktor Frankl experienced in the concentration camps and observed others experiencing provided eloquent and definitive testimony that the drive to find meaning in life is a higher drive. Not only was there little of the sexual perversion common to all other exclusively male confinements, but the sex urge was generally absent in the concentration camps. "Even in his dreams," Frankl found, "the prisoner did not seem to concern himself with sex, although his frustrated emotions and his finer, higher feelings did find definite expression in them." The prisoners' religious interest was "the most sincere imaginable." Improvised prayers and services were held and spiritual life deepened. In a weary march in numbing cold, as he staggered with other prisoners to daily forced labor, Frankl for the first time in his life grasped "the greatest secret that human poetry and human thought and belief have to impart: The salvation of man is through love and in love." And esthetic growth matched spiritual: through moving anecdotes, Frankl illustrates that "as the inner life of the prisoner tended to become more intense, he also experienced the beauty of art and nature as never before."[12] Frankl's insights are a stirring illustration of the human capacity to extract from evil, in this case the unparalleled evil of the Holocaust, a measure of good. To ignore those insights is an insult to the memory of those who suffered, akin to forgetting the horror of the Holocaust itself. As a major force in the maintenance of knowledge, the media are especially culpable for their glorification of sex, as for their celebration of violence.

VIOLENCE IN MEDIA

According to Thomas Radecki, psychiatrist and research director of the National Coalition on Television Violence (NCTV), the average eighteen-year-old American has seen 200,000 violent acts on television, including 25,000 murders.[13]* Much of this violence is gratuitous, having no purpose but to bolster ratings by maintaining the audience's attention. The Arnold Schwarzenegger film *Commando* provides a fairly typical example of the violent story line. An ex-commando, now a loving father enjoying a peaceful life in the mountains, is approached by former associates and asked to kill someone. Loathing violence, he refuses, so they kidnap his daughter and vow to hold her hostage until he completes his assignment. Outraged, our hero puts loathing aside and sets out to save the girl. He begins by

*In 1992 the American Psychological Association published *Big World, Small Screen: The Role of Television in American Society*, which presented the results of a five-year review of research. It corroborated Radecki's findings and also noted that children under age seven have difficulty distinguishing commercials from programs and evaluating the persuasive devices of advertising.

killing the two men assigned to guard him, breaking one's neck and dropping the other off a cliff. Warming to the task, he shoots, stabs, and bombs dozens upon dozens of foes and then returns with his daughter, apparently unaffected by the mayhem, to live in peace. Many other major stars are associated with this type of film/TV drama, including Mel Gibson, Clint Eastwood, Charles Bronson, Bruce Willis, Chuck Norris, and Sylvester Stallone.

These so-called action-adventure sagas are not the only program genre young people are exposed to. There are also violent detective shows and, most popular among teenagers, violent horror films; even the Saturday-morning cartoons, whose audience includes many preschoolers, now average twenty-six violent acts per hour (with individual scores as high as one hundred per hour). This represents a fourfold increase in little more than a decade. All this violent programming, together with violent fiction, heavy metal music, and video games, teach that the ideas our forebears condemned as false and vicious are acceptable and healthy; more specifically, that violent behavior is normal, that the best response to the threat of violence is violence, and that whatever the "good guys" do to their opponents is justified. Add those lessons to relativism's "You create your own truth," selfism's "You are God," and emotionalism's "Trust your feelings," and the result is a frightening propensity to violence.

In discussing his violent film *GoodFellas*, director Martin Scorsese speculated that "maybe we need the catharsis of bloodletting and decapitation like the ancient Romans needed it, as ritual but not real like the Roman circus."[14] It is absurd to contend that the "rituals" of our entertainment can be neatly insulated from our lives, to pretend that there is no relationship between the climate of violence created and maintained by the media and the acts of violence plaguing America. How else can we explain real-life incidents such as people putting glass, cyanide, and razor blades in Halloween treats, one man murdering another over a parking place, drive-by shootings, an eleven-year-old trying to poison her principal so he wouldn't tell her parents she had been in a fight at school, a mother threatening to kill a high school official because her daughter didn't make the cheerleading squad, someone dropping a fifty-two-pound rock off a highway overpass and killing a passing driver, a mother and children voting on whether to kill the husband/father (the ayes had it)? What more plausible reason can we cite for eight teenage skinheads torturing a cat, breaking its back and watching it try to crawl away, donning masks and dancing around it, then killing and mutilating it, and videotaping the whole incident? What more logical cause for a dozen youths walking into a settlement of homeless men, screaming "trick or treat," and attacking them with meat cleavers, bats with nails in them, and lead pipes?

It would be a mistake to think that the only effect of violence in the media is on the people who are influenced to commit violence or on their victims. Dr. George Gerbner, dean of the Annenberg School of Communications at the University of Pennsylvania, points out that those who identify with the victims are also affected. "Those who are exposed to this kind of violence develop an exaggerated sense of fear, anxiety, insecurity, dependence, paranoia and mistrust. Therefore general exposure to a high level of violence cultivates a 'mean world' syndrome, a sense that the world is a very dangerous place in which to live and that you're going to be hurt."[15]

Some defenders of media violence argue that "No one was ever raped by a book or murdered by a movie," which is reminiscent of the NRA's fallacious "Guns don't kill people, people do." Both formulations confuse *influence, instrument,* and *agent.* Ideas represent influences; guns (and other weapons), instruments; and people, agents. A book or movie cannot be the instrument of mayhem, unless it is used to club someone over the head. Nor can it be the agent. But it can, and in many cases unquestionably is, the influence. And that is sufficient cause for concern and for action. Other defenders of media violence simply argue that there is no evidence that the media in any way influence people's behavior.* Since this response has been repeated hundreds, perhaps thousands of times over the

*Harry N. Hollis, Jr.'s sardonic rejoinder rings true: "I can assure you that these same network officials [who deny that violence on TV causes some viewers to act violently] do not say this to advertisers. They don't tell advertisers that TV will not motivate people [to buy products]."[17]

past few decades, it is not surprising that many people believe it. Nevertheless, it is patently false; there is abundant evidence, research-based as well as anecdotal, of media influence on behavior. In 1978 NBC broadcast a movie in which a girl was raped with a mop handle by reform school classmates. Four days later on a San Francisco beach a gang of teens molested a nine-year-old girl in a similar fashion. (The girl sued the network and lost, only because the court ruled the film's producers had not intended to incite violence.[16]) In 1986 in Watertown, New York, a sixteen-year-old boy was convicted of killing an eleven-year-old playmate while acting out a role from the fantasy game Dungeons and Dragons. More recently, in a number of schools around the country, the Ninja Turtles have been banned as a bad influence on children after teachers noted that children's play had become more aggressive, often in direct imitation of the Turtles' behavior. (One shudders to imagine the potential for harm in serial killer trading cards.)

Teenage suicide has been shown to increase following the broadcasting of fictional movies or news stories about suicide. Preschool children have been found to play more aggressively after watching an aggressive film. (Conversely, preschoolers who are shown a television model of sharing are much more likely to share than those who are shown a model of selfishness, regardless of any preaching that accompanies the modeling.) Adolescent viewers of highly violent television content have been found to have "high levels of aggressive behavior regardless of television viewing time, socioeconomic status, or school performance." A comparative study of three Canadian towns before and two years after the introduction of television suggested a clear relationship between television and aggression. An unusually sophisticated study of FBI crime statistics in sixty-eight U.S. cities before and after the advent of television demonstrated that in every case the introduction of television resulted in an increase in the rate of larceny. A pair of intensive studies of children in the U.S. and Finland disclosed a clear correlation between the viewing of television violence and aggressive behavior both immediately and in subsequent years, the second study documenting a significant relationship between exposure to television violence at age eight and serious criminal behavior at age thirty. The authors concluded that "Aggressive habits seem to be learned early in life, and once established, are resistant to change and predictive of serious adult antisocial behavior... Early television habits are in fact correlated with adult criminality."[18] Moreover, they argue, "television violence affects youngsters of all ages, of both genders, at all socioeconomic levels and all levels of intelligence... It cannot be denied or explained away."[19]

A number of scholars have compiled detailed summaries and analyses of available research in the field of TV violence. A 1977 review covered 67 studies; a 1986 review, 230 studies. Both reviews and virtually every research study they covered concluded that there is a clear and significant relationship between the viewing of television violence and antisocial attitudes and actions.[20] "What they [children] see," another researcher wryly observed, "is what we get." As to how what is experienced in the media translates into negative behavior, Leonard Berkowitz, aggression researcher and professor of psychology at the University of Wisconsin, offers the most plausible explanation: "There is no one factor at work, but one of the things that happens is that people get ideas as well as inclinations, and if their inhibitions happen to be weak at the time, these ideas or inclinations can be translated into open behavior."[21]

Anthea Disney, editor in chief of *TV Guide*, reports that a study commissioned by her magazine found on a single randomly chosen day 1,846 separate acts of violence on television. Cartoons were the most violent category, and cable networks averaged three times as much violence as the major commercial networks. Disney argues that TV violence should be treated as a public health issue, as are cigarette smoking and drunken driving.[22] In *Deadly Consequences*, Deborah Prothrow-Stith, assistant dean of government and community programs at the Harvard School of Public Health, suggests that inner-city children may be more susceptible to TV violence because they watch more TV and have fewer male role models.[23] How ironic it will be if white TV moguls prove to be partly responsible for black crime!

The last decade has witnessed not only an increase in media sex and media violence, but also the even more potent combination of the two, pornoviolence. The celebrated film *Silence of the Lambs* and Brett Easton Ellis's controversial novel *American Psycho* are notable examples. Similarly, the album *Mind of a Lunatic*, by the Geto Boys, deals with murder and necrophilia. As columnist John Leo has noted, even the names of contemporary musical groups suggest pathological preoccupation with sex, scatology, and violence. He found thirteen bands named after male genitals, six after female genitals, four after sperm, eight after abortion, one after vaginal infection, ten after various sex acts, and twenty-four disparaging blacks, the disabled, or gays.

Dr. Seymour Feshbach, chairman of UCLA's psychology department, warns of the danger of combining sex and violence: "If you vicariously identify with the characters, you can get a very strong conditioned effect, and the violent act becomes attached to sexual arousal. The cognitive message is, this is okay, people do this. And obviously rape is the more severe form of sex mixed with violence."[24] Anyone unpersuaded of the relationship between media pornoviolence and the escalating incidence of rape in the U.S., now an estimated 1.3 to 2 million offenses a year, would do well to reflect on George Will's searingly logical juxtaposition of the testimony of the alleged assailants in the "wilding" episode in New York's Central Park in which a young jogger was viciously beaten and gang-raped, and the lyrics of the controversial 2 Live Crew album, *As Nasty As They Wanna Be*. The attitudes expressed by the young men, he observes, show eery similarity to the lyrics. The wilding episode and the attitudes behind the song lyrics, Will concludes, testify to "America's slide into the sewer."[25]

The insensitivity of some media executives about these matters is appalling. Time-Warner executives continued to defend their decision to release Ice-T's *Cop Killer* even after police groups protested and called for a boycott of Time-Warner products. Moreover, they claimed to be defending First Amendment rights by their stand. (Apparently the First Amendment guarantee of rights doesn't extend to the life and happiness of the police and their families.) But that was not Time-Warner's only affront to common decency. According to *U.S. News & World Report* the company sent gratis copies of the album to disc jockeys in miniature black vinyl body bags as a "promotional gimmick."[26] There is additional evidence suggesting that the vast Time-Warner empire, which includes HBO, Cinemax, *Time* Magazine, and book- and record-publishing holdings, is insensitive to the growing problems associated with sex and violence. In the spring of 1992 Time-Life ran commercials for a video entitled *Trials of Life*, a close look at violence in the animal world. Against a backdrop of carnivorous stalking, the announcer talks about the struggle for survival and urges viewers to buy the video and "see why they are called *animals*." The commercial does include a warning about the possible inappropriateness of the material for younger viewers, but perceptive viewers will be inclined to regard that qualification more as a sales gimmick than an expression of social concern. In the same year Warner Books published *Sex* and Warner Records released *Erotica* by Madonna and ran an elaborate foldout insert in *Publishers Weekly* featuring a photo of the reclining star, scantily clad and with one hand inserted between her legs. The ad copy promises an "explosive," "electric," "erotic" product that "takes a provocative look at sexual fantasies in photographs and words, as this extraordinary celebrity once again dances to her own beat, presenting a remarkable book of erotic imaginings. . . ." The ad announced a "spectacular six-figure multimedia marketing campaign," which was to include "unprecedented publicity, an extraordinary PR and ad campaign, national print and radio penetration, and full size stand-up [wouldn't reclining be more in character?] Madonna easels and full-color posters."

OTHER HARMFUL EFFECTS

Stimulation of unhealthy attitudes toward sex and violence, though the most obvious harm done by media, is not the only or perhaps the most serious harm. As even a cursory examination of the facts will document, the media also breed passivity and conformity, undermine learning, discourage rationality, subvert standards of excellence, and promote incivility. In their research on the effects of television viewing, Professors Robert Kubey and Mihalyi Csikszentmihalyi have found that while people watch TV, they feel more passive and relaxed, less alert and challenged, and less concentrated on what they are doing than during any other activity with the exception of resting. They have also found evidence of a spillover effect, in which passivity continues for a time after watching TV.[27] To understand why this occurs we need only compare the experience of TV viewing with that of reading.* When we read we are actively engaged with the text. We move our eyes over the page and control our own pace, pausing to ponder a meaningful passage and probe or savor its meaning. The images that fill our minds are constructed by our imagination, not provided by the author. When we view television, we surrender our senses to be stimulated by programmers in ways they determine and control. Laugh tracks, today so sophisticated that they can mix a variety of kinds of laughter to create the illusion of a live audience, prompt us to be amused; applause tracks tell us when to cheer; game-show lights, bells, and whistles dazzle our senses; and background music evokes the desired emotional response. Moreover, program content develops in viewers the expectation of being entertained, shocked, and titillated.

The increase in the number of magazines offering stories of celebrities' private lives and Kitty Kelley-type biographies represents the print media's attempt to meet (and profit from) this expectation. Media executives miss or ignore the fact that young people bring this expectation to the classroom and thus reject meaningful learning. Between 1966 and 1990 the percentage of students who studied in the library dropped from 27.4 to 10.1; those who checked out a book over the course of a year dropped from 51.6 to 26.7.[28] Further, a U.S. Department of Education study disclosed that students' level of performance in mathematics is positively related to the number of books in their homes and the amount of time they devote to pleasure reading; as TV viewing increases, achievement decreases.[29]

In the early 1950s, well before television had come of age, artist Henri Matisse observed that "cinema, advertising, and magazines push at us a daily flood of images which, already made, are to vision what prejudice is to intelligence." Art pro-

---

*Marshall McLuhan, the late communications authority, warned that electronic culture affects us very differently than print culture, undermining thought and judgment and disposing us to accept what we see unquestioningly.

fessor Mark W. McGinnis testifies that television has exacerbated this effect, noting that over the last fifteen years "students' individualism seems to have diminished ..., replaced by a conformity born of having had the same visual experiences." When assignments are unstructured, he has found, students "produce facile variations on commercial imagery, such as the death's-heads, muscle men, and huge-breasted women in heavy-metal motifs."[30]

The media undermine learning in a variety of other ways as well. One is by preventing the development of the advanced attention span required to deal with complexity. The average, relatively uneducated nineteenth-century American's attention span was much longer than that of today's college student; for example, relatively uneducated people listened patiently to Lincoln and Douglas debate for over seven hours in language and syntax that would be considered formidable today. In contrast, contemporary college students often begin to writhe as if in physical pain when a discussion extends beyond five or ten minutes.

From its inception, television programming was geared to a short attention span; but as its domination over American culture grew and more and more people were lured from reading and serious discussion (which extend the attention span) and less able to sustain their interest, programmers have adopted such artificial methods of heightening attention as car chases, explosions, gratuitous scenes of sex and violence, the multiplication of subplots (pioneered by "Hill Street Blues"), and frequent shifts of camera angle and scene. Similarly, advertising agencies have employed more and more desperate measures to maintain viewers' attention during commercials. Subaru for example, floats clusters of words over rapidly changing auto factory scenes, while the narrator reads the words aloud. Other admakers alternate blurred with clearly focused shots. And Pepsi creates excitement in its "Uh huh" series by having the camera bounce to the music, shift between long shots and close-ups, and rapidly change the angles of shots of Ray Charles and his dancers.

The extent to which this downward spiral to lower and lower levels of attention has proceeded is best appreciated by watching an older vintage television drama, such as "Gunsmoke" or "The Waltons." I recently viewed an old "Paladin" episode and was struck with how languorous the pace seemed, much of the show being devoted to a long discussion between Richard Boone and the female lead about the demands of duty and honor. The advent of MTV, with its dramatic and often bizarre visual effects, and a new "program" every three or four minutes, has reduced viewers' attention span still further. One result is that sound bites in political campaigns have had to be reduced from 42.3 seconds (1968) to 8.5 seconds (1988). A couple of centuries ago, when English author Jonathan Swift wrote of a people whose memory was so short they forgot the beginning of a sentence before they reached its end, he was being satirical; it now seems he was also prophetic.

Even programming intended to assist learning often contributes to the attention-span problem. Jane M. Healy, educational psychologist and author of *Endangered Minds*, advances a number of reasons why "Sesame Street" is "bad news for reading," including its focus on looking to the neglect of listening; its rapid movement of images, which discourages sustained attention; its fostering of passivity, which prevents children from learning important "attack skills" in reading; and its emphasis on "empty alphabets" rather than meaning.[31] If television has made it difficult for many baby boomers to muster the tolerance for silence and the patience necessary to become devoted readers, it has made it very nearly impossible for the "Sesame Street" generation to do so. Moreover, it is very likely responsible, in large measure, for the new emotional disorder baffling psychologists— Attention Deficit Disorder (ADD). This malady is characterized by lack of attention, impulsiveness, hyperactivity, lack of inhibition, and inability to control behavior, particularly violent behavior. Five times more boys than girls are afflicted with it. As researchers labor to find a cause and a cure, clinicians are prescribing drug therapy, sometimes combined with psychotherapy. Among the interesting questions that deserve researchers' attention are these: Why has ADD only recently been discovered? Did it exist earlier in the century but simply go unnoticed? If it truly is a new condition, is it possible that the broadcast media's manipulation of viewers' (listeners') attention spans is a causative factor? Does popular culture's emphasis on self and expressing one's feelings aggravate the symptoms of impulsiveness and lack of inhibition? Does the constant exposure to vicarious violence in movies and on television, particularly the cartoons and other programs young children watch, contribute to the symptoms of violent behavior? Is there any correlation between frequent use of video games and ADD? (That boys tend to play such games more often than girls could explain why boys are more often afflicted with this condition.)

Those who have managed to maintain the reading habit are likely to benefit less from it than they should because the media promote an episodic grasp of reality, a condition characterized by an extreme compartmentalization of knowledge that prevents one from using existing knowledge to build new knowledge. Broadcast media bombard us with information, each story limited to thirty seconds or less, and punctuated by totally (and sometimes obscenely) unrelated appeals—AIDS statistics, a teachers' strike, and an airline crash, followed by a hemorrhoid commercial, the sports scores, and a hurricane warning. In an effort to compete, newspapers and newsmagazines employ episodic formats of their own.

When Magic Johnson made his startling announcement that he is infected with the AIDS virus, hot lines were reportedly deluged with calls for information, revealing a lack of understanding that disturbed AIDS workers. "We had thought that we had been giving out this information for years," Dr. Reed Tuckson, the former health commissioner for the District of Columbia was quoted as saying, and everyone wondered where public information efforts went wrong. Surely part of the problem lies in the episodic nature of news reports, and part in the fact that the reigning relativism, selfism, and emotionalism have made listening to others archaic.

Television is inherently nonrational: unlike printed material, its appeal is directly to the senses rather than to (or through) the mind. Although this does not necessitate television's being actively opposed to reason and logic, it has become increasingly so by promoting a relativistic, feeling-centered popular culture. Thus Anheuser-Busch runs the "Why Ask Why? Try Bud Dry" commercial series mentioned in chapter 1 and discourages intellectual curiosity; in his ad for Canon's Rebel camera, André Agassi asserts that "Image is everything" (and by implication substance and integrity are nothing); Mazda's appeal tells us "It just *feels* right"; and Reebok reminds us, "Life is short—play hard." (Our grandparents would have taken the more rational view: "Life is short—*Work* hard.") In addition, lottery ads promote the fallacy that one in fifty million represents favorable odds; a USA network show is titled "Beyond Reality" and a David Byrne concert movie, *Stop Making Sense*; and an actor in a Dean Witter commercial depicts the founder intoning such advice as "We measure success one investor at a time" (who doesn't?) and "Listen not only to what our investors say, but to what they mean." (Is there a difference? Don't investors say what they mean?)

Talk-show guests, drawn almost exclusively from the entertainment field, are allowed to discuss any subject they wish, regardless of their qualifications or lack thereof. Miss America is encouraged to give her views on abortion, the AIDS policy, and the cause of Third World economic plight. In many cases, the host will ritually applaud anything celebrities say, however outrageous or illogical it may be. For example, when rap singer Kool Moe Dee declared that AIDS is a white genocidal plot against blacks, one talk-show host replied, "That's interesting."

Just as radio and television talk-show producers know that outrageous views increase ratings, book publishers understand that such views sell books. That is why the two often collaborate, the latter publishing, for example, improbable works on reincarnation, abduction by extraterrestrials, channeling, or the occult, and the former scheduling the authors on their shows. Fairly typical is the story of astrologer Joan Quigley. When it was disclosed that President Reagan and his wife Nancy sought her astrological guidance, she immediately got a book contract and began appearing on the talk shows, making predictions about Jackie O, Princess Di, and Madonna. More than one editor has told me that "Common sense doesn't sell"* and that gimmicks are more important than substance. Since people

---

*Evidently common decency doesn't either. Annette Funicello claims that a publisher encouraged her to write her autobiography but immediately lost interest when she said she had never been involved in scandalous behavior.

can't buy what is not available, it is hardly surprising that such cynicism and contempt for the public have become a self-fulfilling prophecy.

Because people are imitative, not just in childhood but throughout life, and they consciously or unconsciously pattern their behavior on the models society puts before them, constant exposure to shallow or extreme views can be expected to corrupt people's thinking. For example, when actress Demi Moore explained to *Details* magazine why she decided to nurse her child until she was two years old—"that's a particular philosophy I have . . . allowing her to make her own decisions. *I feel she is a better judge than I am"* (emphasis added)—there undoubtedly were readers who adopted that absurd logic. And when the public is fed a steady diet of nonsense, the incidence of irrational, compulsive behavior can be expected to increase. Such an increase has already occurred—bulemia and anorexia, binge drinking, drug use, and compulsive gambling are all serious social problems. "Drama queens" and "excitement junkies" (both male and female) are reportedly seeking or creating crises in their lives in imitation of the characters in soap operas.[32]

According to author Naomi Wolf, an alarming number of women have succumbed to the irrational desire to meet the artificial standard of beauty idealized by popular culture and so have become slaves to the cosmetic, reconstructive surgery, and diet industries.[33] Wolf's description of the condition is no doubt accurate, and no one should be surprised if the mysterious condition known as "body dysmorphic disorder," characterized by the obsessive delusion that one is unimaginably ugly, were found to be caused by the media's incessant promotion of an artificial standard of beauty. However, Wolf's belief that a male conspiracy exists to rob women of self-esteem and subtly discriminate against them seems far-fetched. The manipulation of women, as of men and children, is more likely prompted by simple greed and disregard for the welfare of others.

Yet another harmful effect of the media is to subvert standards of excellence. Celebrity is capriciously bestowed, sometimes to a genuine achiever, but often to an undistinguished or mediocre one. Take the case of Vanna White. Neither an actress nor an entertainer, she became a celebrity for looking pretty and turning letters proficiently, and celebrity brought her a book contract (perhaps symbolically, *Vanna Speaks* has no table of contents) and a fee schedule of $30,000 per lecture engagement. She receives in an hour what many teachers are begrudged for a year's work. And the unhealthy adulation for celebrities extends to high places. A recipient of the Presidential Award for Excellence in Science Teaching complained that then-President Bush snubbed him and the other fifty award recipients, but managed to find time, a few days later, to greet Bo Derek. The lesson implicit in celebrity-worship is transparent: forget about working to achieve excellence; high-profile mediocrity is just as good.* And lest anyone get the idea of working too hard (and catching up with countries such as Japan), the media provides regular cautions—for example, the *Parade* cover that asks in inch-high letters "Are You Afraid to Have Fun?" and refers readers to a special report by Dr. Joyce Brothers offering advice on overcoming this "secret problem that many suffer."[34]

Standards of *moral* excellence are similarly disparaged, with the same harmful effect. When presidential candidate Gary Hart was found to have had a liaison with Donna Rice, he was out of the political race, but she promptly signed with a talent agent to do articles, photo layouts, television appearances, and even (she hoped) write a book. Donald Trump's now and then consort Marla Maples traded her notoriety for a reported half-million-dollar contract to advertise "No Excuses" jeans. When Sidney Biddle Barrows was convicted of running a brothel, she not only got a book contract for *The Mayflower Madam* and made the rounds of all the talk shows, but became the subject of a TV movie in which she was depicted as the streetwalkers' Mother Teresa. That celebrity led to a second book, *Mayflower Manners*, offering advice for the age of sexual revolution by answering such timely questions as what lines are most effective for picking up one-night stands and who should provide the condoms.

---

*Now there is a network devoted solely to celebrities: the E! Entertainment TV network. One writer called it a "round-the-clock genuflection at the altar of celebrity." Here for twenty-four hours a day celebrities are able to talk about themselves and promote their products. The rule for interviewers is not to ask any awkward or difficult questions.

The list of men and women who attain celebrity and wealth from sin and crime grows daily, and every instance proclaims to young people that what counts is not the way you live your life but what material gain you derive.

No one appreciates the publicity value of moral outrageousness better than the queen of self-promotion, Madonna. Here's one example of her *modus operandi*. First she produces a controversial music video, with hints of lesbianism, group sex, and domination; then she appears on "Nightline," where the video is aired. Appearances on other shows follow, affording her continuing opportunities to advance her gospel of sexuality. When the issue of the controversial nature of the video is raised, she retorts, "What about violence and the degradation of women?" Given that her videos vividly reinforce the male fantasy that all women are asking for it, her answer is as offensive as it is evasive.

Most media representatives support the idea that parents should do a better job of teaching children moral values. Yet, ironically, the media themselves undermine parents' efforts. Andy Warhol exaggerated when he predicted that one day everyone would enjoy fifteen minutes of celebrity, but his basic perception was accurate: modern communications technology has multiplied the number of celebrities contending with parents for children's attention, respect, and admiration.* Thus parents find it increasingly difficult to meet the responsibility of being teachers and role models for their children. As British economist E. F. Schumacher noted,

> If . . . nothing is left for the fathers to teach their sons, or for the sons to accept from their fathers, family life collapses. The life, work, and happiness of all societies depend on certain 'psychological structures' which are infinitely precious and highly vulnerable. Social cohesion, cooperation, mutual respect, and above all, self-respect, courage in the face of adversity, and the ability to bear hardship—all this and much else disintegrates and dis-

*In this context, *celebrities* refers not just to well-known entertainers but to anyone whose name and face appear in print or on television. To children, the argument "Important people are on television; that person (unlike my parents) is on television; therefore that person is important" is logically unimpeachable.

appears when these 'psychological structures' are gravely damaged.[35]

The situation is damaging enough when the celebrities are praiseworthy and are treated so. It is especially destructive when, as is so often the case, they are not. On the same edition of "A Current Affair" that recounted Pee-wee Herman's pathetic affair in the porn theater, a segment had a woman guest discussing the late Sammy Davis, Jr.'s use of drugs, pornography, adultery, orgies, even Satanism! And the treatment was not only uncritical, but bordered on the celebrational. On a "Donahue" show about prostitutes and their children, a woman in the audience asked the prostitutes, "Did you have a high school education?" (They did, and one had even been to college.) Phil asked why the woman raised that question. She replied that when she went to high school, she learned bookkeeping and other subjects that made her employable. Phil then inquired, in that patented mocking tone he reserves for those who value common sense and traditional standards of decency, whether she thought that because she had raised her kids doing honest work, the prostitutes should also. Having made his disparaging point about traditional morality, he walked away before she could answer.

The standard media defense "We are just airing timely issues" (translation: sensationalism sells) rings hollow. Consider the "Geraldo" show that featured Ross Jeffries, author of *How to Get the Woman You Desire Into Bed*, a self-published book available only by phone. The book explains how to use hypnotic language patterns to bypass consciousness and register subconsciously. Although Geraldo challenged and at times ridiculed the author, he nevertheless made people aware of the book, thereby legitimizing and in a sense promoting it. He was also thoughtful enough to provide his viewers with the author's complete telephone number: 1-800-000-STUD. (Geraldo gave the full number.) Consider, too, the kind of news coverage given to even obscure rock musicians when they say or do something outrageous. For example, when a young black performer named Sister Souljah made inflammatory remarks at a Rainbow Coalition gathering, *Newsweek* ran a picture of her on its cover[36] and explained later that they had done so because "she had a lot of people thinking and talking about rap and race."[37] A pathetic excuse. Those who make absurd statements sometimes do get others thinking, but that is no reason to showcase their absurdity. *Newsweek* could have used for its cover a picture of then-presidential candidate Bill Clinton chastising her, or of Reverend Jesse Jackson taking offense at Clinton's statement. Better yet, the magazine could have consigned the story to page 54 and used the cover to highlight a matter of greater importance.

Adding insult to injury, the media blame parents and teachers for the social problems the media have caused. For several decades the media have made the job of parents and teachers considerably more difficult by giving credence to the idea that there is an unavoidable "generation gap" between young people and adults. This idea, advanced by anthropologist Margaret Mead and others and still being disseminated in books, movies, and television shows, is pure bunk. One finds little evidence of such a gap in other cultures—China and Japan, for example—until they become Westernized. And it was not observable in our own culture prior to the mid-twentieth century.* The generation gap idea was canonized in the 1960s and 1970s not because it had merit, but because it fit the anti-authoritarian, iconoclastic mood of the time. The fact that many young people now believe that contemptuous disregard of the lessons of home, school, and church is normal, even heroic, in no way validates the idea of a "generation gap." It merely demonstrates the media's success in making it a self-fulfilling prophecy.

Entertainers enjoy greater visibility in America than ever before, not only in their roles as entertainers or to promote their work, but also as champions of ideas and causes. They deliver commencement addresses and receive honorary degrees, make public service commercials, perform at benefits for disaster victims, and make speeches endorsing political candidates. They are disproportionately represented on talk shows, where they are often encouraged to give their views on matters about which their knowledge is less than superficial. It goes without saying that celebrities have a right to express their

---

*This is not to say that there were no differences of opinion between parents and children, or that rebelliousness was unknown, but that these phenomena were not inevitable or unsolvable, as the generation gap concept suggests.

ideas, and talk-show hosts and planners of functions can be forgiven for engaging people who will draw a large audience. Nevertheless, it is important to recognize the unfavorable consequences of this situation. Because most entertainers are liberal,* the ideas they champion are likely to be the most intellectually fashionable ones, notably relativism, selfism, and the exaltation of feelings. Because the public tends to respond to celebrities with admiration and even awe, their ideas are more likely to be accepted uncritically than are other people's ideas. And because the choice of celebrities for all these occasions of visibility consigns wiser, more informed individuals to *in*visibility, the public is denied access to genuine expertise. Never have the insights of the best and brightest among us been more desperately needed or less accessible. Never have inspiring models of greatness, men and women of accomplishment in the most challenging of life's arenas, been so effectively displaced by mere pretenders.

Critics of the media or of the popular culture the media convey risk disparagement and ridicule. They are commonly branded intellectual Neanderthals, inquisitors, neo-Fascists, or buffoons. When people objected to a nude photo of pregnant Demi Moore on a magazine cover, Mary Hart complained on "Entertainment Tonight," "It's getting so everytime you turn around, someone doesn't want you to see a magazine cover," and proceeded to worry aloud that censorship is on the rise. In a story on the revised movie rating codes (changing the X rating to NC-17), the usually perceptive "60 Minutes" included a clip of the legendary Will Hays righteously fulminating against smut in language that today seems ludicrously stilted; the same story repeatedly showed a scene from an Italian film with a censorious priest previewing a film and ringing a bell to signal which parts were offensive and should be cut. When then-Vice President Dan Quayle suggested that the TV show "Murphy Brown" glorified illegitimacy and denigrated family values, the media went into a ridiculing frenzy. A real TV anchorwoman with an illegitimate child accused Quayle of insulting all mothers in her

---

*In the 1988 election, 76 percent of entertainers' financial contributions went to Democratic candidates.[38]

situation. News shows tabulated Quayle's verbal gaffes and resurrected old Carson and Letterman routines lampooning him.

Several decades ago when moderates warned that a permissive approach toward obscenity would likely lead to the legitimizing of increasingly offensive material, they were ridiculed for being priggish. Today, when time has proved their prediction accurate, they are not (as honesty demands) given credit for their foresight—they are instead chastised for not acknowledging the inevitability of change in moral standards. A case in point: in response to the question of "whether photographs of unorthodox couplings will become standard art-gallery fare" a columnist sniffs, "Of course they will. Opponents of censorship are disingenuous to pretend otherwise. Time always tempers what we consider shocking: the raunch level of 1969's X-rated "Midnight Cowboy" would hardly qualify as PG-13 today."[39] Such responses as these suggest the accuracy of columnist John Leo's observation that the media are often guilty of "cheerleading for the unraveling of the social structure."[40]

Media disdain notwithstanding, it is not a sign of ignorance or artistic deficiency but a mark of responsibility and common sense to be troubled by popular culture's contribution to moral decline. C. S. Lewis, a master of both fiction and nonfiction writing, observed that "the contemporary propaganda for lust [makes us] feel that the desires we are resisting are so 'natural,' so 'healthy,' and so reasonable, that it is almost perverse and abnormal to resist them. Poster after poster, film after film, novel after novel, associate the idea of sexual indulgence with the ideas of health, normality, youth, frankness, and good humour. Now this association is a lie."[41] Common sense and everyday experience continue to support this perspective.

THE ROLE OF ADVERTISING

Throughout this century the advertising industry has portrayed itself in a positive light. While admitting that some of its practitioners might occasionally annoy people with their shrillness or insult their intelligence with a patronizing ad, they have categorically denied that advertising does harm. Contemporary spokespeople perpetuate the tradition. Advertising is "simply salesmanship," employing the same principles of persuasion used in addressing a civic organization, a business conference, or a political gathering, claims advertising executive John O'Toole. He portrays advertisers as people who present information to help the public understand how "the product will solve a problem, make life easier or better, or in some way provide a benefit."[42]

The argument is specious. To begin with, it ignores the distinction between honest persuasion and propaganda. Honest persuasion may sometimes appeal to the emotions, but it does not discourage thought or engage in deception. Propaganda, on the other hand, evokes feelings in order to prevent thought and consciously deceives. The vast majority of advertisements, print as well as nonprint, are propaganda. They manipulate us by appealing to our desires, playing on our insecurities, magnifying our genuine needs, creating artificial needs, and pretending differences where none exist.

Observed impartial *Consumer Reports*, "Since there's little difference in quality between Coke and Pepsi, the soft-drink giants must appeal more to consumers' emotions than to their reason."[43] Advertisers employ every available technological device to make the public suspend their critical evaluation judgment and accept biased testimony (the manufacturer's self-praise) as fact. They also employ the devices associated with propaganda, including "bandwagon," glittering generalities and slogans, and they pay celebrities enormous sums to shill for their products. Rising tennis star Jennifer Capriati, for example, received an estimated $6 million in endorsements in her first year as a professional, compared to $200,000 in winnings. And the greater the recognition, or Q-factor, the greater the payoff: for Michael Jordan, an estimated $11 million annually; for Magic Johnson, $9 million; for André Agassi, $7 million.

Advertisers shamelessly forge irrational associations between their products and popularity, success, sex appeal, and love. Ford Motor Company, for example, ran a 27-by-22-inch double-page ad in *USA Today* for its Mercury Sable. A half-silhouette of a man and woman in suggestive embrace dominated the page, dwarfing the car. (The ad appeared in a number of magazines as well.) The ad copy read, in part: "We dressed in silence. And drove. When we walked in, she said something to the piano player. Next thing, I hear this song we used to love. She takes my hand. We dance. And something that was there before, was back. Only stronger." It went on to say, undoubtedly with calculated ambiguity, "the body has been totally restyled" and "the controls are easier to read and reach."

During the 1991 U.S. Open tennis tournament, a commercial for Gillian dresses was broadcast over and over again for two weeks in prime time. Against a soft brownish-yellow haze a woman in black, legs provocatively raised, dress invitingly short, perched atop a piano while a man clad in a tuxedo played. In the background a voice was heard soulfully singing "When a man loves a woman. . . ." The camera lingered on the woman as she slithered up and kissed him.

A full-page ad for Georges Marciano's Guess jeans pictured a young, nubile blonde woman standing in front of what appears to be a barn door, evoking farmer's daughter associations. Appearing to be clad only in a white shirt and perhaps an undersized bra, but naked from the waist down, she leans forward and smiles at the camera as her breasts spill out into view. The page size is 8 inches by 10 1/2 inches, her body fills about 80 percent of the page, her breasts are 2 inches by 3 inches. Yet the Guess jeans logo is only one-half inch square and almost hidden at the top right of the page. (The name Georges Marciano appears in half-inch letters at the bottom.)[44] What exactly was being advertised?

"Stealth advertising" in movies compounds the industry's characteristic deception. The movie *Teenage Mutant Ninja Turtles* contains a fifty-second commercial for Domino's Pizza disguised as a scene. *Total Recall* featured twenty-eight brand names; *Home Alone*, thirty-one. In one long scene, a medicine cabinet is displayed with the brand names and logos of products clearly visible. In *License to Kill*, James Bond twice lights up a particular brand of cigarettes, and the audience is informed that his girlfriend has resumed smoking after a five-year layoff. These details were reportedly not in the original plot, but were added because a tobacco company paid $350,000. Explains Robert Kovoloff, president of Associated Film Promotions: "There is no greater promotional value—short of a direct endorsement—

than having a major motion picture star use a product in a big budget film."[45]

Though few advertisers would admit publicly that they aim to deceive or that they engage in manipulation, a favorite industry maxim is that ads should "sell the sizzle, not the steak" and that advertisers should establish and maintain an early presence with young people. "It isn't enough to just advertise on television . . . " declares an advertising vice president. "You've got to reach kids throughout the day—in school, as they're shopping in the mall . . . or at the movies. You've got to become part of the fabric of their lives." In 1989 Whittle Communications introduced its controversial "Channel One" program, offering schools free video equipment and ten-minute daily newscasts if students were required to watch two minutes of paid commercials. Within a year an ad agency specializing in school marketing was advising its clients, "Kids spend 40 percent of each day in the classroom where traditional advertising can't reach them," but "now, you can enter the classroom." (Disney, Nabisco, Coca Cola, Eastman Kodak, Kraft, Procter & Gamble, McDonald's, and Kellogg were among those who expressed interest in the arrangement.)[46]

Declared researcher Kenneth Curtis: "To the commercials on television are given the loudest, most far-reaching voice ever enjoyed by a communicator. They are based and designed on the most thorough and sophisticated research into the motivation of human personality . . . and are produced with the most capable, expert talent available. After two years of detailed research into their content, I have concluded that commercials represent an insidious assault on the Christian view of life."[47]

The alcohol industry points to its "know when to say when" commercials as evidence of its responsible approach to advertising. But those ads are outweighed about ten to one by commercials featuring not someone delivering a quiet lecture, but hordes of animated people holding drinks and having fun in a party atmosphere. Still, the industry's claims of responsibility have impressed some observers. Columnist Robert Novak, for example, doubts that teenage males are silly enough to believe that if they drink beer they'll get women, and reasons that if he and his pretelevision age peers drank beer in high school, then TV ads can't be causing drinking among teens today.[48] Such reasoning not only ignores the fact that the drinking of today's teens is vastly different in degree than that of teenagers in the forties and fifties; it also misses the point that advertising's real impact is not at the level of specific action but at the level of attitude and inclination to act.

Because advertisements are designed to sell goods and services, irrespective of the consumer's need for them or ability to afford them, the most commonly used appeals are to *self-indulgence*—"You deserve this"; *impulsiveness*—"Don't delay; act now"; and *instant gratification*—"You'll feel so good." It was such appeals that Reverend Jesse Jackson had in mind when he charged Nike with promoting an "ethos of mindless material-ism" by tantalizing black inner-city youngsters to buy $125 sneakers that most can afford only by trafficking in drugs. Similarly, direct-mail appeals and promotions on college campuses in recent years have resulted in a dramatic increase in students with major credit cards and a corresponding rise in debts that some students cannot pay.[49]

The fact that America's children have seen three-quarters of a million advertisements by age eighteen helps to explain why their heroes are entertainers and celebrities rather than engi-neers, physicians, and scientists; why an increasing number of them have as their life's goal making a lot of money; and why they experience difficulty in any situation demanding the exer-cise of self-control or extended effort.

If advertisers really believe the attitudes they assiduously cultivate in people are confined to buying behavior, they are naive indeed. Attitudes spill over very easily from one circum-stance to another. Thus it is not unreasonable to assert a relationship between the demand for instant gratification and the declining readership of newspapers, despite the abbreviat-ing of stories and the simplification of form. Nor is it difficult to see a connection between impulsiveness and the research revealing that many physicians form their diagnoses in as little as thirty seconds, often before all the symptoms have been identified.[50]

Education consultant Arthur Whimbey offers a personal ex-ample of a similar phenomenon. At age twenty-eight he found himself still making errors in pronouncing unfamiliar words, confusing, for example, *aerobics* with *aerobatics*. Determining that it was not a problem of faulty analysis but of jumping to a pronunciation based on a roughly similar word, he overcame the habit by checking his impetuousness and concentrating on accuracy. Whimbey finds a similar tendency at work in "the way my remedial math and reading students process sentences, paragraphs, and math problems. . . . Their attention flies by without picking up the pertinent elements, interpreting them, and combining them accurately."[51]

What other problems are attributable to advertising's cultivation of self-indulgence, impulsiveness, and instant gratification? Certainly any social problem characterized by a lack of self-control, including spouse- and child-abuse, substance abuse, and such crimes as assault, rape, and murder; and arguably any problem complicated or intensified by impetuousness, such as the school dropout problem, credit card misuse, bankruptcy, teenage pregnancy, AIDS, and suicide. No other single agency in American life, it seems, is implicated in so many of the nation's problems as is advertising—not the home, school, or government. As the late Richard Weaver wrote almost half a century ago, "The metaphysicians of publicity have absorbed the idea that the goal of life is happiness through comfort. It is a state of complacency supposed to ensue when the physical appetites have been well satisfied. Advertising fosters the concept, social democracy approves it, and the acceptance is so wide that it is virtually impossible today, except from the religious rostrum, to teach that life means discipline and sacrifice."[52] Our social problems have grown much worse in the last decade. The evidence implicating the media, including the advertising industry, in those problems is overwhelming. A single observation by a nineteen-year-old, Dwight Chapman, reveals an insight that media defenders seldom grasp. "The first time I heard a St. Ides [malt liquor] commercial," he said, "I heard a whole slew of rappers. When it played again, I realized it couldn't have been later than 9 o'clock, so there were still little kids listening. When you have big-name rappers like Ice Cube and all his cronies talking about 'get your girl in the mood quicker. . .'—little kids believe whatever they hear. And most stores, if you want St. Ides and you're 13 years old, if you have the money, they don't care. It's bad."[53]

Much has been written in recent years about the "cultural elite." The term is unfortunate in that it creates an image of people who think themselves better than others and hold their opinions arrogantly. Though it may be an accurate representation of some individuals, surely the majority of men and women in the media are no less humble, fair-minded, or concerned about their fellow citizens than people in any other walk of life. They did not, after all, *create* relativism, selfism, and the exaltation of feelings. Like most other Americans, they merely grew up in an atmosphere in which these ideas were dominant. If they have developed a stronger allegiance than others to popular culture,* it is only because their professions involve the dissemination (or the dramatization) of ideas. Therefore, they have been more exposed to and influenced by the ideas that have become entrenched and institutionalized in their industry. It is understandable that they feel more comfortable with scripts that reflect the familiar values of relativism, selfism, and the exaltation of feelings, more at ease with people who espouse related ideas, and quicker to endorse those values than to challenge them.

In brief, the goodwill of the vast majority of the men and women who comprise the media is not open to question. Yet this acknowledgement must not obscure the inescapable conclusion that the media have had a number of negative effects on the lives of all Americans, particularly the young. As we shall see in the chapters that follow, they have undermined the traditional morality and religious values that are the foundation of social order and civic virtue; and they have created attitudes that make raising and educating children difficult if not impossible.

*That people in the television and movie industries have such views has been documented by numerous polls; for example, a Center for Media and Public Affairs survey found a divergence between their beliefs and the beliefs of a majority of Americans: 49 percent believe adultery is wrong compared with 85 percent of the general public; 45 percent have no religious affiliation, compared with 4 percent of the general public; 20 percent believe homosexual acts are morally wrong, compared with 76 percent of the general public; 97 percent say abortion is a woman's right, compared to 59 percent of the general public.[54]

SIX

Personalized Morality

I was conducting a faculty seminar at a small Northeastern college on how best to develop students' evaluation and discussion of ethical issues. It is important, I explained, to establish a working principle to which all students can give at least tentative agreement and which can serve as the basis for judgment. I proposed a principle underlying most ethical systems—respect for persons.* Most faculty in attendance nodded vigorously in affirmation, but several members of the philosophy department voiced strong objection, arguing that no principle can be presumed to apply universally.

"I am not recommending presumption," I responded. "Have students challenge respect for persons before accepting it and when it has proved worthy (as it assuredly will), have them embrace it and employ it until they have sufficient reason to question its applicability to a particular case. From time to time, if you wish, have them reexamine the principle."

*This principle and the criteria associated with it—obligations, ideals, and consequences—are detailed in my book *Thinking Critically About Ethical Issues*, third edition (Mountain View, Calif.: Mayfield, 1992). Brief descriptions of the principle and the criteria appear later in this chapter.

The philosophers continued to object. When I invited them to cite an ethical issue in which this principle was not an important consideration, they were silent. Even after I pointed out what their own experience compelled them to confirm—that the typical classroom discussion of ethical issues seldom gets beyond "Well, that's my opinion and I'm entitled to it," and that the principle of respect for persons elevates discussion to a more productive level—they still insisted, to my consternation and that of their colleagues, that no such foundation for judgment and discussion should be established.

These professors of philosophy harbored the prevailing attitude toward morality—that it is purely subjective and that no basis exists, or can exist, for judging the rightness of an issue. Since all values are held to be relative, no one's value system is considered better than anyone else's and individual conscience is considered infallible. Whatever people may feel comfortable doing becomes, by that very fact, morally right for them. The only real moral offense, from this perspective, is to call someone else's behavior immoral. When Sidney Biddle Barrows appeared on a talk-show to promote the sequel to *Mayflower Madam*, for example, and a caller questioned whether her books glamorized immorality, she huffed, "What do you want me to do, take a job in Bloomingdale's?" and the host snickered. The caller's question, though in reality an interesting and relevant philosophical question, was treated as a breach of good taste. Similarly, it is not uncommon for even educated people to argue that parents and teachers should accept children's attitudes and values rather than try to change them. I recently heard a college dean publicly chastise a professor for "making a value judgment."

Values Clarification, the approach to moral education that has dominated American education for the past two decades, reflects this intellectual fashion. It not only rejects the idea of absolute values, but also of objective judgment—that is, judgment based on consideration of the reasonableness of the various viewpoints. There are no "shoulds" or "oughts" in Values Clarification; classroom discussion of ethical issues is designed to give students an opportunity to express their views in an atmosphere of mutual acceptance.* Everyone is considered right, no one wrong; the clash of ideas is banished and serial monologue replaces discussion and debate. At first thought, this view of morality seems to be an expression of fairness, tolerance, and intellectual humility, an eminently wise perspective on questions of right and wrong. Alas, it is actually a variant expression of the same nonsense discussed in earlier chapters. Relativism, selfism, and Romanticism have found their most forceful, belligerent, and absurd expression in contemporary morality. Numerous historical events prepared the way for the triumph of moral relativism: the disillusionment caused by the Depression and World War II; banishment of ethics and esthetics from philosophy on the grounds that all values are feelings, and the subsequent displacement of philosophy by psychology; and the subjectivizing influence of the 1960s, with its anthem that "everything is beautiful in its own way" and its tortured reasoning that since everyone has a right to an opinion, every opinion must therefore be right.

The measure of moral relativism is that no one can maintain it consistently. However heroic people's defense of the view that there is no right or wrong apart from one's perspective, common sense will sooner or later force them to affirm a standard beyond self in one situation or another. The particular situation that triggers the (often fleeting) restoration of common sense is not the same for everyone. For some, it is assaults on the elderly, for others the report of abused animals in puppy mills, for still others a blatant breach of trust. Alan Dershowitz, for example, the well-known law professor and trial lawyer with impeccable liberal credentials, admitted that Woody Allen clearly "crossed a boundary" when he began an affair with Mia Farrow's daughter. As to Allen's statement that he sees no moral issue in the matter, Dershowitz responded that Allen was wrong—that he "ought to" see one.[1]

Given the right issue, those for whom morality is defined by

*Sadly, many psychologists have validated this shallow perspective by telling their patients that emotional problems are caused by "*must*urbation"—that is, by thinking in terms of what one *ought to, should,* or *must* do. Though they may intend only to cure compulsiveness, their approach to therapy undermines an entire academic field—ethics—and transforms the seven deadly sins into the seven life-style choices.

culture rather than self will experience the same sudden return to their senses. Some years ago in Brazil a man shot his wife in the face, killing her because she flirted with another man. He pleaded that he had merely "defended his honor." He was not only found not guilty, but a radio poll revealed that a majority of the people thought his plea valid and defended the verdict. Though I know many moral relativists, I never heard one say, "If that's the Brazilian ethic, then it must be right for them." Nor have I heard anyone saying of the deplorable situation in Somalia, with tens of thousands of children dying of starvation because revolutionaries won't allow food to reach them, "I feel bad about it, but I can't pass judgment on another culture's morality." No, they call the actions of those cruel men barbaric and demand that other nations send troops and end the tragedy. They know that right is right, regardless of who or how many say otherwise.

THE COST OF MORAL RELATIVISM

One consequence of moral relativism is the schizophrenic reaction of alternately praising and denouncing a particular way of thinking or behaving. On an "Oprah Winfrey Show" concerning women who have had affairs with their husbands' bosses, for example, one guest admitted having had over twenty affairs, most of them with superiors at work so that she could get something from them. She explained that her husband is unintelligent and that she doesn't love him now and never did love him. When asked why she married him, she answered, "Because I don't want to support myself and his family can do things for me." Later she added, "I know what I'm doing and why I'm doing it," "I want all I can get out of life," and "I don't like commitments; I like to go out and have fun." Oprah was astounded, saying that she hadn't heard a story like this in all her years of interviewing people. Surprised and outraged by the woman's view, the audience frequently interrupted her with hoots and jeers.[2]

The outrage was understandable, but not the surprise. What the woman was saying was not a great deal different from what numerous writers have been saying in *Cosmopolitan* for decades. In fact, if this woman had worn a more stylish outfit and additional makeup and had tempered her bluntness with a little eyelash-fluttering coyness, she would have passed for the quintessential "Cosmo girl." What shocked the audience, I suspect, was not what she said, but her refusal to wrap her views in the euphemistic jargon of relativism. Though her amorality was lamentable, her freedom from hypocrisy was both refreshing and instructive about the reality of moral relativism.

The capriciousness of public reaction to people's behavior has created considerable confusion about right and wrong. Given the vigorous defense of Andrew Dice Clay's vicious "comedy" and 2 Live Crew's pornoviolent lyrics, Brown University junior Douglas Hann had reasonable cause to believe his shouting of anti-black, anti-Semitic, anti-gay epithets in the dormitory courtyard would be considered protected speech. Instead, he was expelled. (The ACLU's protest to the university may have provided him some small consolation.) Perhaps he got exactly what he deserved and merits no sympathy. Nevertheless, we should acknowledge that in many ways it is a baffling and depressing time to be young. Fifty years ago it was common to hear that "one person can make a difference," usually in the context of parental exhortation. Today those words have lost their power. If there is no right and wrong except what the individual feels, then there is no point in making a difference.

Everyday experience drives home this lesson. A well-known Hollywood celebrity recently admitted that he's never dieted, has never shopped in a supermarket, and hates commercials, yet he accepted $2 million to do a series of healthy eating commercials for a large Italian supermarket chain. (By way of comparison, years after the Civil War, Robert E. Lee, then ill and without income, was offered $50,000 by an insurance company just to use his name. He declined because he believed it was wrong to accept money without earning it honestly.) A Supreme Court justice disclosed that he accepted $140,000 in cash and gifts from a close friend, while serving on the Court at a salary of $118,000. A distinguished senator admitted that he failed to report gifts of more than $14,000 from a man who later pleaded no contest to tax evasion; in addition, friends reportedly loaned him more than $700,000 in a six-year period and then forgave more than $133,000 of the debt. And scandals proliferate—the junk bond scandal, insider trading on Wall Street, the S & L and BCCI affairs, congressional check-kiting, and so on—often presenting the taxpayers with a hefty bill.

The cost of this confusion is greater than monetary; America's moral idealism has been eroded. James Patterson and Peter Kim, authors of an ambitious survey of American attitudes and values, *The Day America Told the Truth*, report that more than 70 percent of their subjects don't have a single hero. Harvard professor of psychiatry Robert Coles states in his book *Children in Crisis* that 60 percent of the children in his survey base their moral standards mainly on self-gratification. Cheating is epidemic, not only in schools and colleges but also in the workplace. Résumé fraud is a significant problem in business and the professions, and the scientific community is concerned about dishonesty among researchers.

In 1970 four out of ten college freshmen said one of their life goals was "being well-off financially" and eight out of ten valued developing "a meaningful philosophy of life"; in 1987 the percentages were almost reversed.[3] An Insurance Research Council survey conducted by the Roper Organization revealed that 23 percent of respondents think it permissible to pad for deductibles, and 20 percent approved of padding claims to recover premiums paid in years for which no claims were filed.[4] And a study of male college students revealed that 44 percent would force a female to do something sexual that she didn't want to do, if they knew they would not be found out or punished.[5] Counselors and police officers report that fewer and fewer young violators show remorse for their offenses.

Many people are wondering why America is plagued by moral callousness and insensitivity. They are appalled and frightened by what they hear on the nightly news. A man chains his wife to concrete blocks, then takes their young children out to enjoy July 4 fireworks. Two teens throw a homeless man off a bridge to his death, even after he protests he cannot swim. A twelve-year-old girl admits that on three occasions she falsely accused her parents of child abuse so that she could get a chance "to be out, to be free and go to parties and stuff" at foster homes and in detention centers. Thieves lurk in cemeteries and steal purses from grieving women. A disgruntled man mails a live grenade to his boss after he is fired. Several dozen doctors receive credit for attending a Colorado seminar on malpractice, even though they spent their time on the ski slopes.

Why are such incidents more and more common today? Why is there an increase in serial crimes whose sadistic perpetrators display no feeling for their victims, show no mercy? Why has the character of child abuse changed over the past decade or so, with four out of five cases now involving sexual abuse as well as violence, and not a few involving bizarre satanic rituals? Because of moral relativism. When people believe there is no standard other than personal preference and whatever they feel like doing is permissible, there is bound to be an increase in immorality. When young people are denied meaningful moral education, the consequence is moral illiteracy. To believe otherwise is irresponsibly naive.

There is a category of logical fallacy known as "slippery slope." The idea, simply stated, is that it is illogical to argue that bad conditions necessarily slide into worse conditions. Liberal intellectuals often ignore the qualifying term ("necessarily") and deny the possibility of progression from bad to worse, arguing in effect against the reality of cause and effect. But the gymnastics of sophistry aside, bad can and often does lead to worse. Dr. Leo Alexander, consultant to the Secretary of War in the Nuremberg trials of Nazi war criminals and a close student of the sordid history of those crimes, notes that the horrors did not spring forth full-blown, but came in small stages. First the chronically ill were "compassionately" killed. Then the category was gradually enlarged "to encompass the socially unproductive, the ideologically unwanted, the racially unwanted and finally all non-Germans."[6] A similar progression has occurred in sexual morality. The elimination of prohibitions against fornication, adultery, and sodomy has led to greater tolerance of all forms of sexual expression, including pedophilia.

The North American Man-Boy Love Association (NAMBLA), for example, is not reticent about its belief that sexual contact between a man and a boy is a victimless crime. A former member of the New York chapter explains: "I don't think the age of consent is an important issue. The thing is that people need to be able to express themselves sexually, even young people. NAMBLA is concerned about gay kids who need to be able to express themselves. And in most of these cases, the boys are just as interested in having sex as the men are." He goes on to say though most members prefer boys who have reached the age of puberty, some prefer young boys and are fond of saying, "When they're 8, it's too late." The former member agrees that "A kid's sexual preference should be immune from parental authority... I believe a 5-year-old child is absolutely capable of deciding—and acting upon—his own sexual preferences. And if the 5-year-old child wants to get involved in a situation with an older man, it's fine with me."[7] That public reaction of this view has gr   ı more tolerant is suggested by the fact that an American Civil Liberties Union spokesman testified before the U.S. Attorney General's Commission on Pornography that his organization opposed the legal restriction of child pornography.*

Respect for law is another victim. The fundamental principle of law is identical to that of ethics—respect for persons. Moreover, it is moral reasoning—the assessment of the point at which one person's action violates the rights of others—that produces laws; and just laws can be distinguished from unjust only on the basis of the quality of that reasoning. By making moral judgment purely subjective, relativism trivializes moral reasoning and undermines the legislative and criminal justice systems. Thus we have been afflicted with such absurd practices as indiscriminately sealing criminal records and thereby inviting sexual deviates, rapists, embezzlers, and armed robbers to escape opprobrium, regain anonymity, and so continue their criminal activities until they are caught again. And foolish laws, like the Texas statute allowing motorists to buy books of five-dollar speeding coupons in advance and to use them when they are caught speeding, seem to be proliferating.

"But who can say what is right and wrong?" relativists are quick to reply, and they assume there is no answer. Yet there is

*The ACLU's positions often reflect moral relativism. According to William Donohue in *The Politics of the American Civil Liberties Union*, the organization opposes laws restricting gambling, some narcotic use, homosexual conduct, pornography, abortion, suicide, the use of metal detectors in airports, and the distribution of child pornography.[8]

an answer: anyone who appreciates the gift of citizenship, values civilization above savagery, and cares about the kind of world we are creating for our children. To pretend that by refusing to make moral judgments we are being objective and neutral is naive. Not to judge is to judge—it is saying that the issue in question is of so little consequence that all views are equally acceptable. There is nothing intolerant or undemocratic about taking a stand on moral issues; on the contrary, the democratic principle that individuals have inalienable rights requires vigilance in acknowledging and safeguarding those rights. It may not be easy to decide such thorny questions as whether drug addict mothers should be prosecuted for addicting their fetuses, whether it is immoral for the United States to sell arms to actual or potential dictators, whether society has a moral obligation to provide health insurance for those who cannot afford to buy their own, or any of the thousands of other moral issues confronting us. But there is no other responsible alternative to deciding.

The tendency to absolve individuals of responsibility for their actions, blaming instead some nebulous villain such as an inherent predisposition to antisocial behavior or dysfunctional family life, is but a reflection of the relativist's refusal to make honest, meaningful moral judgments. Holding individuals accountable for their offenses suggests that people are not animals acting on instinct or blind urge, but moral agents who can choose to behave well if they wish. This idea is anathema to relativists because it implies an objective standard of morality binding on all human beings regardless of their station in life, educational background, personal desires, or fantasies. Far from being undemocratic, this conception is *too democratic* for relativists, who would rather give criminals an excuse ("Society made me do it") than to affirm the idea of culpability. In 1917 the American Psychiatric Association listed 59 forms of mental disturbance; in 1952, 106; today, 292, including "Hypoactive Sexual Desire Disorder," "Self-Defeating Personality Disorder," and "Attention Deficit Hyperactivity Disorder." Sadly, when criminals believe the lie that they are not responsible for their deeds, they resist rehabilitation and instead nurture a resentment that finds expression in more violent acts of crime. The increasing incidence of savage crime reveals the paradox of relativism—by denouncing objective morality, it has proved objective morality indispensable.

The strongest argument against moral relativism is that it cannot be applied consistently without forcing us to conclusions that are manifestly absurd. For example, it forces us to approve, at least tacitly, behavior that simple decency requires us to condemn. Consider some actual cases. In Miami a Cuban refugee was charged with dousing her husband with rubbing alcohol and setting him on fire because he had been acting crazy and refusing to work; she reasoned that by setting him on fire she'd get him into the hospital and get him some help. A father kept his eighteen-year-old daughter chained in the basement because he was afraid she would become a prostitute. (She died when a fire broke out and she was trapped.) A New York City couple allegedly tortured their nine children, ages two to seventeen, by locking them in a dark closet, handcuffing them to metal bars, holding them under water, raping and sodomizing them, and feeding them nothing more than watery gruel. When the children were discovered, they had never spoken to another human being. A philosophy that requires us to say of such cases "if the people involved felt their actions were right, then they were right for them" can hardly be taken seriously.

Not only does relativism imply that terrorism, rape, and child molestation are acceptable if the perpetrator believes they are; it also obliterates the distinction between scurrilous behavior and heroism. During the Holocaust thousands of Gentiles hid Jews, often at the risk of their own lives and those of their families, because they thought it was the right thing to do; others did similarly, but demanded payment from the Jews; still others reported people who did so to the authorities who cooperated with the Nazis and shipped people off to die in the camps. Relativism would have us view these actions as morally equal. In Bogota, Colombia, a wealthy man, Jaime Jaremio, regularly visits the sewer urchins, those poorest of the poor children who live amid three thousand miles of stinking, flowing, typhoid-ridden excrement. Jaremio distributes food and clothing, builds houses for them, and finds them jobs. In contrast, vigilantes (allegedly with the approval of police) kill the children and leave their bodies on roadsides to rot.

The measure of relativism is that it sees no difference between the hand of compassion and the hand of death, between
patriotism and treason, victim and villain, virtue and vice. Relativism regards the homeless Orlando, Florida, man who found
$29,200 in $100 bills and turned it in to the sheriff's office as no
more virtuous than the Savings and Loan manipulators, the
firefighters rushing into a burning building as no more heroic
than the arsonist who lit the blaze, the Albert Schweitzers and
Mother Teresas of the world as worthy of no greater praise
than the Hitlers and Stalins. It denies that serious issues are
worth taking seriously and thus diminishes our humanity. We
need and deserve better than that.

THE KINSEY-HEFNER LEGACY

Sexual morality is only one aspect of morality, but it is an
especially important one because, as we have seen, popular
culture has made it a major part, some would say a fixation, of
modern American life—and because it is a factor in so many
modern problems: divorce, academic failure and dropping out of
school, teenage pregnancy, abortion, venereal disease, AIDS,
child molestation, rape, and sexual harassment. It is widely
recognized that the research of Alfred Kinsey and the *Playboy*
"philosophy" of Hugh Hefner played an important role in the
sexual revolution. But there have been relatively few analyses
of the nature of that role and its relation to these social problems. For this reason, the research of communication specialist
Judith Reisman, though unheralded, must be counted among the
most important of our time.

Dr. Reisman, president of the Institute for Media Education,
has meticulously analyzed the twin volumes that ushered in the
sexual revolution—Alfred Kinsey's *Sexual Behavior in the Human Male* (1948) and *Sexual Behavior in the Human Female*
(1953)—and traced their effect on the lives of several generations of Americans and people of countries influenced by our
culture. Her findings call into question much of what has been
taken for granted about sexual behavior for half a century.
Kinsey, she concludes, was far from the objective scientific
observer he is usually pictured as. Rather, he knowingly used

biased samples and tolerated, perhaps encouraged, the sexual molestation of children for his scientific "studies."

At least one-quarter of the sample in his study of male sexuality, Reisman alleges, were prisoners. Presumably, incarceration resulted in homosexual experience in prison for some of them. Further, most if not all of the high school boys Kinsey claims to have surveyed were from a group with an unusually high (if dubious) incidence of homosexual experience. During his research, she notes, Kinsey "appears to have directed experimental sex research on several hundred children aged 2 *months* to almost 15 years. These children were orally and manually stimulated to orgasm over periods as long as 24 hours by a group of nine sex offenders, some of whom were 'technically trained' . . . These orgasm tests on children constituted Kinsey's experimental child sex research database." A number of pediatricians with whom Reisman consulted speculated that the children would not have submitted to such "experiments" unless they were held or strapped down.[9]

Kinsey's study of female sexuality, Reisman alleges, was similarly flawed and no less objectionable. His planned use of volunteers in the study was shown to be unscientific by the respected psychologist Abraham Maslow. Maslow had established that volunteer data would, if uncorrected, sharply inflate the numbers of women reporting unconventional sexual behavior. Yet as Maslow revealed years later in a letter to a friend, Kinsey's reaction was to refuse to publish Maslow's findings or even to mention them in his books. "All my work," Maslow noted, "was excluded from his bibliography."[10] From the data Maslow had warned him against using, Kinsey and his followers concluded, among other things, that incest can be satisfying and enriching and that the only reason children get upset from sexual contact with adults is because of the prudishness of parents and legal authorities.[11]

Kinsey, Reisman charges, did not approach his research with an open mind but had a very clear personal agenda. He wanted to establish that *exclusive heterosexuality is abnormal and results from conditioning and inhibitions; that sex between a man and a woman is no more natural than sex between two men, a man and a child, or a man and an animal; and that bisexuality should be the norm in human sexual expression.* And the conduct of his research ensured that these would be his scholarly findings.

Cognizant that Hugh Hefner had been strongly influenced by Kinsey, Dr. Reisman undertook a comprehensive study of *Playboy* (and of its competitors, *Penthouse* and *Hustler*) and the "philosophy" it has espoused since its first issue was published in 1953. Parroting Kinsey, she notes, *Playboy* has taken a stand against chastity, marital fidelity, and the Judeo-Christian view of morality, and in favor of early sexual experimentation. This view has been openly espoused from the beginning. The December 1953 issue ran an article on virginity that included these lines: "Most men realize that virginity is an unpleasant little matter to be disposed of early in life . . . you are actually doing the girl a service. Some may suggest that you are trying to deprive them of something—trying to take from them a cherished possession. This is nonsense."[12] The January 1963 issue included a section that lauded the viewing of pornography by boys and girls, suggested ways to get girls drunk and seduce them, and advised readers they could get virgins to have sex by promising marriage and then leaving them waiting at the church. *Playboy* and its competitors, Reisman points out, have consistently found humor in the seduction, manipulation, and even rape of young women and girls.

Reisman traced *Playboy*'s inclusion of increasingly objectionable themes over the years. A few of the examples she cites will suggest the tone and emphasis: naked toddlers soliciting sex from sisters and mothers; the gang rape of little Dorothy by the Straw Man, the Lion, and the Tin Man; Alice in Wonderland talking about performing oral sodomy on the Cheshire Cat; and the seven dwarfs voting on whether to gang rape Snow White. A February 1970 Valentine's Day cartoon collection depicted children being sexually assaulted. In one, Little Boy Blue held a whip and prepared to torture a little girl who stood bound and gagged, wearing high heels, garters, and black stockings. Nine little angels romped nearby, two of them copulating.

From 1957 to 1984 Santa Claus was depicted in *Playboy* 329 times, Reisman found. In some cases he was associated with liquor and/or drugs and with violence, but in the largest number of cases (170) he was associated with sexual activity, including orgies. These included adultery, pimping, sex and minors, and bestiality. *Not once, Reisman notes, was Santa depicted in "benevolent/altruistic" activity!*[13] She also explains (here speaking of *Playboy, Penthouse*, and *Hustler*) that though she tabulated nearly a thousand scenes of child-adult sex, compared to about thirty scenes of youthful peer sex, in nearly forty years of publication she found not a single cartoon, photo, or illustration that celebrated the beauty and wonder of birth. "Never was it hinted," she explains, "that all experiences pale before the birth of a child born of the love between a woman and a man. Never was a child displayed within a religious framework, as a 'child of God,' to be treasured, cherished, beloved, and protected."[14]

"Celebrating a self-centered Eros," Reisman concludes, "*Playboy* institutionalized the war between women and men, waging a forty year assault against marriage, the family, and heterosexual love."[15] In addition, she charges that

> *Playboy* and its imitators in magazine, film, television, dial-a-porn, advertisements, and other media are sadosexual training manuals for juveniles. The charge is that these materials teach and have long taught young and old that the "girl next door" can be used in perverse, harmful ways for films and fun—even if she or he is a small child, and that [a female's] "no" means "yes." The charge is that sex materials in the home often lead to sexual abuse of children by kin and/or to a broad range of other emotional and physical problems.[16]

The relevance of Dr. Reisman's research and conclusions is undeniable. The physical, sexual, and psychological abuse of children is epidemic in America. Every day 7,300 cases of abuse are reported; every day four children die from that abuse. The great majority of abusers begin molesting others when they are teenagers, in some cases preteens, and many are never cured of this behavior.[17] If Reisman is correct, the dramatic increase in the number and character of child abuse cases cannot reasonably be attributed to better reporting or to the fact that the abusers were themselves abused. As with other sexual problems, the escalation of child abuse is in part traceable to the erroneous views Kinsey published and Hefner disseminated.

The unparalleled impact of the "sexual revolution" in the span of less than fifty years is explained by its convergence with two other phenomena—the popularization of relativism, selfism, and the exaltation of feelings; and the explosion of the entertainment and communications media that give expression to all these views. This convergence is reflected in the U.S. Navy's Tailhook scandal and in sexual harassment in the workplace, in the increasing incidence of rape and other sexual violence, in the epidemic of sexually transmitted disease, and in the divorce rate. It is most dramatically reflected in the controversy over abortion.

THE ABORTION ISSUE

The descriptors that opposing sides in the abortion debate have chosen for their positions are loaded terms and contribute to the climate of hostility that exists. "Pro-choice" implies that people who oppose abortion want to force their values on others and deny them their constitutional rights.* "Pro-life" suggests that people who support abortion are malicious murderers whose next cause is likely to be infanticide. Both notions are false. Neither side has cornered the market on sincerity and integrity. This is not to say that both sides are right. Since they are diametrically opposed, logic poses only two choices—either one is right and the other wrong or each is partly right. Being wrong, incidentally, is not synonymous with being evil. In any case, substituting neutral terms—"pro-abortion" and "anti-abortion"—represents a small but worthwhile step toward reasoned discussion.

When conservative thinkers err, it is usually in the direction of absolutism; when liberal thinkers err, it is usually in the opposite direction, relativism. The reason that the legal victory in *Roe v. Wade* went to the liberal thinking pro-abortionists is not that their position was philosophically superior, but that then as now relativism, selfism, and the exaltation of feelings domi-

---

*Students of irony will note that people who deny free will generally are pro-choice on abortion.

nated popular culture. It is fashionable to classify Supreme Court justices as *politically* rightist, leftist, or centrist, and that is not unreasonable. But there is a more fundamental and, in this case, meaningful classification: the justices are *human* and therefore are influenced by the dominant themes of their culture. It is both foolish and unhistorical to believe that the latest decision is necessarily better than the one it displaces. Progress is possible, but so is regression. A nation or an entire civilization, no less than an individual, can make a tragic mistake.

Was *Roe v. Wade* a triumph of common sense, or of uncommon nonsense, or some mixture of the two? The answer cannot be found in emotional polemic, but only in dispassionate examination of the central questions: What is the nature of the abortive act? Is the fetus a living being? If so, is it a *human* being? Is it reasonable to classify abortion as a right, constitutional or otherwise? Is the issue of abortion a matter of gender— that is, a woman's issue and therefore one in which men have no business becoming involved? Is it a private matter in which government interference is inappropriate?

The most neutral, scientifically accurate description of the act of (nonspontaneous) abortion is *the induced expulsion of a nonviable fetus*. It is unquestionably a destructive act, but not every act of destruction is wrong, so we must inquire as to just what is being destroyed. The scientific answer is a living being, of the species *homo sapiens*. To say a fetus is not a living being is an expression of biological illiteracy, though it is not at all unreasonable to wonder when that living being is properly classified human. The answer here is not quite so clear-cut. In centuries past biological knowledge permitted the conclusion that the fetus became human at some specific moment *in utero*, for example the time of implantation or the time of first movement, known as "quickening." Philosophers and theologians were generally comfortable with this view. Contemporary biology, however, confirms that the genetic blueprint is established at conception and that this astoundingly individuating "document" contains an entire compendium of characteristics and predispositions. Moreover, biology establishes that the process of growth and decay, the life of an individual, is an unbroken continuum from conception to death.* Logic invalidates the pro-abortionist challenge, "Prove to us that the fetus is a human person." The burden of proof is never on those who affirm scientific knowledge and common sense—it is always on those who deny it.

The abortion issue is essentially a question of rights, but it is not the simple matter pro-abortionists claim—in other words, not merely a matter of a woman's reproductive rights. The argument that "One can do as she wishes with her own body" misses the point that a fetus is not its own mother—it is attached to, not identical to, its host. First and foremost, the issue is a question of whether the human person in the fetal stage has any right to "life, liberty, and the pursuit of happiness." Next, it is a question of when, if ever, the rights of the mother (or for that matter the father) of the fetus are to supersede the rights of the unborn human person. Instead of setting forth their arguments for denying rights to the unborn, pro-abortionists have ignored the question altogether and framed their position in terms of the politically correct, but philosophically shallow, terms of *choice* and *diversity*. There may be a case to be made against granting any rights of the unborn, including a class of rights subordinate to those of the mother (though I doubt it). But there is surely no justification for ignoring such a crucial matter, nor for accusing those who insist on its discussion of being intolerant or unintellectual.

The question of fetal rights is as essential to resolving the abortion issue as the question of Afro-Americans' rights was to the slavery issue. Because it is a human question, it concerns both men and women, and people of all races and all perspectives. More and more of late, pro-abortionists have been attempting to silence those that disagree with them. They say that men do not bear children, so men have no business talking about the issue. And they demand that anti-abortion commercials, like the Arthur S. DeMoss Foundation series "Life: What

*The continuum idea did not arise with modern science. Almost 1800 years ago Tertullian, the Carthaginian theologian, argued that "prevention of birth is premature murder, and it makes no difference whether it is a life already born that one snatches away or a life that is coming to birth that one destroys. The future man is a man already. *The whole fruit is present in the seed*" [emphasis added].

a Beautiful Choice" be banned from the air. (The series attacks no one, but merely offers warm and gentle praise for people who, when faced with a difficult decision, decide to "make an extra place at life's table.") Such attempts to subvert honest debate are every bit as offensive as anti-abortionists blocking access to legal abortion clinics. They trivialize the issue and violate democracy.

Under the best of circumstances, it is difficult to admit we are wrong, no matter how substantial the evidence against our view. But when the reigning view is that everyone creates his or her own truth, self-esteem should be unconditional, feelings are a valid moral standard, and sexual repression is harmful, right and wrong become strictly personal matters and evidence loses its force. People will believe whatever they feel comfortable believing. And the belief that a pregnancy may be terminated if one wishes is a preeminently comfortable belief.

A REASONABLE MORAL STANDARD

The first characteristic of a reasonable moral standard is that it helps people recognize moral goodness and greatness. An Ann Landers reader wrote to describe a love story she was privileged to witness. For eight years an old man cared for his wife, a victim of Alzheimer's. He visited the nursing home each day and tenderly, lovingly fed, bathed, and dressed her. Even though she no longer recognized this husband of half a century, he paused to groom his hair and adjust his tie before he entered her room. Filmmaker Pierre Sauvage, who was born and hidden in the French town of Le Chambon-sur-Lignon, returned there as an adult to probe the story of the five thousand inhabitants of the poor farming town who had saved five thousand Jews from extermination. In his film, *Weapons of the Spirit*, he recorded his findings. When he asked the townspeople why they kept the Jews hidden all that time despite the danger, they replied simply that their Jewish neighbors needed help, adding, "It's a normal thing to do." (Themselves a minority, these Huguenots had earlier helped refugees from the Spanish Civil War and had taken urban children in during a medical emergency.) Their pastor, André Trocmé, a pacifist, led them, saying: "We will resist without fear, but also without pride and without hate." And resist they did, as did a dozen surrounding communities who followed their example. There was not a single betrayer among them.

History is filled with such stories: Socrates speaking the truth even though it would condemn him; Martin Luther proclaiming "Here I stand, I can do nothing else"; Lincoln issuing the Emancipation Proclamation; Gandhi meeting the violence of imperialism with nonviolent resistance. But their power to inspire us depends on our acknowledgment that the actions they describe are higher, finer, and nobler than the alternatives.

Another characteristic of a reasonable moral standard is that it employs criteria more substantive than personal preference. All responsible moral discourse presumes such a standard. The presumption may be explicit, as before and during Operation Desert Storm, when discussion raged over whether it constituted a just war. Among the questions asked then were: Is the cause just? Is President Bush acting in the best interests of the American people? Have peaceful alternatives been pursued first? Will the good achieved outweigh the harm done? But more often the standard is implied. The Simon & Schuster editors decided to suspend publication of Bret Easton Ellis's *American Psycho* because its content outraged them. But the basis of their outrage was not that the book offended their personal standards of taste; otherwise, their action would have been unremarkable. They decided that the book is a moral outrage for reasons above and beyond personal taste.

Similarly, when animal-rights activists protest the traditional way of training greyhounds to race, they are not expressing their personal taste; they are saying that it is a moral abomination to release a live rabbit whose legs have been broken so that it emits a sound of terror and the dogs, in their excitement, run faster to reach it and tear it to shreds. In addition, they argue that the trainers' answer—"It's no one else's business what we do"—fails to address the moral question.

The only way we can expect people to listen to our ideas is to appeal to something binding on all individuals, regardless of personal preference—indeed, something that applies to all cultures. In 1991 France's highest court outlawed surrogate motherhood, stating that it violates a woman's body and improperly undermines the practice of adoption. "The human body," the court maintained, "is not lent out, is not rented out, is not sold." Notice that the court did not say "The Frenchwoman's body" but the *human* body, meaning all people at all times and all places. It is precisely this perspective that underlies the United Nations' condemnation of such practices as slavery, debt bondage, and forced prostitution. And the European Court of Human Rights decision that branded the law against homosexuality a breach of human rights was not limiting its application to Europe, but extending it to all countries. What these and similar positions have in common is their view that because all humans share a common nature, cultural differences should not enter into moral judgments. Saying this does not mean it is easy to escape our own cultural bias when examining other cultures, but only that is possible. (If it were impossible to get beyond the moral viewpoint of our own culture, then no German could ever have opposed Nazism and no one could ever convert to another religion or political philosophy.) Nor is it saying that all judgments of other cultures are necessarily informed or reasonable or that they should be made capriciously. It merely affirms that such judgments are proper and reasonable to make.

A reasonable moral standard also affirms the existence of evil, the reality of free will, and the importance of developing one's conscience. Many relativists regard the distinction between good and evil as unnecessary, an archaic holdover from our Puritan heritage. There is no evil, they say, merely different moral philosophies. But the distinction remains necessary despite their rejecting it. Evil is an obvious reality. As sociologist Peter Berger has noted, "There are certain deeds that cry out to heaven. These deeds are not only an outrage to our moral sense, they seem to violate a fundamental awareness of the constitution of our humanity. In this way, these deeds are not only evil, but monstrously evil."[18] Hitler's extermination of nine million people comes immediately to mind, as do Stalin's slaughter of thirty million Russian peasants and the case of Georgia Tann, a leading adoption expert in the 1940s and well-regarded lecturer on the subject, who was secretly a kidnapper and became wealthy by stealing and selling more than five thousand babies. Protected by a powerful politician, she obtained children by misleading ignorant people, using welfare agencies to take children from parents and brazenly advertising nationwide.[19] Another case is the forty-year experiment in Alabama conducted by the Public Health Service (1932–1972), which used two hundred black men in an experiment in which their syphilis was untreated without their knowledge so that the researchers could learn the effects of untreated syphilis on the human body. (At that time more than a few racists were still arguing that black bodies were not properly classified as human.) Yet another example is the 1.5 million elderly people who suffer abuse, often at the hands of their own children, including neglect, physical, psychological, and emotional harm, and financial manipulation. These examples illustrate the wide variation possible along the scale of evil. But whether millions are affected, thousands, or only a single individual, the reality of evil is undeniable.

Over the past century the concept of free will has been eroded in America. Psychiatrist Thomas Szasz, the bane of the promoters of psychobabble, traces the process of this erosion. Freud termed the belief in free will "unscientific" and stressed that it "must yield to the demand of a determinism whose rule extends over mental life." Freud was well aware of the implication of this view; in the index volume of Freud's collected works, Szasz points out, there is not a single reference to *responsibility*. As a result of Freud's influence, virtually every action that used to be considered morally wrong or sinful, including murder, is now considered by at least some psychiatrists to be a sign of sickness, specifically of personality disorder (unless, of course, it has crossed the line from disapproved to approved behavior, as has promiscuity). The criminal has been viewed as victim rather than victimizer; temptation and choice have been replaced by "intrapsychic conflict"; and the domain of psychiatry has been enlarged from "the study of insanity to the study of interpersonal and intrapersonal relations," thus embracing "virtually every discipline and field of study other than the hardest of hard sciences" and covering *every problem in living*.[20]

In stark contrast to Freud, Viktor Frankl offers a psychology of responsibility that regards human beings as moral agents who possess free will and can therefore choose their behavior. He wrote, "Man is never driven to moral behavior; in each instance he decides to behave morally. Man does not do so in order to satisfy a moral drive or to have a good conscience; he does so for the sake of a cause to which he commits himself, or for a person whom he loves, or for the sake of his God."[21]

The individual conscience is not, as relativists would have us believe, infallible. Because conscience may be strong or weak, sensitive or insensitive, actions cannot be right or wrong merely because one's conscience says so. In many people conscience is so undeveloped or manipulated that it serves merely to justify their desires and actions. "I did that before, so it must be all right to do it again." Speeders, drunken drivers, unfaithful spouses, and robbers often believe themselves to be blameless. Before it can guide us morally, conscience must be trained, and training must start in the realization that conscience is fallible and self-deception is an ever-present danger. Values Clarification (VC), as we have seen, is a dominant form of moral education, but it is worse than none. Young people need to make moral decisions and to evaluate them. They need to learn how to analyze their moral reasoning and hear the criticisms of morally knowledgeable adults. VC denies them this. Its emphasis is nonjudgmental acceptance of everyone's views, and therefore it denies the reality that because ideas often clash with one another, evaluation and judgment are unavoidable.

The theory of moral development that underlies VC and many other contemporary ethical approaches is based upon the work of Jean Piaget and Lawrence Kohlberg. Essentially it argues that children go through clearly defined stages of moral development. But Michael Schulman and Eva Mekler, in reviewing the research on moral development, have found ample reason to challenge Piaget and Kohlberg. According to Schulman and Mekler, children reason and act more morally and act less egocentrically than Piaget acknowledged. Moreover, Kohlberg's tests of moral development really measure verbal sophistication rather than morality; Kohlberg has never been able to demonstrate that children treat people any differently as they progress through what he claims are the stages of moral development.[22] The great danger in stagism is that it implies a validation. A teacher observing a child behaving badly is tempted to say, "Oh, he's just in that stage and will eventually come out of it," rather than guiding the child to understand that his action is morally unacceptable.

At first thought it might seem difficult to teach anyone to be thoughtful of others and respectful of their rights. But it is really not. One study demonstrated that the feelings of empathy for others can be produced in people merely by changing their focus as they listen to an interview. By concentrating on the feelings of the person involved, rather than on the facts of the case, they became more empathetic.[23] The only real impediment to teaching our children to act ethically is the popular doctrine of moral relativism. Why do so many otherwise perceptive people embrace this shallow view? One reason is that they fear the extreme of absolutism. (This fear is not entirely without foundation. Throughout history absolutism has worked great mischief.) Another is that modern philosophers such as Bertrand Russell have aroused suspicion about metaphysics. Russell and others asked the worthy question, "How does one get from an *is* to an *ought*?" But they asked it rhetorically, with their minds closed to the possibility of bridging the chasm. However, there is an answer: we get from *is* to *ought* in the same way we cross other intellectual chasms, by reasoning. This is not an easy way, but it is a real one, and in fact the only one that our human condition permits. By refusing to accept reason as a valid path to moral knowledge, modern philosophers unwittingly contributed to our present dilemma—the popular rejection of any *ought*, including those of simple courtesy and law. And they have persuaded some of their followers—I have in mind the professors of philosophy I spoke of at the beginning of this chapter—to forget that the purpose of raising questions is to answer them and that ethics is not an academic parlor game but a subject vital to the conduct of our lives.* Jacob Bronowski, biologist, philosopher of science, and author of *The Ascent of*

---

*The situation recalls Thomas Hobbes's observation that one distinguishing characteristic of human beings is "the privilege of absurdity to which no living creature is subject, but man only. And of men, those are of all most subject to it that profess philosophy."[25]

Man, finds it "particularly sad that philosophy has remained remote from any genuine inquiry into the human mind and the dilemmas of personality. At a time when young [people] hunger for principles to guide their lives, philosophy has been preoccupied with forms of analysis in which, it rightly assured them, there surely are [no guiding principles] to be found."[24]

Like absolutism, relativism is an extreme view. But more importantly, it is the *reigning* extremism. Despite the repetitive warnings of popular culture about the imminent danger of repression and inhibition, the fact is that our age is governed by moral permissiveness and laxity rather than scrupulousness. If it were otherwise, then the dominant response to the AIDS epidemic would have been for abstinence, monogamy, and sexual fidelity, or at least masturbation rather than "safe" sex. Only the most intransigent (and addleheaded) permissivism would place sexual license above life itself and respond to a deadly, incurable plague with a thin sheet of breakable latex!

Fortunately, there is a moderate position between the extremes that is at once a corrective of each. This view is natural law philosophy. It is abhorrent to relativists because it challenges relativism. Yet many of the ablest thinkers have subscribed to some variation of it, including Confucius, Aristotle, Cicero, Thomas Aquinas, John Locke, Thomas Jefferson, and Abraham Lincoln. Natural law philosophy has been negatively and unfairly stereotyped in the media, notably during the confirmation hearing of Supreme Court Justice Clarence Thomas. It may be accurately summarized as follows:

> We don't create our own morality any more than we create our own reality; rather, we learn or discover the objective morality binding on all human beings that arises from our common human nature, irrespective of differences of class or station or culture. We learn right and wrong by God's revelation, human reason, or both. Individually or collectively through our culture, more or less insightfully, we develop interpretations of that morality and enshrine them in tradition. Due to the complexity of life, many of the moral situations confronting us pose exquisite dilemmas that resist easy disposition. Because interpretations will vary and human beings are fallible, analysis and dialogue will always be necessary.

The rule that circumstances can alter cases safeguards natural law philosophy from extremism. This principle makes it possible for the natural law ethicist to reason that while cannibalism is generally a moral abomination, an airplane crash survivor in the Andes Mountains who cannibalizes a dead companion when no other means of self-preservation are available in a hostile terrain far from safety is not morally culpable; and to argue that a drunken driver who kills a pedestrian is guilty of a more serious offense if he knowingly drank more than his limit and had had previous convictions for drunken driving; and that while any sexual assault is objectionable, one in which age or condition rendered the victim helpless, and the assaulter was in a position of trust, is even more blameworthy. This principle also makes it possible to distinguish between situations in which people act freely and those where their free will is compromised through coercion or compulsion, as in the case of someone who, at gunpoint, is made to perform an immoral act.*

Our country has been immersed in moral relativism and selfism for so long that many Americans doubt that any other moral perspective is possible. They have heard so many alarmist warnings about the dangers of absolutism that they cannot imagine a society speaking in a single voice on fundamental moral issues without sacrificing individuality and creativity. The falsity of this view was never more evident to me than when I visited Singapore several years ago as an education consultant. Having spent the previous twenty-seven years in American classrooms, I was not well prepared for the experience. When I entered a classroom, usually with the principal, all activity would stop, the students would rise and say in unison, "Good morning, principal. Good morning, sir." Eager learners and animated participants in class discussion, they were nevertheless scrupulously courteous toward their peers and their teachers. When I met with students individually and in small groups, they were shy at first, an understandable reaction on meeting an

*As this explanation implies, judging an act to be morally right or wrong is very different from judging the person who commits it. Thus there is no contradiction in regarding homosexuality as immoral and yet supporting gays' civil rights. (Technically, there are no gay rights or "straight" rights, but only civil rights for citizens who are gay or "straight.")

Occidental stranger from a foreign land; but what struck me was not their shyness but their attentiveness when I spoke and the obvious respect that shone in their eyes.

My experiences outside the schools left me equally impressed. Not only did I learn that Singaporeans enjoy the freedom to walk the streets of the city late at night without fear of being accosted, but I encountered dozens of indications that Singaporean culture is kinder and gentler than American, to borrow a phrase. Once, standing at a busy intersection at midday, I asked my host why out of hundreds of people there was not a single jaywalker. She replied that the police not only gave out tickets but also put people's pictures in the newspaper, and no one would want to have his or her family shamed in that way. On another occasion, at a social gathering, a middle-aged woman told me that she and her brothers and sisters often argued over whose house their parents would visit for weekends. As an American, the first image that came to my mind was of each sibling offering a dozen excuses why he or she couldn't take the parents that weekend. But she went on to explain that *each sibling wanted to have the parents visit.*

How are such qualities to be accounted for? And how should we explain the hard work and commitment to excellence so often found among Asians in general and most embarrassingly documented in the academic test scores of recent Asian immigrants to this country? Should we credit genetic superiority? Hardly. Morally responsible qualities are simply valued enough that home, school, and all other agencies of the culture cooperate in cultivating them in children and encouraging them in adults. Research has shown that at about age three all children begin to distinguish right from wrong and feel shame when they violate moral rules. Only in an environment where there are no standards (or they are not followed) do they react otherwise.[26] Also, once children believe there is an ideal to measure up to, their natural desire for competency makes them want to measure up to it, and they are disappointed when they do not.[27] When an ethics program teaching specific moral values was added to a Los Angeles school district, the results were dramatic. One year after its inception, major discipline problems such as fighting, using drugs, and possessing weapons decreased by 25 percent; minor problems such as tardiness decreased by 39 percent; unexcused absences decreased by 18 percent. Moreover, virtually every aspect of student behavior improved and the number of students on the honor roll increased.[28]

TEACHING MORAL VALUES

If we are ever to solve this country's social problems, we must acknowledge the moral bankruptcy of our time and the culpability, not only of parents and teachers, but most of all of the media. We must also take responsibility for creating an environment that nurtures morality in children and adults. This responsibility originates in the realization that the moral law is a requirement that arises from our human nature and therefore is binding not only on religious people but on everyone. It is a matter of the spirit and consequently, as Socrates and many other thinkers outside as well as within the Judeo-Christian tradition have argued, its importance transcends material and physical concerns. This does not mean that religion-based morality should be ignored; on the contrary, it should occupy a place of honor in the educational system and in the general culture. To pretend the Ten Commandments are somehow irrelevant to moral living is a violation of common sense, the consequences of which are evident in our mounting social problems. But what principles and standards will be acceptable to the American people, whose racial, religious and ethnic origins are so diverse? The first principle, central to virtually every ethical system, philosophically or theologically based, and acceptable to all people of goodwill, is *respect for persons*. As Errol E. Harris has noted, it entails three requirements: "First, that each and every person should be regarded as worthy of sympathetic consideration, and should be so treated; secondly, that no person should be regarded by another as a mere possession, or used as a mere instrument, or treated as a mere obstacle to another's satisfaction; and thirdly, that persons are not and ought never to be treated in any undertaking as mere expendables."[29]

Since every significant human action occurs, directly or

indirectly, in a context of relationships with other people, the criteria for deciding whether an action honors or violates the principle of respect for persons are *obligations, ideals,* and *consequences*. Obligations range from formal agreements to the demands arising from relationships; thus there are business and professional obligations and obligations of marriage, parenthood, citizenship, and friendship, among others. Ideals are varieties of excellence that help us demonstrate respect for others and achieve greater harmony with them. Among the ideals found in many cultures are the following: justice, fairness, tolerance, compassion, loyalty, amity, peace, truthfulness, trustworthiness, courage, fidelity, moderation, humility, integrity, empathy, forbearance, purity, respect for legitimate authority, perseverance, and self-reliance. The practical and theological virtues—prudence, temperance, justice, and fortitude; faith, hope, and charity—are also ideals. And the Golden Rule is actually a cluster of ideals, including cooperativeness, civility, kindness, and dependability. Consequences are the beneficial or harmful effects that result from an action and affect the people involved, including the person taking the action. Some consequences are physical; others, emotional or spiritual. Some occur immediately; others, much later. Some are intended; others, unintended. Finally, some are obvious; others, subtle. For example, at first consideration the failure to pay one's bills would seem to affect only one's creditors, but it actually has a far-reaching ripple effect that reaches millions of people: the total cost of such delinquency in this country is estimated at $60 billion annually, or about $200 per person.[30]

Popular culture's notion of "different moralities for different people" notwithstanding, the list of moral considerations in the previous paragraph is hardly controversial. Most Americans would affirm many or even all of them. Where controversy often arises is in the application of those considerations to specific situations. The reason is simple. Obligations sometimes conflict with one another, or with ideals, and the consequences of an action may not be all good or bad, but mixed. When this occurs, there is room for disagreement over whether an action is, on balance, moral or immoral. Should doctors be required to submit the names of AIDS patients to U.S. health officials? Is it morally acceptable for a principal to pressure teachers to grade leniently? Is it morally acceptable for Jehovah's Witnesses to violate their consciences and accept blood transfusions? Such complex moral questions require careful analysis.

This assertion may sound identical to the relativistic "situation ethics," but it is not. "Circumstances alter cases" has been accepted by ethicists and moral theologians for centuries. Taking another person's life, for example, violates God's commandment. Yet there is a tremendous moral (and legal) difference between self-defense and premeditated murder. The error of "situation ethics" is in acknowledging *nothing but* circumstances—that is, denying such general prohibitions as the Ten Commandments. For Jewish and Christian ethicists the Commandments are the starting point and the continuing reference point of analysis.

With young children, parents and teachers should cultivate what philosopher Alfred North Whitehead called "the habitual vision of greatness" by introducing children—through books, films, oral anecdotes, and personal contact—to men and women whose example provides inspiration to moral living. Such individuals include not only well-known heroes, but also people whose deeds are more modest—the retired man who does volunteer work at a hospital, the woman who distributes food to shut-ins, the child who faithfully gives part of her allowance to the poor. Though extolling virtue is valuable at all ages, in the teenage years parents and teachers should guide students to examine more complex ethical questions and to make sound moral judgments. Since modeling is a powerful kind of teaching, parents may wish to let even young children hear them engage in this kind of discussion so that they become familiar and comfortable with it long before they can engage in it themselves. The discussion should not focus on feelings or preferences, in the relativistic manner of popular culture, but instead on the obligations present in the situation, the relevant ideals, and the consequences of actions. If obligations or ideals conflict, the question of priorities should be addressed. Ultimately, analysis and discussion should identify the most moral course of action. Here are two examples of the kinds of issues that are fruitful to discuss. The first was widely reported in the news; the second is hypothetical.

In 1983 a mentally unstable man called an Alabama TV newsroom and threatened to kill himself. The station notified the police, then dispatched a camera crew to the scene. The crew reportedly stood by, filming, while the man doused himself with lighter fluid and lit first one match, then another, in an unsuccessful attempt to ignite himself. They moved in to stop him only after he tried a third time and succeeded. The television station subsequently ran the film footage on the air. One member of the crew explained later, "My job is to record events as they happen." Did the crew behave ethically?

When Sally's father was gravely ill, he called her to his bedside and said, "I'd always hoped I'd see you graduate from college and go on to become a physicist, but I know death is near. Promise me one thing—that you'll keep on studying hard and become a physicist." Sally was deeply moved. "I will," she responded; "I swear to you I will." Her father died shortly thereafter. Now it is two years later, and Sally is ready to graduate from college. But she will not become a physicist. She has decided to go to law school. Is she guilty of any moral wrong?

The range of questions that can be posed directly or in the manner shown above is limitless. For example, is it ethical to share copyrighted software with a friend? To perform potentially harmful tests on laboratory animals? To write a composition for someone to submit as her own? To embellish your résumé? To turn in a friend you observed stealing? To repeat a story you promised not to repeat? To market serial killer trading cards? The history of every academic discipline is filled with specific moral issues that have challenged its practitioners in the past and continue to do so today. These provide an excellent way for teachers to help students of all ages become more morally discerning and more skilled in making ethical judgments, outcomes that cannot be reached by mere exposure to the names and ideas of famous ethicists. (It must be emphasized that the judgment I am referring to is not the relativistic "all views are equal" but the determination of which view is most reasonable in light of the relevant obligations, ideals, and consequences.)

Moreover, when the issues discussed arise from the subject

matter itself, students' evaluation and discussion of them does not displace "course content"—it reinforces it. There will not always be complete agreement about the most moral action. Nevertheless, moral discourse will be productive if it occurs in the context of the conviction that some actions are more ethical than others and if good people strive to find the most moral response to life's challenges. It is precisely this conviction that has been seriously eroded in the latter half of this century. Its restoration will require the combined efforts of every agency in society—home, school, church, business and the professions, and especially the entertainment and communications media.

SEVEN

Fashionable Religion

It would seem that a relativistic age would be overflowing with tolerance for religious believers, particularly since polls consistently show that faith in God is still an important value for most Americans. Yet intolerance, suspicion, even outright hostility toward religion is the norm. Sometimes the attitude is thinly veiled, as when a talk-show host introduces the first half of a show by asking ominously, "Should the Bible rule your bedroom?" and the second half with a breezy "Sherre Hite takes our sexual temperature."[1] But it is often blatant, as when *Newsweek* disparaged believers for using "sulfurous ads" and "evangelical sallies" to advance a "righter-than-thou social agenda" and further characterizing them as "a new breed of bluenoses," "the morals squad," "artbusters," and "stiff-necked moralists" engaged in "righter-than-thou" and "inflammatory" activities.[2] What horrible offense did religious people commit to warrant these slurs? They objected to the use of their tax dollars to support such "artistic" works as a photograph of a crucifix in a bucket of urine and a bust of Jesus made up as a drag queen!

If depictions of religion were at one time too syrupy, popular culture has certainly overcorrected the lapse. Bing Crosby's genial Father O'Malley has been replaced by an assortment of hypocrites, seducers, child molesters, mobsters, and even murderers in clerical garb. Reverent treatments of Christ and His followers have been displaced by vile ones: *The Last Temptation of Christ* presents Jesus engaged in crucifying someone else and Mary Magdalene bedecked with tattoos. Film critic Michael Medved charges that an "overt and pervasive hostility to religion and religious values" has taken root in Hollywood. The explanation for this change, he argues, is not that the public wants movies that portray religion as hypocrisy or mental aberration; indeed, anti-religious films usually lose money while films like *Chariots of Fire* and *Tender Mercies* do well. Rather, it is that Hollywood decision makers are out of touch with mainstream America.[3]

Hostility toward religion is not confined to art and entertainment: it may be observed in everyday life. In 1990 the Middle States Accrediting Association demanded that Westminster Theological Seminary in Philadelphia put women on its board or risk losing its accreditation—this despite the fact that the seminary is a Presbyterian institution and one of their religious tenets prohibits the ordination of women. In recent years churches and temples have been broken into and vandalized. Church services have been disrupted, parishioners pelted with condoms. In New York City's St. Patrick's Cathedral the sacred host was desecrated by a group of gay rights activists angry over the Catholic Church's opposition to their cause. In most of these cases the ACLU and other guardians of the First Amendment remained uncharacteristically silent.

CAUSES AND EFFECTS OF HOSTILITY

Popular culture's disparagement of religion is no coincidence. It is the continuing, heightened expression of what philosopher William Barrett terms "the effort to undermine in one way or another the spiritual status of the human person."[4] By 1900 the passion for science created by Darwinism succeeded in purging from the university supposedly nonscientific matters such as love, charity, loyalty, and faith; the extension of this purge eventually deleted the subject of religion from history textbooks.

Positivist philosophers and their psychological counterparts, the behaviorists, expressed a similar passion in renouncing the metaphysical and transcendental and consigning spiritual inquiry to meaninglessness. The field of sociology was conceived and nurtured in that same passion: Lester Ward, its father, also founded the National Liberal Reform League that aimed to oppose "all forms of superstition," especially "the leading doctrinal teachings of the so-called Catholic and Evangelical Protestant churches," and to achieve "the triumph of reason and science over faith and theology."[5] But Freudianism has proved to be an even greater foe to religion than scientism. Like Marx, Freud saw religion as an opiate, but one with its roots in unconscious desires. In his reductionist view, religious belief has no basis in reality, but is the mere projection of human delusion. Psychiatrist Thomas Szasz, not a religious believer himself, attacks this Freudian fanaticism, noting that "medical psychiatry is not merely indifferent to religion, it is implacably hostile to it. Herein lies one of the supreme ironies of modern psychotherapy: it is not merely a religion that pretends to be a science, it is actually a fake religion that seeks to destroy true religion."[6]

The stereotypes of religion that pervade American culture today—the believer as buffoon or self-deluding hypocrite* or frightened slave of sexual inhibition or Fascist bent on taking away the rights of others—are simply the popular expression of the pseudoscholarly notions of scientism, positivism, behaviorism, and Freudianism. This link to ideas vaguely thought to be scholarly explains why religious insults are considered acceptable even by those who decry slurs about race, ethnicity, and gender. Religious people seem to *deserve* such treatment. The stereotypes, of course, are misrepresentations of reality and

*The strangest charge of self-delusion is that "secular humanism" exists only in religious believers' imagination. When a religious writer refers to secular humanism and its atheist agenda, many liberal intellectuals deny there is such an -ism and agenda. Yet it is a matter of historical record. The *Secular Humanist Manifesto* was published in 1933 by philosopher John Dewey and others. Even today the American Humanist Association makes no secret of its existence. At one time presided over by Isaac Asimov, it claims five thousand members and has a newspaper and a publishing house (Prometheus Press) to promote its atheistic views. One of its spokesmen, Paul Kurz, often appears on television talk-shows.

are easily refuted by a cursory reading of history: the early Christians facing the Romans' lions courageously, the great religious thinkers originating the principles America is founded upon, the Protestant reformers challenging the Roman Catholic Church, the Pilgrims risking their lives in the name of freedom—these examples and countless others suggest the unfairness, indeed the foolishness, of dismissing religious belief so summarily. But the mischief done by these stereotypes goes far beyond slander. Media bias against religious believers has conditioned the public to dismiss the *ideas* of religious believers. Meanwhile, with a deep bow to relativism, the media provide a platform to celebrities to speak on any subject they wish, their ignorance notwithstanding. Consequently, when writing for a popular magazine such as *Parade* or speaking on a television talk-show, astronomer Carl Sagan can slide from the area of his training into philosophical and theological matters without raising eyebrows. Meanwhile religious philosophers or theologians are denounced for speaking within their own areas of expertise, if indeed they are allowed to do so.

A typical example of Saganism is *Parade*'s excerpt of the book *Shadows of Forgotten Ancestors: A Search for Who We Are*, authored by Sagan and his wife, Ann Druyan. Not only was the story featured, but a picture of the authors adorned the cover. In the space of a little over two pages, the authors manage to pontificate on several fields outside their competency, including religion, epistemology, anthropology, and ethics. They manage to dismiss and ridicule the entire history of philosophy and theology in a single sentence: "Most of the philosophers conventionally adjudged great thought that humans are fundamentally different from the other animals—because of an immaterial 'something' [the soul], for which no scientific evidence has been produced, that resides somewhere in the bodies of humans but in no one else on Earth." They go on to discuss examples of animal intelligence and leap to the outrageous conclusions that "human scientists cannot do as well as preadolescent chimps" on a technological task, a monkey who learned to wash sand off sweet potatoes is "a primate genius, an Archimedes or an Edison" of monkeydom, and a group of macaque monkeys "seem exemplary in their moral grounding and their courageous resistance to evil." Readers are advised to be proud of their simian heritage and to strive to lift their ethics to that standard.[7]

When rock stars speak about religion, the politically correct response is quiet acceptance or the incantation of "Well, if it's meaningful to him..." For example, Glen Benton, the leader of the rock group Deicide, acknowledges that his Satanism is not a gimmick but a religious conviction—he really worships the devil. Here are some of the thoughts he shared with a newspaper reporter: "I've never been influenced by anybody. I don't walk in people's footsteps. It's between me and Satan himself. I wake up every day and know who I am. My life is miserable. It's my own wish. Misery and anger create the music we do." Also, "I don't tell people to kill themselves in my lyrics—they're based on voices that have told me to kill myself."[8] We're not supposed to question his credentials (or his sanity). Yet if a priest or minister mentions Satanism, albeit from a different point of view, we are supposed to snicker, roll our eyes, and think him out of order. Even a secular academician risks scorn when making such a charge, as University of Denver professor Carl Raschke made after researching the increasing incidence of crimes in which Satanism is a factor. ("Satanism," he writes, "is terrorism. It is the gestation of a permanent terrorist subculture in America that will bring the random violence and political intrigues of the Old World at last to the new."[9])

This culture-encouraged irrationality has ushered in the quasireligious movement known as "New Age," a broad category covering a variety of beliefs, including trance channeling, healing with crystals, reincarnation, out-of-body experiences, altered consciousness, and UFO abductions. The great irony is that the same people who dismiss Judaism and Christianity as archaic uncritically embrace superstitions shown to be shallow nonsense millennia ago! The range of such nonsense is breathtaking. Linda Evans and Joyce DeWitt claim to be guided by an entity named Mafu from the seventh dimension, last incarnated in A.D. 79 in Pompeii. (A talk-show a few years ago featured one such entity, I believe it was Mafu, speaking through the slumped body of its medium. When the entity used the plural form *phenomena* in a sentence calling for the singular *phenomenon*, I felt the satisfaction any former English teacher would on realizing that usage problems exist in other "dimensions" as well as our own. Misery loves company.) Shirley MacLaine and J. Z. Knight are guided by Ramtha, a 35,000-year-old master from Atlantis. A sample of his wisdom: "God is within." (Speaking of age, astrologer Linda Goodman claims to have studied astrology since a billion years before Atlantis. That's matriculation!) A Stanford University professor teaches a graduate school business course that incorporates zen, yoga, tarot cards, chanting, and "dream work."

The Franklin Mint ran a full-page ad in *Parade* for The Crystal Ball, "presented by Jeane Dixon." The copy read, "For centuries the crystal ball has been said to foretell the future . . . to chart one's destiny. And now, this wondrous orb of fable and fortune can be yours. Hold it in your hands. Feel its awesome power. Launch yourself on a journey of discovery that will last a lifetime . . . if you dare." Former actress Corinne Calvet reportedly provides hypnotherapy to the stars. She is quoted as claiming to have helped a male playboy overcome his inability to sustain a romantic relationship: "I regressed him back to the 1800s. He discovered he had been a girl then—a girl who had been in love with her father." Singer Dionne Warwick hosts an extended commercial for Linda Georgian's Psychic Friends Network. A new branch of feminist literature, known as the "goddess movement," reveres prepatriarchal female deities and ancient pagan goddesses. Among the works in this category is Diane Stein's how-to book, *Casting the Circle: A Woman's Book of Ritual*, demonstrating how moon rituals, candle magic, circle rituals, and other aspects of witchcraft empower women by strengthening self-awareness and personal power.

Lloyd Strayhorn, a well-known numerologist, appearing on a nationally syndicated talk-show, explained that certain numbers are associated with specific planets (nine with Mars, four with Uranus, and so on) and that a person's number governs his or her life in profound ways. For example, a number six person is more susceptible to nasal conditions than most. Why do stores price items $5.99, $6.99, and so on? I would have said it's because at first thought we see $5 rather than $6 and so are more inclined to buy. Wrong. Strayhorn explained that it's because the number nine is a human sign, bespeaking great vitality, so we are subconsciously attracted to it. Audience members gave him their first names and the month and day of their birth (no year necessary), and he told them about their health, abilities, educational attainment, success with the opposite sex, and so on. And he informed the audience that the number of letters in a movie title governs the degree of its success. Not only did the host refrain from asking what seemed a reasonable question, "Are you for real?" but he thanked him profusely for appearing and referred to numerology as "a spiritual platform from which to understand [oneself]."[10] As G. K. Chesterton once observed, "When people stop believing in God, they do not believe in nothing—they believe in anything."

In contrast to the tolerance toward New Age religion, popular culture is generally intolerant of Judeo-Christianity. As New York University professor Paul C. Vitz and others have noted, some history textbooks omit references to the Reformation and discuss groups such as the Pilgrims and occasions such as the first Thanksgiving as if they were purely secular. Religious symbols are prohibited from schools and public property, and prayer is banned not only from school classes but graduation ceremonies as well. The Supreme Court's decision against invocations and benedictions in *Lee v. Weisman* (1992) was well publicized. Not so well publicized were the two prayers offered by Rabbi Leslie Gutterman that caused the original lawsuit to be filed. Those prayers are as follows:

Invocation

God of the free, hope of the brave:

For the legacy of America where diversity is celebrated and the rights of minorities are protected, we thank You. May these young men and women grow up to enrich it.

For the liberty of America, we thank you. May these new graduates grow up to guard it.

For the political process of America in which all its citizens may participate, for its court system where all may seek justice, we thank You. May those we honor this morning always turn to it in trust.

For the destiny of America we thank You. May the graduates of Nathan Bishop Middle School so live that they might help to share it.

May our aspirations for our country and for these young people, who are our hope for the future, be richly fulfilled. Amen.

Benediction

O God, we are grateful to You for having endowed us with the capacity for learning which we have celebrated on this joyous commencement.

Happy families give thanks for seeing their children achieve an important milestone. Send Your blessings upon the teachers and administrators who helped prepare them.

The graduates now need strength and guidance for the future. Help them to understand that we are not complete with academic knowledge alone. We must each strive to fulfill what You require of us all: to do justly, to love mercy, to walk humbly.

We give thanks to You, Lord, for keeping us alive, sustaining us, and allowing us to reach this special, happy occasion. Amen.

How these carefully worded nondenominational prayers, for which no one in the audience was required to stand or bow his or her head, and to which no one needed to say "Amen," can be viewed as exacting religious conformity is difficult to understand except as a manifestation of irrational hostility toward, and/or fear of, religion. As Justice Antonin Scalia argued, in a dissenting opinion joined by three other justices, there is no evidence that these prayers in any way violated the Constitution. In fact, he observed, they were "so characteristically American they could have come from the pen of George Washington or Abraham Lincoln himself. . . ." Not so surprisingly, in the same year that the highest court in the land passed down this decision, a major public university paid $4,200 for a photograph by Andres Serrano. The photograph enlarged the nascent genre by depicting a small plastic copy of Michelangelo's *Pietá* submerged in a tank filled with urine and cow's blood. (Has Serrano mentioned to his therapist his preoccupation with urine?) The work will be displayed in the art department's gallery.[11]

Popular culture's hostility toward religion has given millions of people a distorted view of the role of religion in society. They have been conditioned by the media to admire those who speak out against acid rain, the slaughter of whales and dolphins, the extinction of the snail darter, and the destruction of Brazilian rain forests, but to be suspicious of those who speak out against abortion. (Perhaps the media would be less tolerant of environmentalists if their cause were more explicitly associated with religious belief.) They have been persuaded to be unconcerned about the effects of violence and the glamorization of promiscuity in films and on television, and to accept unquestioningly the advertising industry's propaganda for impulsiveness, self-indulgence, and instant gratification, yet to be positively phobic about schoolchildren's repeating words such as, "Father, we thank thee for the night/And for the blessed morning light/For rest and gladness, loving care,/And all that makes the world most fair./Help us to do the things we should,/To be to others kind and good./And all we do in work or play,/To grow more loving every day."

The public have been made to feel comfortable when the word *God* is used to damn but not to bless, with *Jesus* as an expletive but not as a term of reverence. They have learned to accept expressions of love of art, science, music, and literature, but to grow nervous when someone expresses love of God. Many of the same parents who object to a crucifix in a city seal or logo, to the expression "so help you God" in courtroom oaths, and to an athletic team's pregame prayer think nothing of sending their kids to a Satanic Death rock concert. Parents have more to fear from irreverence than from reverence. For that matter, the philosophical debate over such issues as separation of church and state is hardly aided by popular culture's conditioning of the public to mindless approval of secular religion. Both social progress and the safeguarding of America's unique political heritage depend on the willingness to listen to diverse views and to judge them fair-mindedly. By cultivating hostility to religion, the media unwittingly undermine the very social values they mean to advance.

THE FAILURE OF RELIGIOUS PEOPLE

Religious people are often so busy pointing out the faults of the media that they fail to recognize their own failure to dispel the spiritual confusion that has been deepening for half a century. The failure is shared by both liberal and conservative religionists, though for different reasons. Stung by the hostility of the general culture toward them and their faith, liberals have sought to convert the world through accommodation. As their ancestors incorporated pagan customs to make their religion more accessible and conversion more appealing, they have integrated secular ideas with their religious beliefs. Because it has seemed more reasonable to speak the language people were familiar with, they have stopped speaking of things the world regards as unpleasant, such as sin, remorse, and redemption, and have spoken instead of creating one's own truth, self-esteem, and fellowing one's feelings. Their intention is laudable—to restore a religious perspective in American society—but their reasoning is flawed, for they neglect to ask the crucial questions, "Are these beliefs compatible with our religion?" "Does our embrace of these ideas represent an essential surrender to secularism?" and "Does the world in its present dilemma really need less of the traditional religious message or more of it?"

This philosophy of accommodation with secularism pervades liberal religion. In 1991 the Presbyterian Church published *Keeping Body and Soul Together*, which called for a redefinition of sin to reflect "the changing mores of our society." (Religion writer Kenneth L. Woodward commented that it read like "a sermon on Eros prepared in the heat of politically correct passion.") Book titles from religious houses include *Love Yourself, The Art of Learning to Love Yourself, Loving Yourselves, Celebrate Yourself, You're Something Special, Self-Esteem: You're Better Than You Think, Talking to Yourself: Learning the Language of Self-Affirmation,* and *Self-Esteem: the New Reformation*. A Williamsville, New York, minister distributed condoms at a Sunday worship service. And preachers exhort people to feel good about themselves and to pray for the grace to accept themselves as they are: "We must view ourselves as uniquely wonderful, intrinsically valuable," writes Robert Morey.[12] Here is a passage from a church bulletin, composed no doubt by a well-meaning pastor in explication of Luke 4:31–36:

> The one possessed is full of self-hate and self-loathing. The mirror of his soul shows ugliness. He cannot love himself because he seems so unlovable. But the possessed man comes to Jesus who offers him unconditional love. Jesus gives it freely. The miserable man upset the spellbound listeners in the synagogue. He was unlovable. His evil spirit made rude noises. Jesus quieted that noise and touched the man at the point of his anguish. In effect Jesus told the man, "I love you. I trust you. You are not ugly. You are a masterpiece of God." Jesus gave him what we would call a good external feedback about himself. In the warmth of Christ's affection, the man believed this was true. So began the healing that led to wholeness and freedom.

> O Father of the human family, create love in all human hearts. You created all people in your image. Shine again through the mirror of all human souls so that they can see the masterpiece which you created, and so with proper self love, go on to fill the rest of the world with the creative generosity with which you began it. Amen.

Now compare this to the original passage in Luke: "Now in the synagogue there was a man who had a spirit of an unclean demon. And he cried out with a loud voice, saying, 'Let us alone! What have we to do with You, Jesus of Nazareth? Did You come to destroy us? I know who You are—the Holy One of God!' But Jesus rebuked him, saying, 'Be quiet, and come out of him!' And when the demon had thrown him in their midst, it came out of him and did not hurt him" (vv. 33–35). *There's not a hint of self-esteem doctrine here.* The pastor had obviously drunk too deep of the cup of selfism and read its message into Luke.

The liberal surrender to secularism is even evident in some seminaries. When *New York Times* reporter Ari Goldman took a year's sabbatical to study religion at Harvard Divinity School, he found to his dismay a heavy dose of "religious relativism." Among his professors, it seemed, homophobia was considered a greater sin than sodomy. As a Jew, he sought to understand

Christianity better, but he was disappointed. A course in Catholicism that promised an examination of how Catholics balance church/state issues proved to be "an unrelenting attack on the anti-abortion agenda of the Catholic church." As a result of his experience he concluded that at Harvard Divinity School, "the Bible can be picked apart, examined, debated, and condemned, but never, never accepted at face value as historic fact."[13]

However well-intentioned liberal accommodaters may be, their initiative has been doomed from the start. Even if relativism, selfism, and the exaltation of feelings were wise counsel, thoroughly compatible with Christianity, the propagation of New Age faith is not likely to lead people to Christ. But those beliefs are neither wise, as we have seen in earlier chapters, nor compatible. If we create our own truth, what need have we of the Ten Commandments? If we already participate in the divine nature, what need have we of salvation? What would we be saved from? *Our own perfection?* If whatever we feel like doing is acceptable and nothing is a sin, what point was there in the incarnation, crucifixion, and resurrection?

Prophetically, psychiatrist Viktor Frankl warned of this folly thirty years ago. "As soon as we have interpreted religion as being merely a product of psychodynamics, in the sense of unconscious motivating forces," he wrote, "we have missed the point and lost sight of the authentic phenomenon. Through such a misconception, the psychology of religion often becomes psychology as religion, in that psychology is sometimes worshiped and made an explanation for everything." The liberal attempt to modernize religion represents a lack of faith in the genuineness of people's search for God, a lack of faith in the power of the Holy Spirit to inspire them to respond, or both. Now as always, the proper role of the church is to tell people not what they want to hear or what is fashionable, but what they need to hear.

Although religious conservatives have managed to avoid the errors of liberals, their response to the hostility of the general culture has been equally unfortunate. They have become inordinately suspicious of intellectuality and in their defensiveness have retreated to a communal ghetto from which it is impossible to provide meaningful witness. If the liberal response to the modern world has been *reckless accommodation*, the conservative response may be characterized as *reckless renunciation*. Confronted by secular humanism, many conservative Christians proclaim all humanism anathema. Appalled by rationalism, they denounce rationality and regard the mind as part of our animal nature. Offended by scientism, they reject science as inimical to religious belief. This siege mentality is responsible for their withdrawal from dialogue with non-Christians and for their classifying as enemies many people who in fact share their essential values and beliefs—for example, men and women who accept both science and religion, and religious (as opposed to secular) humanists. It also accounts for their opposition to educational initiatives such as the critical thinking movement, which actually is their children's best protection against the manipulation of popular culture. Sadly, this mentality renders people more vulnerable to dishonest televangelists, who disguise their hypocrisy and greed in biblical quotations and false piety.

The conservatives' ceding of humanism, rationality, and science to secularism is both ironic and tragic. It is ironic because historically Christianity has been the champion of all three. Thomas Aquinas's baptizing of Aristotelean philosophy made Christianity preeminently a religion of faith *and* reason and ushered in both Christian humanism and the age of science. Medieval science was unparalleled in its intellectual energy and scope.[14] It is, of course, true that Martin Luther rejected the Catholic intellectual tradition, taking "St. Paul without his hellenism, and St. Augustine without his Platonism," and reconceptualizing faith as "no longer a human participation in the Divine knowledge, but a purely non-rational experience—the conviction of personal salvation."[15] But that fact does not alter the earlier historical record. The ceding of reason to secularism is tragic because it conveys the message that religion is irrelevant to economic, social, and educational affairs. Secularists may believe they have more respect for the human mind than do religionists, but they are mistaken, for they assume that the mind is reducible to matter. To a certain extent, conservatives have themselves to blame when their contributions to public discourse are routinely ignored. What their pride sees as other people's hardness of heart is more often *the logical conse-*

quence of their belief that faith and reason are mutually exclusive. For conservatives to expect nonbelievers to entertain their ideas solely on the basis of their zeal for them is presumptuous.

Reason is not exclusively a secular enterprise. Moreover, secular reasoning about human affairs is often flawed in ways religionists are uniquely qualified to expose. For example, Bishop Fulton Sheen answered the secularist assumption that the theory of evolution disproves creation with this eminently logical reasoning: "The vaster vistas which scientific evolution have opened in no way affect creation, any more than the invention of machinery affected the necessity of manufacture. The how of a process never dispenses with the explanation of the why."[16] How much more effective is this response, sound reason defeating unsound, than the pathetic attempt of some fundamentalists to explain away fossils. And how much more effective would religious believers be in exposing the shallowness of equating humans and animals if they raised the question, as scientist/philosopher Jacob Bronowski did, that if human beings are no more than animals, why aren't rats and pigeons writing books about B. F. Skinner? Or consider the effect if they adopted this playful yet powerful argument of G. K. Chesterton:

> That an ape has hands is far less interesting to the philosopher than the fact that having hands he does next to nothing with them; does not play knucklebones or the violin; does not carve marble or carve mutton. People talk of barbaric architecture and debased art. But elephants do not build colossal temples of ivory even in a rococo style; camels do not paint even bad pictures, though equipped with the material of many camels'-hair brushes. Certain modern dreamers say that ants and bees have a society superior to ours. They have, indeed, a civilization; but that very truth only reminds us that it is an inferior civilization. Who ever found an ant-hill decorated with the statues of celebrated ants? Who has seen a bee-hive carved with the images of gorgeous queens of old? . . . It is exactly where biology leaves off that all religion begins.[17]

Would that Carl Sagan had read less of Huxley and more of Chesterton!

Innumerable issues remain mired in secularistic and materialistic nonsense. False ideas are misdirecting people from lives of virtue and service. Meanwhile many of the very people entrusted with disseminating spiritual wisdom are refusing to appeal to the minds of their neighbors, minds God fashioned to be responsive to that wisdom. Consider the pivotal issue of free will versus determinism. Secularism increasingly tends to deny the former and affirm the latter, with such devastating effects on morality and law as transferring responsibility for actions from wrongdoers to society in general and eroding the concept of accountability for one's life. Determinism is logically untenable; everyday reality forces even the most ardent of its champions to deny it a hundred times a day. Every time they say "Please pass the salt" or "Thank you for your courtesy" they are acknowledging that the other person is not compelled to act but has a choice. Given the fact that many religious liberals have been infected with relativism, we might well expect conservatives to seize the initiative and remind the world of these contradictions. Alas, they are more often found reminding the world that human beings are wretches in the sight of God, their works and deeds counting for nothing. Though this message does not explicitly deny free will, it trivializes it and thus aids and abets determinism.

Many conservative Christians would object, of course, claiming that they are merely being faithful to the Bible, accepting it literally and resisting the temptation to interpret. But they are mistaken on both counts. Biblical references to faith and works are complex. Some speak of *works* as being inconsequential compared to *faith*, whereas others stress the importance of *works*. For example, in Matthew it is written "Not everyone who says to Me, 'Lord, Lord,' shall enter the kingdom of heaven, but he who does the will of My Father in heaven" (7:21). And James argued that faith without works is dead (2:14–26). Although it is possible to argue that one passage is more significant than another, or that one person's view is more accurate or reasonable than another, neither of these ideas challenges the fundamental fact that all readers of Scripture are engaged in interpretation and that the effort to interpret accurately is not only unavoidable but wholesome.

The world would be better served if liberal and conservative religionists could overcome the pride that divides them and prevents them from joining forces to guide America out of the spiritual wasteland of secularism. For liberals this means acknowledging the folly of trying to change other people's thinking by *adopting* their thinking, and demonstrating the relevance of their religious convictions to economic, social, and educational problems. (Those who have lost touch with those convictions will first have to rediscover them.) For conservatives it means overcoming their unwholesome suspicion of the human mind and reclaiming the ancient religious view that the mind is a spiritual reality composed of intellect and will; that though the intellect is clouded and therefore prone to error, it is nevertheless capable of apprehending truth; and that though the will is weakened by original sin, it is capable of responding to grace. In other words, though we are sinners, we are nevertheless created in the image and likeness of God: and our minds are the defining characteristic of that image. If both sides could accomplish these tasks, they might in time integrate their theological views. For example, instead of continuing the endless and profitless debate over faith versus works, they might agree that though salvation cannot be earned by what we do in our lives, nevertheless what we do is the outward manifestation of the faith within us and in that sense the measure of our faith.

WHAT RELIGION OFFERS

The idea that religious faith strengthens a society is neither new nor radical. Thomas Jefferson believed that the continuation of the liberties Americans enjoy depends on the realization that they are a gift from God.[18] Alexis de Tocqueville, French statesman and observer of our nation in its early years, saw religious faith as vital to society. "In ages of faith," he wrote, "... [people] repress a multitude of petty passing desires in order to be the better able to [satisfy] that great and lasting desire which possesses them... This explains why religious nations have often achieved such lasting results; for whilst they were thinking only of the other world, they had found out the great secret of success in this."[19] The relationship between freedom and responsibility is delicate and complex; when the balance between the two is not maintained, as Viktor Frankl warns, freedom "threatens to degenerate into mere license and arbitrariness."[20] But to whom or what is responsibility directed? Surely not to self, for it is the urges of self that are most in need of direction and control. Responsibility to the community is better, though dependent on the uncertain willingness of individuals to subordinate self-interest to the greater good. The most compelling argument can be made for responsibility to God, and that is precisely why a society that nurtures religion is more cohesive, stable, and productive. Doing one's job for the glory of God, whether that job is studying in school, making automobiles, selling clothing, or being a homemaker, is a greater spur to excellence than doing it for materialistic ends.

Arnold Toynbee, the renowned modern historian, notes that in disintegrating societies the gap between classes (such as, it would seem, the widening gap in America today) is caused by the breakdown of the "social ethos." The process of disintegration, he observes, instills in people the notion that social evils are external to them and therefore outside their control, a notion that enjoys wide currency today. In sharp contrast to this perspective, Toynbee argues, the Judeo-Christian sense of sin is liberating, having "the effect of a stimulus because it tells the sinner that the evil is not external after all, but is within him, and hence subject to his will." Consequently, "the member of a disintegrating mundane society who has learned that self-fulfilment is won by self-surrender in God has a surer hope, and therefore a deeper happiness, than the merely 'once-born' member of a society that is still in growth. . . . "[21]

Having long been brainwashed by popular culture to regard religion as repressive and inimical both to personal growth and democratic principles, many people sincerely believe that religion not only doesn't speak to their problems, but actually creates social problems. They would be surprised to learn that scholarly research indicates otherwise. Sociologist David Martin explains: " . . . When you get rid of religion, all those evils that you thought were associated with religion reappear, just as strongly and sometimes even more forcefully. So they were inherent possibilities of social life as such, not characteristics specifically associated with religion."[22] Studies done by atheists and agnostics, as well as by religious scholars, document that "the more religious youth are, the less likely they are to be involved in drugs, alcohol, premarital sex" and that "religious people can cope with physical illness and death better than non-religious people."[23] Concerning the allegation that religion obstructs personal growth, professor Paul C. Vitz points out that the concept of a *person* was created by early Christian theologians and adds that, unlike the concept of an *individual,* the idea of *person* calls for a commitment beyond self.[24]

Americans need to rediscover the truths that guided their ancestors, truths popular culture has obscured. They need to understand, for example, that the Judeo-Christian view that God created the universe (by evolution or otherwise) is not just a pious myth without intellectual substance. It is primarily an argument whose premises, supporting evidence, and conclusion deserve to be compared with counterarguments and judged on their reasonableness. Though space does not permit that comparative analysis to be undertaken here, this much can be said: the religious argument has not grown less compelling during the twentieth century but more so. Every momentous achievement of humankind in this most remarkable of centuries gives eloquent testimony to the capacity of the human mind. People speculate about an artificial intelligence that will rival or surpass the average human being's intelligence as if it would somehow diminish the human mind. But any such intelligence will be a further triumph of the human mind. And every such triumph, past, present, and future, gives additional support to the conclusion that the universe originated not in mindless matter but in awesome intelligence.

The communications media have promoted the notion that science and religion are incompatible. This advocacy is almost never accomplished by direct action, but rather by the process of selecting which authors to publish and which guests to feature on news- and talk-shows. Media people may not have any personal bias, but the way the categories "science" and "religion" are defined and segregated ensures that scientists who affirm the compatibility of science and religion are excluded from consideration. The prevailing assumption, unconsciously held, is that anyone who would make such an affirmation is not a genuine scientist. The public is thus prevented from the realization that many distinguished scientists argue that on key scientific issues, the facts permit *and sometimes favor* the traditional religious perspective. Concerning the "Big Bang" theory of the origin of the universe, for example, Robert Jastrow, director of NASA's Goddard Institute of Space Studies, says that science can't tell whether the universe was created from nothing or whether matter existed before the Big Bang because whatever properties may have existed previously would have melted down. "Thus," he explains, "according to the physicist and the astronomer, it appears that the Universe was constructed within very narrow limits, in such a way that man could dwell in it. This result is called the anthropic principle. It is the most theistic result ever to come out of science, in my view."[25]

On the subject of biological evolution, which is widely assumed to have disproved the Judeo-Christian belief in the origin of human life, British scientist Chandra Wickrahasinghe offers sharply conflicting testimony. The research that she and Sir Fred Hoyle did led them to the conclusion that biological conditions were never suitable for life to have formed on earth. The "organic soup" that modern biology says was the basis of life could never have been present, in her view. She concludes that Darwinism is fatally flawed, explaining, "there's no evidence for any of the basic tenets of Darwinian evolution. I don't believe there ever was any evidence for it. It was a social force that took over the world in 1860, and I think it has been a disaster for science ever since." Moreover, she regards contemporary evolutionists as "very arrogant and dogmatic people" who are acting in "defiance of science" because the scientific method opposes their conclusions. Genuine science, she says, supports "some miraculous property of life that's either explained in terms of a statistical miracle or in terms of an Intelligence intervening. It's one or the other."[26]

Science historian Stanley L. Jak argues similarly. He writes, " . . . The emergence of life on earth is, from the purely scientific viewpoint, an outcome of immense improbability. No wonder that in view of this quite a few cosomologists, who are unwilling to sacrifice forever at the altar of blind chance, began to speak of the anthropic principle. . . . The universe may have after all been specifically tailored for the sake of man."[27]

It is commonly assumed that modern physics has delivered the most decisive blow against traditional religion.* Yet the distinguished physicist Henry Margeneau, once a colleague of Albert Einstein, explodes this myth. For centuries, he explains, scientists scoffed at St. Thomas Aquinas's view that the universe was created by God from nothing, but relativity and quantum mechanics have demonstrated that Aquinas's view is not unreasonable. Margeneau notes that the leading scientists, the people who made the greatest scientific contributions—he specifies Eccles, Wigner, Heisenberg, Schroedinger, Einstein, and Jastrow—have all been religious in their beliefs.[29]

According to popular culture, the traditional Judeo-Christian view of human nature is hopelessly outdated. But even casual comparison of that view with the modern secular view reveals its greater reasonableness. The Judeo-Christian view holds that human nature is flawed and humans therefore have a *tendency* to commit moral wrongs.** The secular view is that it is flawless and there are no moral wrongs, only different preferences or "life-styles." As America's social problems grow, the religious view is more and more compelling. Every headline reporting a crime, every statistical report assessing man's well-established inhumanity to man, adds further evidence. Secularists are pathetically inconsistent when they dismiss the Ten Commandments as archaic and in the next breath call for more stringent laws to protect them from assault, murder, and mayhem. And they are intellectually irresponsible when they dismiss the power of prayer as a means of shaping people's lives for the better. Consider a single example, the prayer of confession at the

*It has also been assumed that modern physics disproved the idea of a reality independent of the human mind. This assumption reinforced relativism. But Mortimer J. Adler demonstrates that the assumption is unwarranted. He likens the classic experiments in subatomic physics to the situation of a pool in a hermetically sealed house. Its water, undisturbed for centuries, is placid. Then people enter the house, jump into the pool, creating turbulence, and proceed to describe the water as inherently wave-filled and fluctuating.[28]

**The traditional view is sometimes misconstrued to mean that human nature is evil. Some, notably Calvinists, have taken that position. But the mainstream view is that humans are not depraved but only *deprived*.

beginning of the Roman Catholic Mass: "I confess to almighty God, and to you, my brothers and sisters, that I have sinned through my own fault in my thoughts and in my words, in what I have done, and in what I have failed to do...." It doesn't take a great deal of reflection to conclude that this prayer, if sincerely expressed and acted upon, will produce more caring parents, more respectful children, kinder neighbors, more diligent students, better workers and citizens, and thereby a better society.

Whether the power of prayer is defined as spiritual, in the mystical sense, or merely as psychological, is beside the point; the power itself is obvious, as is the fact that it would help to solve the plague of lawlessness afflicting America. Secularists have every right to oppose prayer, despite these realities, and to argue instead for more police, larger prisons, and rehabilitation programs that persuade convicts to feel good about themselves and their actions. But they should be honest with themselves and the public and admit that they are motivated by stubborn allegiance to antireligious bias and not by logic. And they would do well to buy additional insurance!

On no contemporary issue is the Judeo-Christian perspective more demonstrably superior to the secularist view than the issue of sexuality. Here, as with the other examples, this conclusion requires no leap of faith, but only a dispassionate consideration of the evidence and the application of common sense. The traditional religious view is that sexual expression should be reserved for marriage and therefore that premarital and extramarital sex are wrong. The important question is not whether this ideal is difficult (no reasonable person would deny that, especially in today's sex-sodden culture) but whether it is worthy, and that is best answered by considering the impact it would have on society if it could be achieved. If teenagers were not sexually active, girls would not experience unexpected pregnancies and the trauma of deciding whether to undergo an abortion or deliver a baby they lack the maturity to nurture. The school dropout rate of both boys and girls would be reduced and they would, arguably, earn better grades. Those who encourage teenage sexuality are often incredibly naive, ignoring as they do the loss of concentration on schoolwork that occurs when teenagers become sexually active.

Three decades ago Arnold Toynbee made an insightful and, it appears, prophetic observation about youthful sexuality in Western society. He noted that Western preeminence in recent centuries can be credited to two developments: an analytical rather than a worshipful approach to tradition; and lengthening the education of the young by postponing their sexual awakening. He noted that we have recently departed from that wise precedent and have lowered the age of sexual experience "to a veritable Hindu degree" even as we have prolonged the process of education, making it virtually impossible for our young people to keep learning uppermost in their thoughts. And he warned that our educational expectations for the young will be futile unless we prolong "the age of sexual innocence."[30] The events of the last thirty years have proved Toynbee's words all the more sagacious.

Since marital infidelity is a significant factor in divorce, if married people remained faithful to their vows, there would be fewer divorces. Thus many children as well as parents would be spared the pain and suffering associated with the dissolution of a marriage. With fewer single-parent families, the welfare burden of Aid to Families with Dependent Children would be lessened, as would the problems experienced by latch-key children. Stronger marriages would likely increase parental attention to the upbringing of children, and that attention would have a favorable effect on teenage behavior. The incidence of uncivil, disrespectful behavior of teenagers toward adults would tend to decrease, as would the incidence of teenage crime. Finally, fidelity within marriage, when combined with abstinence before marriage, would dramatically reduce sexually transmitted disease, including genital warts, herpes, chlamydia, gonorrhea, syphilis, and AIDS. How woefully inadequate, by comparison, is secularism's campaign for condoms that, even when conscientiously used, have a 15 percent or greater failure rate.

It would be utopian to expect a majority of Americans to once again embrace the ideals of premarital abstinence and monogamy overnight; such a change will take years, perhaps a generation or two. But it makes perfect sense to work toward that ideal because any advance will reap significant gains for the individuals themselves and for the country. Despite all these reasons for transforming popular culture's hostility toward religion into support for religion, many people are likely to resist that transformation out of fear that European history will be repeated on this continent and that religionists will gain too much power and use it to deprive others of their freedoms. Their fear is not without foundation; it is entirely possible that, given the right conditions, the scenario that haunts them could become a reality. Unfortunately, they are so absorbed in fearing this remote, highly unlikely danger that they are missing the *dire reality* that Americans are losing their religious heritage and the social cohesiveness it guarantees. In researching his book *The Spiritual Life of Children,* Harvard psychiatrist Robert Coles found that "many children are ashamed of their spirituality, afraid of being mocked by the secular community, afraid that others will see them as absurd, foolish, or superstitious." The same phenomenon, he believes, is occurring among adults.[31]

How great is America's need to reclaim its Judeo-Christian heritage? In the view of American Enterprise Institute scholar Robert Nisbet, very great indeed.

> If there is one generalization that can be made confidently about the history of the idea of progress [in the West], it is that throughout its history the idea has been closely linked with, has depended on, religion or upon intellectual constructs derived from religion . . . It was belief in the sacred and the mythological that in the beginning of Western history made possible belief in and assimilation of ideas of time, history, development, and either progress or regress. Only on the basis of confidence in the existence of a divine power was confidence possible with respect to design or pattern in the world and in the history of the world . . . But it is absent now, whether ever to be recovered, we cannot know.[32]

EIGHT

Mindless Education

Reports of the woeful academic deficiencies of American students continue to alarm concerned citizens, and with good reason. When compared with young people from other nations, American youth score close to last in biology, math, chemistry, and physics. Although the number of illiterates may be modest, the number of functional illiterates is disturbingly high. Whereas it is common in many countries for students to become fluent in a second language, many American high school graduates have failed to master their own language. Moreover, for more than a decade employers have been lamenting the lack of problem-solving and decision-making skills in their workers. Their laments were, in fact, the catalyst for the educational reform discussion that began with the publication of *A Nation at Risk* in 1983 and continues to this day. Long before incautious Japanese leaders questioned the quality of the American workforce,* Robert Reich and other political economists estimated that only one in five U.S. workers is skilled enough to meet world competition. Nor is it a secret that corporations spend over $35 billion

*In 1992 some Japanese leaders suggested that America's loss of competitiveness in world markets was due to the laziness and incompetence of American workers. Many Americans expressed outrage at the charge.

annually in efforts to overcome the educational deficiencies of their employees.

The popular view is that the deficiencies of today's students are solely attributable to negligent parenting and incompetent teaching. This is the view not only of pundits and cracker-barrel educational philosophers, but (lamentably) of some serious and credentialed contributors to educational reform. This view rests on the assumption that home and school are the only significant influences on the lives of children. As we have seen in previous chapters, that assumption may have been warranted earlier in this century, but it is definitely not warranted today. Popular culture is a greater influence on most young people than home, school, and church combined. This has been the case for more than thirty years, and the influence is increasing. If there are more negligent parents today than a couple of generations ago, and that may well be the case, it is because today's parents were influenced by the relativism, selfism, and exaltation of feelings that dominated the 1960s, 1970s, and 1980s. If there are more incompetent teachers, and there probably are, the cause is the same. Nor is incompetence found only among educators. There are arguably more incompetent doctors, lawyers, businesspeople, and elected officials than there were a couple of generations ago.

THE EFFECTS OF POPULAR CULTURE

Scapegoating parents slanders the many conscientious parents who give their children good example and teach them well and then have their hearts broken when their children quit school, become addicted to drugs, or engage in criminal activity. Likewise, scapegoating teachers slanders the many teachers who are doing a heroic job under unfavorable conditions, devoting hundreds of extra hours every year to preparing creative, lively, relevant adventures in learning, only to find their students unresponsive. As we noted in chapter 1, one of the most significant yet neglected facts in the discussion of America's educational and social problems is that the efforts of the best parents and teachers are often little more effective than the efforts of lazy and irresponsible ones. The reason is simple: the lessons of popular culture contradict those of home and school. America's educational (and social) problems are essentially problems in attitude. Sometimes the attitudes are directly expressed, but more often they are merely implied by the way students act toward parents, teachers, and others. Often they are so subtle that students are not even aware they have them.

The attitudes most evident in students who have trouble at home and in school are a direct reflection of the values promoted by popular culture. Relativism teaches young people that they create their own truth, so they naturally form the attitude that there are no right answers in school or in life, so there is no need to listen to others. Further, since their opinions are "right for them," they don't bother to defend them with reasons or evidence—they just expect teachers and other students to respect their views. And if they aren't "into" an academic subject, then they conclude that it has no value for them. Selfism teaches young people that they are already unique and needn't undergo any process of becoming (self-improvement). Having been told over and over that everyone has his or her personal "style," they regard teachers' and parents' guidance as a violation of their personal sovereignty. This attitude poses an insurmountable barrier to learning, particularly the learning of language skills. People who believe that the way they speak and write is a special mark of their individuality are likely to be content with whatever domain of barbarism they inhabit and therefore unenthusiastic about mastering the conventions of grammar, syntax, and usage. Zealous for their "rights," they want to be approved as they are, not educated.

Having been persuaded by the culture that they should follow their feelings, many young people do just that. Instead of regarding their feelings as tentative assessments, subject to testing against reality, they take them as absolute truth (an ironic twist in a relativistic age). Hence, if they feel their parents and teachers are being unfair to them, then it must be so. If they feel their classes are boring and irrelevant to their lives, then that is the case. If they feel a classmate or some passerby on the street offended them on purpose, that person is necessarily guilty. And if they feel, as popular culture virtually guarantees, that they are the equals of their parents and teachers in every way, they see no need to behave toward them or any other adults with respect or deference. Accordingly, they feel no compunction about speaking to older people in the same tone and often same vulgarisms they use with their peers. There is a pathetic innocence about the *in*subordination of the young; they have no understanding of that offense because the root concept of *sub*ordination is meaningless to them.

Popular culture's incessant preaching that right and wrong are matters of personal preference has created in young people the attitude that they needn't abide by rules and standards. "Who's to say what's right and wrong?" translates to "I'll do as I please." It is this attitude more than any deficiency in their teachers that accounts for the unruliness and disruption that is the norm in many schools. Whereas earlier generations of students acknowledged the school's authority to establish regulations and their obligation to obey them, many of today's students assume it is their constitutional right to wear hats in class, shout crude remarks to one another, run in the halls, interrupt others when they are talking, and harass people they dislike, teachers as well as peers, in and out of school.

The habit of relying on feelings and impressions rather than thoughts plays a significant role in reading problems. In a study that probed the difference between good and poor readers, professors Linda Phillips and Stephen Norris of Newfoundland's Memorial University had a group of sixth graders express what went through their minds as they read a paragraph. They found that whereas both good and poor readers formed impressions from the first sentence, only the good readers remained flexible and revised their first impressions in light of later clues to meaning. The poor readers maintained their first impressions and ignored later clues. The authors conclude that, since good reading requires accurate comprehension, the habit of implicitly trusting first impressions prevents students from becoming proficient readers.[1]

These negative attitudes, which may be summed up as a profound indisposition to learn from parents and teachers, are the principal cause of today's educational deficiencies. But they are not the only cause. As we noted in an earlier chapter, modern programming and advertising practices prevent students from developing a mature attention span and create in them the expectation of being entertained. As a result, they are unable to deal with material that cannot be learned instantly but demands extended concentration. Since even moderately challenging problem solving or idea analysis is beyond their reach, many students writhe and squirm and cast nervous glances at the clock when class discussion of an idea extends beyond a minute or two; others become narcoleptic. Moreover, the episodic format of much of the programming they watch on television, *including the news,* conditions them to see whole subject areas and even individual facts as separate and discrete. They consequently lack the habit of looking for connections among ideas, a habit that is central to all learning and indispensable to creativity.

Predictably, students lack insight into their condition. Their perception is that of the little child in the cartoon who looked up earnestly at his teacher as she finished writing "A, B, C, D, E, F, G" on the blackboard, and said: "I hope that's about all of them. I'm beginning to lose interest." To them school lessons seem interminably long and incredibly boring, their teachers (and parents) hopelessly dull. One can understand *their* failure to see that popular culture has manipulated their minds and sowed discontentment with people who really care about them. But it is not so easy to understand how people in the media and analysts of social and educational phenomena have been blind to the role of popular culture in America's predicament.

THE INTERNAL PROBLEM: PESSIMISM

So far we have been speaking of the external problem, popular culture. There is also an internal problem, the philosophy of pessimism that has corrupted education throughout this century. "The fundamental history of humankind," philosopher William Barrett rightly noted, "is the history of mind."[2] Classical education was aimed at developing students' powers of mind, but modern education is based on a reductionist view of the human mind. Before examining that view, it is helpful to explode the "standards" myth, which holds that prior to the 1960s we had rigorous, exacting educational standards and that reform can be accomplished by merely rejecting permissivism and reviving the old standards. It is true that educators have become permissive during the last several decades and that the effect has been to undermine standards and trivialize learning. Raising standards must therefore be a part of the educational reform effort.* Nevertheless, merely returning to the standards of fifty or a hundred years ago will not solve our educational problems because those standards were not meaningful or productive of excellence then and would not be now. If students of the 1940s and 1950s were more literate and more knowledgeable than their modern counterparts, it is not so much because the educational standards were better then as because the culture reinforced, rather than opposed, the lessons of home and school. Consider this description of a Harvard education in the mid-*nineteenth* century:

> Our professors in the Harvard of the "fifties" were a set of rather eminent scholars and highly respectable men. They attended to their duties with commendable assiduity, and drudged along in a dreary humdrum sort of way in a stereotyped method of classroom instruction. But as for giving direction to, in the sense of shaping, the individual minds of young men in their most plastic state, so far as I know nothing of the kind was ever dreamed of; it never entered into the professorial mind. This was what I needed, and all I needed—an intelligent, inspiring direction; and I never got it, not a suggestion of it. I was left absolutely without guidance.... No instructor produced, or endeavored to produce, the slightest impression on me; no spark of enthusiasm was sought to be infused into me.[3]

What passed for rigor and meaningful education then and thereafter was the educational philosophy of individuals such as William Rainey Harper, first president of the University of Chicago, a philosophy characterized by historian Page Smith as providing for the student nothing more than "difficult, laborious, and unrewarding tasks to perform and insisting that he carry them out properly, and, above all, punctually."[4] Such "stan-

---

*Talking interminably about raising standards, of course, is not synonymous with raising them. Specific changes must be made in teaching. Examples of those changes appear later in this chapter.

dards" may be better than none at all, but they fall far short of what students deserve and need to function now and in the coming century.

Pessimism, the continuing evil within American education, has its roots in John Locke's rejection of the medieval conception of an active mind composed of intellect and will. Locke, a seventeenth-century English philosopher, argued that the mind is passive rather than active, a "blank slate" upon which experience writes. British and American philosophy have continued in this tradition, which carries the implication that the role of the mind is to receive information but not to act upon it.* Since the time of Darwin, science has tended to dismiss metaphysical and spiritual realities and therefore has further weakened the idea of an active, purposeful mind, as did Freud's belief that conscious mental activity is less interesting and trustworthy than unconscious and the behaviorists' reduction of mind to matter. All these historical developments set the stage for the proximate and efficient cause of educational pessimism, the work of the psychometrists who popularized the IQ test in the United States. Ignoring the warnings of the test's inventor, Alfred Binet, that the test did not measure higher-order thinking skills and was not designed as a general measure of intelligence, these individuals used it to advance their elitist agenda. They believed that intelligence is inherited, that most people are intellectually deficient, and that nothing can be done to alter a person's level of intelligence. These convictions they sought to prove by various means, most notably through Harvard professor Robert Yerkes' IQ test, which was administered to 1,750,000 Army recruits during World War I. Though badly designed and flawed in application (it classified illiteracy and unfamiliarity with the English language as mental deficiencies), at the time it was heralded as the definitive study of human intelligence. Among its absurd conclusions: that the average mental age of northern European Caucasians is 13; of southern and central European Caucasians, a little over 11; and of people of color, under 10.5.[5]

This study, as well as other psychometrist initiatives, did

---

*In contrast, continental philosophy followed G. W. Leibnitz's conception of the mind as dynamic.

monumental mischief. It reinforced racism. It prompted Congress to rewrite immigration laws and discriminate against Italians, Greeks, and Poles, among others. It confirmed the prevailing view of business leaders that the average worker lacked the mental capacity to contribute ideas to the company, a view that eventually led American industrialists to reject Edward Deming's insights. In contrast, the Japanese welcomed those ideas, incorporated "quality circles" and other strategies for giving workers a sense of proprietorship over their jobs, and thereby gained an advantage they still enjoy. (The whimpering of Lee Iacocca and certain other business leaders about unfair trade practices demonstrates, sadly, that they still don't understand the nature and extent of their error.) Yerkes's study also reinforced the contempt in which advertising industry held the public and provoked the steady stream of insults to American intelligence that has comprised advertising from that time to this.

The worst effect, however, was on education. Accepting the psychometrists' view of human intelligence as unassailable fact, educational leaders decided that the classical goal of education—a sound mind in a sound body—was unachievable. Since the masses were morons (the term enjoyed scientific status at that time), and since teaching them to inquire, analyze, solve problems, and make decisions was an exercise in futility, educators reasoned that education should concentrate on stuffing minds full of information. Thus did pessimism produce mind-stuffing, with its three *R*'s of Receiving, Recalling, and Regurgitating information. After reigning for almost a century, this philosophy permeates every aspect of education. Courses and curricula comprise blocks of factual material. Textbooks are designed to convey that material to the reader; teacher-designed and commercial tests, to measure students' recall. The dominant, and in many cases the exclusive, classroom method is lecturing about the material to facilitate memorization.

So entrenched is mind-stuffing that teachers are forbidden to question its cherished assumptions. One such assumption is that learning consists only of possessing information. Students are routinely assigned to "gifted" classes on the basis of grade-point averages or IQ test scores, despite the fact that those high averages reflect little more than obedience and concentration (virtues, to be sure, but not the only or the most important ones) and that IQ tests do not measure skill in creative or critical thinking, reflectiveness, or insight. Class size is allowed to rise well beyond reasonable numbers because research supposedly documents that learning is as effective in classes of fifty students as in classes of fifteen. The flaw in all such research is that the "learning" it measures is nothing more than memorizing facts. This research, the foundation of state and local educational funding formulas, is thus relevant to mind-stuffing *but completely irrelevant to mind-building*. Lecturing may impart information, but it cannot provide the guided practice students need to master the habits and skills of higher-order thinking. And it is precisely those habits and skills that people need in their careers and their personal lives.

The unfortunate effects of mind-stuffing in education reach far beyond the classroom. Even before the advent of television, the medium of radio celebrated such walking encyclopedias as the Quiz Kids, but television game shows institutionalized this phenomenon; consider the enormous popularity of the game built on the game-show concept, Trivial Pursuit. Today it is widely, though erroneously, assumed that intelligence consists merely of possessing a lot of information, that the more facts a person has at his or her command, the greater his or her intelligence. Similarly, it is believed that the Intelligence Quotient (IQ), as its name implies, is an index of overall intelligence. That explains why Mensa, the organization open only to people with high IQs, is considered prestigious and why Marilyn vos Savant, who boasts the highest recorded IQ score (230), was given a magazine column, "Ask Marilyn," in *Parade*. Typical reader questions include, "Which is more important, quality or quantity?" "Can one's spirit communicate with oneself and be aware of it?" "All my life, I've believed if men refused to fight, there would be no wars. All my life, I've been told it's not that simple. Why not?" The idea is that with that high an IQ, the fortuitously named Savant must know everything about everything, including science, philosophy, and theology, whether or not she has ever studied the subjects. Her celebrity even got her a book contract. (It is curious that with such amazing powers of mind she didn't write *Brain Building* alone, but had a co-author, Leonore Fleischer.)

The formula implied in this phenomenon, that having facts equals being intelligent, has resulted in the affliction I call *informania,* the irrational conviction that we necessarily act wisely when we are well informed and, therefore, that the prescription for every social problem is to give more information. When the teenage pregnancy rate rises, as it has steadily in recent years, it is assumed that teens lack information about sex. No one seems to be wondering why teen pregnancy was so much lower fifty years ago when there was no sex education in school and precious little at home. So classroom time is diverted from reading and writing to the mechanics of sexual intercourse. The same informania is evident in the reaction to drug abuse, rape, bigotry, AIDS, and a host of other social problems. It is assumed that the only explanation for these deplorable conditions is ignorance of the facts and that the cure lies in a campaign to provide information *rather than in training in reasoned judgment and responsible behavior.* One ironic effect of informania is that the media's appetite for sensationalism can be classified as a public service, thus guaranteeing that the graphic reports of serial killings, bizarre sexual liaisons, and celebrity scandals will continue to aggravate the social problems they ostentatiously deplore.

By keeping students docile, passive, and accepting of whatever lessons they are given, mind-stuffing in the schools has contributed to mindlessness in everyday life. That kind of education is little more than "a state-controlled manufactory of echoes," to borrow Norman Douglas's excellent phrase. It tells students what to think rather than teaching them how to think; prepares them to recite names and dates and places without drawing meaning, significance, and wisdom from what they learn; and ultimately leaves them incapable of meeting the challenges of life and vulnerable to the manipulations of scam-artists and demagogues. It creates poor workers, poor spouses, poor parents, poor citizens.

Pessimism about the human mind and its legacy of mind-stuffing and informania have not gone unchallenged. Throughout this century there have been visionaries—people such as the much misunderstood John Dewey,* Alfred North Whitehead, Jean Piaget, Robert Hutchins, and Mortimer Adler. But their message has been largely ignored. Moreover, most of the current educational reform initiatives fail to address pessimism and the mind-stuffing and informania it has spawned. Some place their hope for educational reform in the expanded use of computers and satellite TV links. These new technologies certainly have the potential to, respectively, make lessons more vivid and increase the quality of educational service to remote areas. Nevertheless, their advocates generally accept the pessimistic credo that intelligence cannot be raised, thinking cannot be taught, and the sole aim of education is to cram minds with information, so they are certain to place the new technologies at the service of mind-stuffing.** Joseph Weizenbaum, MIT professor and pioneer in the development of the computer, is among the harshest critics of the notion that the computer will be the salvation of education:

> A new human malady has been invented, just as the makers of patent medicine in the past invented illnesses such as "tired blood" in order to create a market for their products. Now it's computer illiteracy. The future, we are told, will belong to those familiar with the computer. What a joke this would be if only it didn't victimize so many innocent bystanders ... I think [the computer] inhibits children's creativity. In most cases the computer programs kids and not the other way around. Once they have started a program, the computer may leave them a few degrees of freedom, to be sure, but on the whole it will tell them what to do and when to do it ... The introduction of the computer into any problem, be it medicine, education, or whatever, usually creates the impression that the grievous deficiencies are being corrected, that something is being done. But often its principal effect is to push problems even further into obscurity—to avoid confrontation with the need for fundamentally critical thinking.[6]

*I am referring here to Dewey's emphasis on teaching the processes of thinking, not to his theological presuppositions.

**This is not an indictment of these educators, but only a description of reality. Teachers typically teach as they have been taught. Having been victims of mind-stuffing themselves, seldom if ever encountering any other approach, it is understandable that they assume it is the best approach.

The most recent educational panacea is Christopher Whittle's Channel One, a television show that brings to the classroom news programming and advertisements for food and clothing. Even if such programming is successful in stimulating students' interest and increasing their knowledge, like other programming it is almost certain to prevent their attention spans from developing, maintain passivity and an episodic grasp of reality, and reinforce advertising's values of impulsiveness, self-indulgence, and instant gratification. In this case, the medicine not only doesn't cure the disease: *it is the disease.*

The movement for national testing of student learning, arguably the most powerful educational reform initiative, is similarly flawed. Admittedly, the idea seems reasonable enough, given our national obsession with the quantitative. It aims for a uniform measure of achievement, comparing student performance in the smallest towns and the largest cities from Maine to California and thereby ensuring accountability and lifting students to achievement. But on reflection, one must wonder at the tail-wagging-dog logic that regards testing the solution to the problems of teaching. Gregory Anrig, president of the Educational Testing Service (ETS), has remarked on the foolishness of continually pulling up the carrot to see if it is still growing; and another critic of rampant testing, varying the metaphor, pointed out that *one doesn't fatten cattle by weighing them!* A number of crucial questions about national testing are being ignored. Will the level of the test be the politically expedient lowest common denominator or excellence? If the former, then what will prevent teachers from simply teaching to the test and denying students real learning challenges? What kind of achievement will be measured? Mere possession of knowledge or application of knowledge to solve problems, analyze issues, and make decisions?

What the proponents of testing evidently do not realize is that despite years of research and experimentation, no comprehensive test of thinking skills (creative plus critical plus reflective) exists, that currently the best test of reasoning is the Watson-Glaser Critical Thinking Test, which was developed in 1941 and has significant limitations. The central dilemma, possibly insurmountable, is that national testing demands an easily scored instrument—in other words, an objective test—and such a test does not allow students to demonstrate ingenuity, flexibility, insight, judgment, and other desirable qualities of mind. For this reason, if national testing becomes a reality, it will almost certainly reinforce mind-stuffing and doom the efforts of the visionary mind-*builders* in education.

THE INADEQUACY OF EXISTING REFORMS

The most ambitious educational reform program has been the Bush administration's America 2000 plan.* By the year 2000, it projected the following achievements: all children will start school ready to learn; at least 90 percent of all high school students will earn a diploma; U.S. students will be first in the world in science/math achievement; every adult will be literate; and every school will be free of drugs and violence. The plan for accomplishing these objectives included setting high standards in five core subjects (English, mathematics, science, history, and geography), establishing a system of national examinations called "American Achievement Tests" and a parental choice program that would let parents apply vouchers or tax credits to religious or private schools, and offering increased federal aid to schools that pass the test of accountability by demonstrating increased student achievement. The overall cost in fiscal 1992 alone approximated $690 million.

The designers of America 2000 deserve a great deal of credit. They recognized that American education is in serious difficulty and needs comprehensive overhaul; cosmetic changes and fine tuning simply won't do. They articulated clear goals, including replacing the smorgasbord curriculum with a substantive core curriculum and increasing time on task and homework,** and gave hope to the many educators who have long supported meaningful reform. Yet America 2000 was not without weaknesses. One was its failure to make a clear distinction

---

*At this writing, President Clinton's educational reform plan, "Goals 2000: Educate America," is essentially an extension of the Bush plan.

**The average Japanese elementary school student spends an estimated seven hours a day doing homework; the junior high student, nine; the high school student, eight; the college student, five. In contrast, American students spend little or no time on homework.

between mind-stuffing and mind-building. The simple fact, amply documented in research,[7] is that the same mind-stuffing model that dominated educational practice earlier in the century continues to dominate it today. Never adequate to students' needs, this model is woefully inadequate today. Rather than restore and reinforce mind-stuffing, we should replace it with mind-*building*. The emphasis in teaching, in other words, should not be on telling students what to think, but teaching them how to think—that is, guiding them to weigh and consider ideas, see implications, follow an argument to its logical conclusion, integrate knowledge, and apply creative and critical thinking to solve problems and make decisions. This change will not represent a return to an earlier standard but the creation of a new standard and will require significant modifications in classroom methodology, administrative policies, and assessment practices.

A considerably more serious error than faulty historical perspective was America 2000's implicit and uncritical assumption that parents and teachers are responsible for young people's academic deficiencies. To be sure, this idea was not presented as baldly as Iacocca expressed it: He accused teachers of "massive consumer fraud" (see p. 21 for the quotation). America 2000 more gently advised, "Parents and teachers should encourage children to study more, learn more, and strive to meet higher educational standards." The fact that reveals the assumption is America 2000's assigning the business community the most prominent role in reforming education by establishing the New American Schools Development Corporation. This organization, which has been compared to the World War II Manhattan Project that produced the atomic bomb, was supporting educational research and awarding hundreds of millions of dollars to private and public agencies engaged in the search for educational remedies. The reasoning underlying America 2000, too politically explosive to express forthrightly, seemed to be, "Since no problem can solve itself, and parents and teachers are the problem, our best hope lies in the business community."

In fairness to the designers of America 2000, it must be acknowledged that the educational establishment has a long tradition of resistance to meaningful reform and that business has a legitimate interest in this issue. After all, one in four workers is functionally illiterate, and few possess a satisfactory level of problem-solving and decision-making skill. Also, given the scope of the challenge and the resources of industry, there is wisdom in involving the business community in educational reform. Yet the authors of America 2000, like many other educational reformers, ignored a crucial fact: the main cause of America's educational (and social) problems is neither poor parenting nor poor teaching but popular culture, and the main sponsor of popular culture is the business community. *The profound and potentially tragic irony in assigning business the leadership role in educational reform is that business itself (albeit unwittingly) is largely responsible for the media practices that obstruct learning.*

A MORE COMPREHENSIVE REFORM

There are two essential requirements of effective educational reform. The first is to reaffirm the root meaning of *education.* The Latin verb from which the term comes, *educare,* means "to lead out of." Out of what and to what? Out of ignorance and to understanding and wisdom. The very notion of ignorance presupposes a reality beyond the self, an objective reality that is what it is regardless of what people think or feel about it, a reality about which there are right answers and wrong, shallow views and profound. In our age, reaffirming this meaning of education necessitates opposing relativism, which acknowledges no distinction between ignorance and wisdom, and opposing selfism and the exaltation of feelings, which impede learning. Education depends, above all, on both faith and intellectual humility—faith that there are truths worth knowing; intellectual humility in acknowledging that we do not yet fully know them.

The other requirement is to replace pessimism with optimism—affirming that intelligence is not fixed, but can be increased by nurturing the attitudes, habits, and skills associated with effective thinking.* There is ample evidence that such optimism is not misplaced, that the quality of students' reason-

---

*Interestingly, the Japanese have had that optimistic view of their children. That is undoubtedly why teachers provide more time for creative problem solving and move more freely between the concrete and the abstract in their lessons.[9]

ing and judgment can be improved, and even that imaginativeness and originality can be taught.[8] It is also well documented that providing regular, guided practice in using thinking to solve problems and resolve issues leads to greater mastery of course material—including factual information—than does mind-stuffing. Canada's McMaster University College of Medicine discarded the entire lecture system and substituted a tutorial system in which students grapple with actual clinical problems. They must decide for themselves what they will need to know to solve each problem and how they can best acquire that knowledge. In the process of acquiring it, they discover the relevant physiological, biological, and behavioral principles formerly taught by rote. A similar curricular reform has been effected in the Netherlands' University of Maastricht Medical School, and the results in both institutions have been so impressive that other medical schools, including Harvard's, are following their lead. Students learn more and remember it longer, and fewer fail or drop out of the program.

Problem-based education has proved itself at other levels of education as well. Jim Pollard, former chairman of Spokane Community College's police science department, used it in his freshman and sophomore classes. In several national competitions they finished first four times and second three times *against students from schools as prestigious as the University of California, Berkeley, and the University of California, Davis.* An Arizona high school teacher who attended one of my teaching seminars a few years ago told me he had used this approach in his history class, and students who had previously failed traditional history classes performed as well as the gifted students who were assigned to the class. Second-, third-, and fourth-grade teachers use this approach at the Prairie School in Racine, Wisconsin, and a heart surgeon expressed amazement at the maturity of the questions and depth of understanding of the human heart it produced in his second-grade son. After a classroom lesson on the heart, the boy was asking him more profound, more mature questions than were posed by many of his adult patients. Professor Ilma Brewer of the University of Sydney, Australia, conducted an unusually detailed study in her science classes. During a ten-year period she gradually changed the emphasis from simple recall of information to comprehension/application and found that learning improved dramatically.[10]

Even under poor learning conditions, young people do much better at thinking tasks than skeptics believe. Ann Cook, co-director of New York City's Urban Academy, received a call from a Reuters reporter, who asked whether she could assemble some students to watch President Bush's education speech so that the reporter could interview them. Since the school lacked a cable TV hookup, she took six teenagers, ages fourteen to eighteen, to a neighborhood bar. Not the best conditions for thought and analysis, to be sure, especially since the bar patrons were talking, addressing comments to the television set, and mimicking the president. After the speech, she took the students to a back table for the interview. What followed amazed both Cook and the reporter. The students gave a forty-five-minute "*tour de force,* insightful comments backed up with evidence and verbatim references." They raised important questions, too, such as how the president planned to accomplish his goals, and why, if education is so important, he devoted only a single speech to it. One student criticized the president's call for national testing. Most testing, he commented, measures "what you remember, not whether you can apply what you learn to everyday life."[11]

After a decade of educational reform, there is no dearth of worthwhile ideas for improving American education. In a sense, there are too many. Before faculty can implement the ideas the last visiting expert enthusiastically detailed, a new expert arrives to extol a different approach. The best way to avoid the inevitable sense of frustration and defeat this situation produces would be to have a five- or ten-year moratorium on reform proposals, during which time teachers could sort out and implement the best ideas. Since such a moratorium is not possible, researchers, faculty developers, and administrators should turn their efforts to *integrating* the best reform ideas into a single approach so that faculty can revise their teaching with the assurance that the changes they make today will not be obsolete tomorrow. Among the excellent ideas this approach should incorporate are the inquiry, discovery, and case-study methods; writing across the curriculum; values instruction (not to be confused with Values Clarification, whose flaws are noted in chapter 7); collaborative learning; problem-based education; and the one element upon which all the others depend, instruction in creative and critical thinking.

It is necessary here to address an objection some educational reformers have raised, the idea that thinking instruction, rather than being a solution to our educational problems, is instead a primary cause. E. D. Hirsch, Jr., is a chief spokesman for this view. Hirsch rightly notes that many students lack basic knowledge of history, geography, and current events, among other subjects. He defines knowledge as a "network of information" (or "cultural literacy") and believes that thinking skills are subject-specific and thus not transferable from subject to subject. "What distinguishes good readers from poor ones," he argues, "is simply the possession of a lot of diverse, task-specific information." In Hirsch's view, the answer to America's educational problems is "more surveys [i.e., survey courses] that cover large movements of human thought and experience." And he charges that the critical-thinking movement denigrates facts and "injures the cause of higher national literacy."[12] To begin with, Hirsch's definition of *knowledge* is unfortunately narrow. As Stanford epistemologist Lee Shulman notes, there are three kinds of knowledge—*propositional knowledge,* more commonly termed facts; *case knowledge,* historical situations and events; and *procedural knowledge,* the thinking strategies and protocols used to interpret and apply the other kinds of knowledge to new situations and events. This view explains why so many educated people, filled to overflowing with factual information, are nevertheless abysmal problem solvers. In addition, if thinking skills are themselves a dimension of knowledge, it is difficult to see how they can be an impediment to knowledge. Given the continuing knowledge explosion in every field, thinking skills (procedural knowledge) are arguably more important than ever.

Hirsch's idea that thinking skills are subject-specific, not original with him, is clearly erroneous. *The human mind, after all, preceded the college catalog.* In other words, the division of knowledge into the present disciplines and departments is relatively recent and can hardly be said to limit the human minds that invented it. Furthermore, a moment's reflection will reveal that there is remarkable similarity in the way people in every field speak about good and bad reasoning. From anthropology to zoology, the lexicon of logic has a single set of terms: hasty conclusion, oversimplification, unwarranted assumption, non sequitur, and so on. And the strategies for avoiding or detecting such errors have similar application in every field. At least to this extent, thinking is generic rather than subject-specific. Finally, Hirsch's claim that critical-thinking instruction is responsible for cultural *illiteracy* ignores a crucial fact. Researchers from Charles Silberman (*Crisis in the Classroom,* 1970) to John Goodlad (*A Place Called School,* 1984) and Ernest Boyer (*College: The Undergraduate Experience in America,* 1987) confirm that despite the publicity it has received and the number of educators who affirm its importance, critical thinking has found its way into very few curricula. The cultural illiteracy Hirsch rightly deplores is at root an attitudinal problem, and it is caused more by popular culture than by teachers.

Should thinking instruction displace traditional subject matter? Decidedly not. As former Secretary of Education William Bennett has written:

> Solid and meaningful years of study means the study of the essentials of these disciplines. Acquiring "skills" should not come at the expense of acquiring knowledge. Students should finish high school knowing not just the "method" or "process" of science or history; they should actually know some science and history. They should know fractions and decimals, and percentages and algebra and geometry. They should know that for every action there is an equal and opposite reaction, and they should know who said "I am the state" and who said "I have a dream." They should know about subjects and predicates, about isosceles triangles and ellipses. They should know where the Amazon flows, and what the First Amendment means . . . They should know how a poem works, how a plant works, and the meaning of "If wishes were horses, beggars would ride."[13]

They should know all these things and, of course, a great deal more.

Thinking instruction, as I am defining it, does not affect what is taught in a course, only *the way it is taught*. Geography, history, literature, philosophy, science, and mathematics should occupy a prominent place in the curriculum.* But they, and other subjects, should be taught as dynamic intellectual challenges rather than as dusty collections of inert facts. Every academic subject represents an extended sequence of triumphs of the human mind. Every subject deserves a context that recreates its inherent drama, a context calculated to excite students' interest and enthusiasm for learning. Given the ravages of media attention-maintaining devices, more and more students require such a context in order to learn. This is not to disparage American students but to acknowledge an unpleasant reality. The desire to learn is strong in humans, even in the most deplorable living conditions. In the Palotaka camp of the Sudan, for example, filled with young boys who have traveled hundreds of miles to escape starvation, adults conduct school three hours every other day. Though there are few books and no writing materials, and teachers and students must miss classes to forage for food in the forest, the boys display an enthusiasm for learning that is often lacking in more fortunate students.[14] The resistance to learning evident in many American youth reflects their conditioning rather than any inherent indisposition.

Teachers must begin by streamlining their courses—in other words, by separating key principles, concepts, and information from interesting but less important course material. This task is vital because the knowledge explosion in every field has bloated course material to unmanageable proportions, and because students tend to forget indiscriminately, often remembering trivia and forgetting important matters. As Theodore Sizer is fond of saying, "less can be more": teaching fewer things and reinforcing them in many and varied ways ensures mastery of essentials. Next, teachers must transform passive learning into active

---

*A good case can be made for shifting emphasis from social studies to history, not only because mastery of any field requires historical perspective, but also because practical wisdom is dependent on knowing the lessons of the past. Psychiatrist Carl Jung warned, "The present tendency to destroy all tradition or render it unconscious could interrupt the normal process of development for several hundred years and substitute an interlude of barbarism...A predominantly scientific and technological education, such as is the usual thing nowadays, can also bring about a spiritual regression and a considerable increase of psychic dissociation."[15]

learning by ceasing to tell information and instead guiding students to think creatively, critically, and reflectively about problems and issues so that they can discover essential information for themselves. What is learned through inquiry and discovery is less likely to be forgotten; and even if some of it is forgotten, the intellectual skills acquired in the process will remain.

Historically, textbooks have promoted rote learning. Professor Oscar Handlin offered this description of textbooks in the 1950s:

> With few exceptions [the textbook] is dogmatic and dull, an obstacle rather than an aid to learning . . . Excellent illustrations and maps, thoughtful design and layout, and good paper and binding are characteristic of today's publishing. But there has been no alteration in the basis assumption of the text that learning consists of remembering and that the function of the book is to supply the material to be remembered . . . Generally, publishers, authors, and teachers follow one another in a frustrating circle that strengthens the pattern. The publisher is constrained by the market to turn out books for existing courses; the author writes what will be published; and the teacher shapes his course by the available texts. The result is endless imitation.[16]

Four decades after Handlin made that observation, most textbooks still serve mind-stuffing rather than mind-building, providing mountains of information for students to remember for the examination but no challenge to students' thinking. Here is a typical, abbreviated example of a textbook treatment of an important event in psychology. (The treatment is no different in other subject areas at every level of education.)

> In 1973 Haney, Banks, and Zimbardo conducted an experiment in which randomly assigned college students played the roles of prisoners and prison guards. They were not told how to behave. Very quickly the "prisoners" became distressed, helpless, and apathetic. Some developed psychosomatic illnesses; others became angry and rebellious. Half begged to be released after a few days. Some "guards" were kind; others, "tough but fair." But a third became cruel. Though they were permitted to choose their approach to maintaining order, they chose to be abusive, often for no reason. One tried to keep a "prisoner" in

solitary confinement all night without telling anyone because he thought the experimenters were "too soft." Critics of the six-day experiment say it was too artificial to be meaningful. Zimbardo, the designer, argues that it demonstrated the way people in real life play their "roles."

An interesting case, but what challenge does it present to students? None at all. Students are told all the essential information rather than being challenged to apply their creative and critical thinking. All that remains for them to do is to memorize the facts for the examination. Compare that approach with the mind-building approach, in which the students would wrestle with the problem before being introduced to the psychological research.

What makes some people kind and others cruel? Is it the values their parents imparted, peer pressure, or some other factor? Would a person who is basically kind dramatically change if placed in an unusual situation? What experiences or observations support your view? Devise an experiment that tests whether people change when placed in an unusual situation.

How much more inviting and intellectually engaging this approach is. Students have an opportunity to ponder the matter, reflect on their experience, apply their ingenuity, and express their thoughts in writing and/or class discussion. Later, when the teacher introduces the research study, they will appreciate its significance, be able to discuss it more intelligently and animatedly, and very likely remember it longer. If teachers let textbook publishers know that they want this format in textbooks, and will no longer accept less, they will eventually have their way. But in the meantime, they will have to create their own material by recasting textbook material as shown and by reading in their fields and watching the news for relevant problems and issues. In accounting, students might be given a tax problem that requires reading certain sections of the tax law and deciding how they apply to the particular case, then making the necessary calculations on the tax return. In literature, they might be given a poem or short story and asked to determine its particular strengths and weaknesses and overall quality, without knowing whether a professional or an amateur wrote it. In philosophy, they might be given a current legal issue and asked to decide what philosophical (for example, ethical) considerations are involved and what decision would best honor them. In science, they might address a challenge faced by a modern epidemiologist, forensic specialist, or physicist. The possibilities are endless.

Testing for thinking must reflect these different materials and methods.* Examinations should be constructed in such a way that students do not just present answers, but also detail the thought process that produced the answers, so that teachers can identify thinking strengths and weaknesses and provide appropriate guidance. So-called objective tests, which in reality may be as subjective as any other test, tend to penalize thinkers by affording no way to raise a thoughtful question, express an insight, present an interesting scenario, pursue an implication, note a contradiction, or add a qualification. Such tests also encourage teachers to teach for the test and students to focus on memorizing textbook answers. Portfolios of students' work, debates, exhibitions, and experiments are among the most promising alternatives to objective testing, but are likely to be resisted because they are less efficient and do not lend themselves to national norming. For the foreseeable future, the best way to achieve a reasonable balance between effective and efficient testing is to include problems and issues on tests and to require students to explain the thinking behind each true/false and multiple-choice answer. The highest grades should be reserved for students who demonstrate the possession of relevant information, the ability to think creatively and critically about problems and issues, and skill in expressing their thoughts clearly and effectively.**

---

*Gregory Anrig, president of the Educational Testing Service, is critical of America's preoccupation with testing. "It is . . . distressing," he says, "that we are so obsessed with accountability, just obsessed. That's why there is so much testing. Most of it is for accountability purposes." He adds that the demand for instant analysis and measurement often leads to misleading test results.[17]

**In *Teaching Thinking Across the Curriculum* (New York: Harper and Row, 1988), I elaborate on this and many of the other suggestions advanced in this chapter.

THE COST OF GENUINE REFORM

Mind-building, though vastly superior to mind-stuffing, is considerably more expensive. Classes must be smaller so that every student has frequent opportunities to express his or her thoughts and receive individual attention in developing thinking, speaking, and writing skills. Though there is no magic number for class size, twenty is a reasonable maximum. Since many schools and colleges exceed this figure by 50 percent, some by 100 percent, many more teachers will be needed, and they must be allowed to focus on their teaching. Japanese teachers spend half their working time developing lessons and improving themselves professionally so that they can be better teachers.[18] American teachers must be freed from nonteaching duties so that they can make a comparable investment of time. (One way to reduce the cost of hiring more teachers and more nonprofessional staff to take over nonteaching duties is to streamline the educational bureaucracy and reassign administrators to the classroom.) Also, since few teachers have learned or even observed the methods proven successful in teaching students how to think, workshops must be made available to help them master these methods. They must learn, for example, to yield center stage to students, to cease being "answer persons" and instead guide students to answer their own questions and become their own best critics. And they must develop the habit of asking questions that elicit creative and critical thinking and promote reflection, questions such as, What do you think about this matter? Why do you think this? What evidence do you have? What objections might others raise to your view? Which of those objections have merit? What revision of your thinking would make it more reasonable?

Some would argue that America cannot afford this kind of investment in education, but the truth is just the opposite. We cannot afford to *deny* our young people the necessary preparation for adult life in a free and increasingly technological society. Building an educational system that honors by its deeds the proposition that every human being, regardless of race, creed, or socioeconomic position, has the potential to be a creative, critical, reflective thinker would benefit the country in a number of ways. It would guarantee the vital career skills business leaders have been urging educators to develop for almost fifteen years. It would provide the foundation of mental health—rational thought—and thus spare millions of people from the crippling maladjustments and neuroses that cause them pain and destroy their relationships with others. It would enable people to recognize the shallowness of relativism, selfism, and materialism and resist manipulation by others, notably the spokespeople of popular culture. Finally, it would raise the level of decision making by the electorate and thus ensure that the governance of the country is entrusted to honest, intelligent, competent leaders.

NINE

Reforming
the Culture

"We have entered on a new phase of culture—we may call it the Age of the Cinema—in which the most amazing perfection of scientific technique is being devoted to purely ephemeral objects, without any consideration of their ultimate justification. It seems as though a new society [is] arising which will acknowledge no hierarchy of values, no intellectual authority, and no social or religious tradition, but which will live for the moment in a chaos of pure sensation."[1] In the more than thirty years that have passed since historian Christopher Dawson wrote those words, popular culture has advanced the condition he described far beyond what anyone could have imagined. It has revolutionized the socialization of young people. Though home, school, and church are still expected to prepare them for responsible adult life with its demands of career and citizenship, the entertainment and communications media have made it impossible for these agencies to succeed and have generated a host of social problems that threaten America's future.

By promoting the idea that the proper goal of life is having fun and instantly gratifying every desire, the media have led many people to settle for mediocrity rather than excellence, refuse to accept the challenge of learning, shirk the responsibilities of citizenship (such as voting), and take an irresponsible attitude toward self-destructive actions such as excessive gambling and the irresponsible use of alcohol and drugs. By encouraging self-indulgence and impulsiveness and supporting moral relativism, the media have not only created the present climate of incivility, but also aggravated the problems of sexual harassment and rape, spouse and child abuse, robbery, hate crimes, murder, and suicide.* Moreover, they have made promiscuity acceptable and thereby made illegitimacy rampant** and sexually transmitted diseases, including AIDS, epidemic. Finally, by deprecating religion, they have reinforced materialism and destroyed the spiritual ideas that have provided the foundation for social harmony throughout the history of the republic.

These effects have been most dramatic among the young. A 1990 study revealed that young adults aged eighteen to twenty-nine not only watch TV more than others, but prefer shows about scandal and celebrity. It also found that this generation "knows less, cares less, votes less, and is less critical of its leaders and institutions than young people in the past." Their disengagement reflects disinterest more than disillusionment. Another study published at about the same time by People for the American Way echoes these findings, noting that the focus of this generation is on their rights, with little recognition of their responsibilities. This study cited one case of a twenty-four-year-old woman who, when asked to define citizenship, said it is the right not to be harassed by the police; she cited as a violation of her rights a security guard's insistence that she and her boyfriend stop using their cigarette lighters at a concert.[2]

We do not have to embrace nonsense ourselves to be affected by it. All of us pay in various ways for all the ignorance, apathy, and irresponsibility of others. Our taxes are increased to support expanded welfare programs; we are charged higher premiums for health and accident insurance; we suffer fear and anxiety about our own safety and that of our loved ones; and we bear

---

*According to the National Bureau of Economic Research, the suicide rate for ages fifteen to nineteen more than tripled between 1960 and 1988; the homicide rate for the same group almost tripled.

**Among blacks the rate of illegitimacy has doubled in the past two decades to 64 percent; among whites it has tripled to 18 percent.

the inestimable loss of the talents of millions of people deceived by popular culture to squander their lives. Popular culture is undeniably the ebbing tide that lowers all ships.

Several years before the outbreak of hostilities in World War I, Rollo Walter Brown, an American college professor, visited France to find the answer to a question that had long absorbed him: Why was it that, while the average educated American lacked basic facility with the English language, virtually every French man or woman, regardless of educational level, wrote and spoke graceful, correct French? During his visit he not only examined curricula and instructional materials and observed teachers and students at work in the classroom; he also studied community life. And he found, as common sense could easily predict, that the reason the French spoke so well was that *every agency of the culture actively promoted love and respect for the mother tongue.* French literary masters such as Maupassant were revered by teachers, parents, government officials, and journalists. Young students were given passages from the masters to copy in their notebooks; older students were encouraged to imitate their literary styles. Writing and public-speaking contests enjoyed a popularity matched in our culture only by athletic events. Villages vied against one another in competitions.[3]

If contemporary American popular culture supported traditional social, intellectual, and moral values the way French culture supported language education, our educational and social problems would certainly not be as numerous or as formidable as they are today. Moreover, since popular culture enjoys an influence in people's lives unparalleled in history, its support is essential to the success of any social or educational *reform* that is undertaken. America's future will assuredly depend on our degree of success in reforming popular culture, and that success will be possible only through the cooperative effort of artists, scholars, the print and broadcast media, educators, government agencies, and families. Many people are unaware of the need for change. They acknowledge the need to save the planet's physical atmosphere, but not its social atmosphere; they appreciate the importance of people's physical health, but not their intellectual and spiritual health. Those who understand these matters must raise the consciousness of those who don't, appealing both to their altruism and enlightened self-interest, helping them see that refusal to accept inconvenience and voluntary curtailment of our rights for the greater good of the nation is a virulent form of racism.

The basic goal of reforming popular culture should be to free it from the dominance of relativism, selfism, and the exaltation of feelings, to regain and enlarge the vision of greatness, to establish the highest human values.* Our emphasis should be on the *common* humanity of all people, whether male or female, young or old, abled or disabled, white, black, or Oriental, homosexual or heterosexual, religious believer or atheist, as well as on the interdependency of individuals and nations. Each social agency has its own unique opportunities to contribute to this reform.

THE CHALLENGE TO ARTISTS AND SCHOLARS

It is understandable that the artistic and scholarly communities regard protests against art with suspicion. Historically, such protests have more often than not been fired by the ignorant desire to suppress whatever is new, different, or unfamiliar. But history does not deny the possibility of *internal* as well as external threats: contemporary artistic currents could conceivably retard rather than advance, debase rather than elevate, the arts. Since discussion of ideas is a healthy activity and it is nowhere written that the community of artists and scholars must agree on everything, artists and lovers of art should feel as free to condemn pseudoartists who trivialize art for the sake of some private political agenda or self-aggrandizing publicity as they are to condemn censors. Moreover, they should be able to endorse some taboos without being labeled traitors to their calling. Unfortunately, there is considerable pressure in the artistic and scholarly communities to defend everything that calls itself art or at least to remain silent while the party line is advanced.

In an essay defending Brett Easton Ellis's indefensible novel

*The term *family values,* which became a political point of contention in the 1992 presidential campaign, unfortunately widened rather than narrowing divisions and degenerated into a debate over the definition of *family.* A focus on *human values,* with its suggestion of applicability to all people and every age, avoids that unproductive debate.

American Psycho, for example, Harvard professor Anne Bernays admits that the novel lacks a plot, has a shapeless central character, suffers from an excess of trivial detail, and desperately needs a complete reworking by a "master [editorial] hand." Nevertheless, she sees the controversy it caused as comparable to that over the coarseness of language in *Huckleberry Finn.* To Bernays the central issue is one of taste; she expresses ire at the "moral watchdogs" who "want your taste to be like theirs" and proclaims that "Today's 'unhealthy,'* 'lurid,' and 'outrageous' are tomorrow's ho-hum," without pausing to consider what our society will be like at a time when Easton's descriptions are "ho-hum."[4]

Typically, the unqualified defense of artistic expression goes beyond the artist's right of free speech; it also implies a right to tax dollars to support artistic expression. Professor Ellen T. Harris of MIT, in an essay offering condescension thinly disguised as artistic instruction, explains that there are four ways to dislike art, only one of which is good. The bad ones are to ignore it, to refuse to finance it, and to condemn the artist. The good way is to dislike it. "Art that we dislike is not necessarily bad, immoral, or even difficult," she writes, completely ignoring the corollary that what we like is not necessarily good, moral, or easy. She then quickly adds that we must not confuse disliking with rejecting. Displaying noteworthy disregard for the issue and exquisite tolerance for other people's pain, Harris describes Andres Serrano's depiction of a crucifix submerged in urine as "a very large and stunning photograph of a crucifix bathed in a golden light."[5] In Harris's view, if a work shows mastery of form, it should be eligible for support with the public's tax dollars, even if it attacks the taxpayers' most deeply held beliefs; denying any artist the dole is censorship.**

---

*This was the word critic Roger Rosenblatt had previously chosen to characterize *American Psycho* in *The New York Times Book Review.*

**It is curious that though defenders of public support for controversial art are generally staunch advocates of separation of church and state, few seem willing to acknowledge that public funding of antireligious art is a violation of that separation, or that making people pay for mockery of their beliefs is a violation of their religious freedom similar to the violations that drove our forebears to this country. Moreover, tax support of assaults on others' beliefs at a time when many Americans lack food, clothing, and shelter is obscene.

At the risk of rejection by their peers, all artists and scholars are expected to affirm Bernays's and Harris's view that literary affairs occupy some Olympian height, far above such mundane affairs as everyday human behavior. Such writers have a knack for making the word *moral* sound vaguely distasteful and for ignoring the obvious questions "Does 'art' ever work mischief in society?" and "If so, does society have any recourse?" But since these questions are not only serious and practical, but also classically philosophical, it is irresponsible to ignore them. Surely some painters, composers, sculptors, writers, actors, and photographers reject the party line and share the perspective of the many Americans who believe that people's physical and spiritual welfare is more important than art. They realize that precisely because art has the power to humanize or dehumanize, substance outweighs form. Thus they reason that certain of Robert Mapplethorpe's photographs, however brilliant the technique they display, should be withheld from public exhibition.

Similarly, many artists privately acknowledge that artistic freedom of expression does not imply any entitlement to public funding, and they are well aware, often from sad personal experience that the awards made by the National Endowment for the Arts (NEA) can reflect a peculiar and biased perspective. In recent years, for example, the NEA funded Marlon Riggs's cinematic celebration of homosexual life, an Ann Arbor artists' show that included drawings of a man clubbing a two-year-old with a mallet and a man performing a sex act on himself, and Karen Finley's performance art, in which she covers her partly nude body with chocolate. Yet it denied funding to acclaimed religious sculptor Frederick E. Hart.

Though they do not say so publicly, many artists deplore the use of art to disparage other people's beliefs and convictions, acknowledge their responsibilities as well as their rights, and reject the notion that creativity thrives best when free of all restrictions.* They understand that what sustains creativity is not license or easy federal funds but a social climate that dis-

---

*Architect Fay Jones, for example, stresses the positive value of limitations, explaining that he got his perspective from his mentor, Frank Lloyd Wright. Jones says, "If somebody says, 'Go build the most beautiful building in the world,' it's hard to get a

courages superficiality and rewards artistic pursuit of excellence, a climate that is lacking today. For the past three decades there have been fewer and fewer restrictions on form and content in the arts, yet creativity is less and less in evidence. Former Federal Communications chairman Newton Minow, who in 1961 referred to TV as "a vast wasteland," reiterated that judgment in 1986. And Loring Mandel, a distinguished screenwriter and winner of numerous Emmy awards for his TV dramas, claims that most of today's programming pollutes our minds and betrays us, lying to viewers about the meaning of life and their humanity. Other artists who share Mandel's assessment should join him in protesting the debasement of art from within. Because they are less likely to be labeled ignorant and censorious, their endorsement of such worthy ideas as columnist Nat Hentoff's recommendation for reforming the NEA would be influential. Hentoff proposed that the NEA devote most of its funds to providing art teachers and materials for schools that lack sufficient budgets for art, as well as providing grants to artists to visit schools and share their expertise and enthusiasm.

The academic establishment, like the artistic establishment, tends to pressure its members to embrace relativism and secularism. Concerning censorship, it is fashionable to ask questions such as, "Who can say what is moral and immoral?" "Where would we draw the line?" and "Who judges the judges?" and then to assume that the answers are, respectively, *no one, nowhere,* and *no one.* Equally fashionable is the schizophrenic alternating between lamenting some social problem and then being outraged when someone identifies its cause or proposes a cure. One is supposed to be concerned about issues, but not so concerned as to seek their resolution, as Professor Amitai Etzioni of George Washington University recently learned. Disturbed by extremism of both the right and the left, Etzioni established a moderate journal, *The Responsive Community: Rights and Responsibilities,* for the discussion of vital social

handle on it. Is it going to be in the mountains? The seashore? On a lake? In the desert? Is it a church? A school? Limiting, limiting, limiting—that's part of the process. It's like in writing: If you can say it in two words, it's better than if you say it in five."[6]

issues. When he advocated national service and drug testing, he was branded authoritarian and moralistic; when he supported highway checkpoints to catch drug dealers and gun control as reasonable governmental actions, he was accused of opposing the fourth and second amendments to the Constitution.[7]

George Orwell once observed, "There are some ideas so preposterous that only an intellectual could believe them." Preeminent among today's preposterous ideas is the notion that ideas don't matter and there is no connection between the preaching of popular culture and the very real problems we face. As we have seen, ideas do matter, and there is a clear connection between popular culture's message of relativism, selfism, and the exaltation of feelings, on the one hand, and social and educational problems on the other. A teenage boy persuaded by the culture to seek instant gratification for his desires meets a teenage girl who has been made to feel that virginity is archaic, and they become sexually involved. Because both have been conditioned to impulsiveness, and the sex urge comes upon them without warning, they seldom use a contraceptive. She becomes pregnant and decides to keep the baby, but self-indulgence prevents him from accepting the responsibilities of parenthood. A jobless high school dropout, she is left to raise the child alone. She goes on welfare and moves to an undesirable section of town, where her child grows up in an atmosphere of drug addiction and crime with a mother whose frustration and anger over her situation is directed at her child. The same kind of progression, sometimes as obvious as this and sometimes more subtle, occurs with other social problems.

There is nothing benighted or priggish about being concerned over the erosion of moral standards and seeking its real causes. Both common sense and responsible scholarship demand it. In *The Lessons of History,* distinguished philosophers of history Will and Ariel Durant cautioned that "the sex drive in the young is a river of fire that must be banked and cooled by a hundred restraints if it is not to consume in chaos both the individual and the group."[8] And Arnold Toynbee, arguably this century's greatest authority on the rise and fall of civilizations, affirmed the contribution of relativism and selfism to moral decay.[9] Scholars who share these views must overcome their fear of being branded bourgeois and unsophisticated and challenge their extremist colleagues. Among the most important contributions they can make is to restore respect for reasoned judgment.

Many academicians have grown so reliant on statistical data that they demand final proof before they change their minds about an issue. This affliction—call it *statistitis* for want of a better name—makes them react to social problems as tobacco executives do to the medical questions concerning smoking. They vow to wait for the mother of all research projects to settle the question, finally and absolutely, and refuse to admit, even to themselves, that certitude is likely to arrive too late, if indeed it ever arrives. More reasonable, prudent people and societies, on the other hand, realize that there is no moratorium on tragic effects as research inches laboriously toward ultimate answers. Therefore, while remaining open to new evidence, they make interim decisions on the basis of *probabilities*—that is, the possibilities best supported by the available evidence, such as those presented in this and the previous chapters. The most important of those probabilities are as follows:*

- What people see and hear influences their thoughts, attitudes, values, and actions, often in subtle ways even they are unaware of; and the more popular those ideas, the greater their impact.
- For years the media have promoted numerous shallow and downright erroneous ideas—notably, that truth is relative, that self-indulgence is better than self-control, that feelings are more trustworthy than thoughts and impulsiveness is more individualistic than restraint, that celebrity automatically confers wisdom, that possessing material things brings happiness, and that promiscuity and violence are natural.
- The very form and structure of contemporary media, particularly television, cause problems. By inducing passivity and conformity, they stifle creativity; by preventing the development of a mature attention span, they deny people the concen-

*Some of these conclusions may qualify as not merely probable, but certain. I have in mind particularly the conclusion about the harm done by violence, which is documented by virtually every one of the hundreds of scholarly studies that have been completed. For these, the classification of "probable" is an understatement.

tration needed to succeed in school and in careers; by being episodic and fragmented, they promote superficiality and thwart excellence.

- For all of these reasons, the media make it difficult, if not impossible, for parents and teachers to do their jobs. Virtually every social problem plaguing America today is traceable mainly to the negative influence of the media.

If more members of the community of scholars acknowledged these ideas as probabilities (or even as interesting possibilities), rather than dismissing them as right-wing fantasies, the discussion of America's social and educational problems would be enriched.

THE CHALLENGE TO MEDIA

George Gerbner, dean emeritus of the Annenberg School of Communications, argues that "television is a religion beyond the dreams of emperors and priests because its ministrations are subsidized by a levy on the price of all goods and are invited to entertain in every home in the land."[10] Television is without question the greatest shaper of attitudes and values. But the other media also have greater influence than home, school, and church. And where there is power there is responsibility. That parents and teachers should be held accountable for the education of children is eminently reasonable, but the idea applies with equal force to the men and women of the entertainment and communications media, including radio and television producers, talk-show hosts, station managers, and network executives; the editors and publishers of newspapers, magazines, and books; and music industry officials.

People in the media need to see through the shallow rationalization that they merely "give the public what the public wants." In fact, they give the public what *they think* the public wants, and that view is governed by a misconception about human nature, contempt for people's intelligence, or both. For example, an editor once told me that he didn't accept proposals for books designed to develop intellectual skills because "people who don't think clearly aren't able to sit still and concentrate long enough to read a book that will teach them to sit still and concentrate." If the media had more faith in the higher part of human nature—the reaching for truth and meaning, the yearning to do good and be better than we are, the capacity to understand complex realities—they would be less fixated on offering frivolity, sensationalism, and titillation. I have heard publishers justify their rejection of self-improvement books that stress traditional values with the argument "common sense doesn't sell." Of course it doesn't: people cannot buy what is not available.* If uncommon nonsense is all that is available, people will buy it and day by week, month by year, the pessimism of publishers will become a self-fulfilling prophecy, and common sense will become more and more difficult to sell.

Many broadcasters and publishers fail to realize that they are as much creators of public taste as servants of it. Writers who enjoy eating learn to produce not necessarily what they prefer to write, but what the networks and publishing houses will buy.** Historian Michael John Sullivan, for instance, reportedly began writing a historical treatise on the Harding presidency, but found book publishers unreceptive to the project, so he changed his focus to White House bedroom antics and produced *Presidential Passions,* an account of presidents' love affairs.[11] In a very real sense, Sullivan did not create that book; the contemporary philosophy of publishing did. And that same philosophy guides talk-show staff to seek out the offbeat, the bizarre, the outrageous. Anyone who commits a shocking act quickly finds agents of "Inside Edition," "A Current Affair," "Maury Povich," "Donahue," "Oprah," and "Geraldo" camped on his or her doorstep, checkbooks in hand, trying to outbid one another; and the more reprehensible or grisly the deed, the higher the

---

*This does not mean that the public would joyously welcome an end to debasing entertainments; habit dies hard, and if the downward slide has taken half a century, surely the upward climb will not be instantaneous.

** Despite their vocal defense of freedom of speech and the free exchange of ideas, commercial publishers are surprisingly unreceptive of books that challenge the dogmas of popular culture. This book was rejected by a number of large publishing houses, as were the books by psychologist Judith Reisman mentioned in chapter 6—*Kinsey, Sex, and Fraud* and *"Soft Porn" Plays Hardball.* And according to Carol Tavris, a similarly silent prohibition is practiced by otherwise reputable scientific journals concerning well-documented challenges to the prevailing notions about gender.[12]

bidding. This philosophy, and not America's reputation as a haven for freedom, explains why Salman Rushdie, Robert Mapplethorpe, and Andres Serrano have been more successful than many more talented individuals. It also explains why error so often smothers truth—for example, why books and articles continue to perpetuate the myth that expressing anger dissolves it a decade after Carol Tavris's *Anger: the Misunderstood Emotion* demolished it.

As America's social problems multiply, the media devote more and more space to reporting them, often in sensational ways that glamorize and exacerbate them. Ironically, they fail to notice that they are a significant cause of the problems. Research reveals that prime-time fictional TV is drenched in alcohol: one study found that 64 percent of 195 shows contained some reference to alcohol and included 8.1 drinking acts per hour. Since the drinkers tend to be regular characters rather than occasionals, and upper class, attractive, and glamorous, the implicit message serves more to encourage drinking than to discourage it, even in the case of drinking to solve personal problems.[13] Nationwide surveys reveal that 57 percent of high school seniors, 52 percent of sophomores, and 31 percent of eighth graders drank alcohol in the month prior to the survey; and 32 percent of the seniors, 16 percent of the sophomores, and 13 percent of the eighth graders had five or more drinks during the two weeks prior to the survey.[14] Former Surgeon General Antonia Novello claims that binge drinking is a factor in campus crime.

"Unfortunate is the youth who does not know the pleasure of the spirit and is not exalted in the joy of knowing and the joy of beauty, the enthusiasm for ideas, and quickening experience in the first love, delight and luxury of wisdom and poetry," writes philosopher Jacques Maritain.[15] The media have the power to grant this knowledge and experience to our children. All they need do is end their affair with sensationalism and amorality, celebrate goodness, service, and character, and encourage people to pursue excellence. To begin with, they can stop rewarding outrageousness, iconoclasm, and criminal behavior with publicity. Andrew Dice Clay's offensive comedy, Madonna's morality-mocking videos, and 2 Live Crew's sexually terroristic lyrics don't have to be treated as news; they can as easily, and much more wisely, be ignored. Social register madams such as Sidney Biddle Barrows don't have to be given book contracts and lionized in TV dramas; they can be consigned to obscurity and thereby taught that crime does not pay. The long parade of exhibitionists, spouse abusers, child molesters, self-proclaimed "sex addicts," and other morally corrupt individuals whose stories pollute the broadcast and print media can be left in the anonymity they deserve. This change will undoubtedly reduce "copycat" antisocial behavior, and it will certainly spare the public constant exposure to degrading spectacle.

Secondly, the media can shift their news emphasis from entertainers to achievers in other walks of life. The amount of time now devoted in the broadcast media, and space in the print media, to the lives of actors, actresses, and rock musicians is completely out of proportion to their contribution to society. When they are not using the time and space to promote their latest film or album, they are blathering self-indulgently on matters they know little or nothing about. The impression created in the minds of the young is that entertainers deserve greater respect and admiration than teachers, health care workers, scientists, theologians, historians, and others whose achievements are more numerous and meaningful to society. There are tens of thousands of lively, articulate men and women of genuine accomplishment who can provide informed opinions and insights on vital issues and inspire young and old to excellence. Whatever glitter might be lost by focusing on these people rather than entertainers would more than be compensated for by the increase in substance and motivation to excellence.

Dramatic shows can also be revised to show the richness and complexity of life. The vast majority of TV and cinema drama is either trite or contrived. Consider a fairly typical television plot. While murdering a man, a woman is videotaped by a tourist passing by on a riverboat. The killer enlists the help of the police chief, her lover. But rather than doing the logical thing and locating the tourist, ransacking her room, and finding the tape, she engineers a kidnapping and runs around Paris with her fellow gunmen, shooting up the streets and a couple of apartments with Uzi machine guns. In the course of the chase, the detective is shot in the arm, and as he tries to escape, falls and breaks the arm. Does he then go to a doctor to get it set? No. He instead has the tourist, now smitten with him, set his arm in an alley. Though in terrible pain he manages to kiss her... [16] Much TV and film drama is similarly contrived. Take out the scenes of people rolling around in bed and outside the plot; take away chase scenes and explosions; take away punching/kicking/ shooting/stabbing, and there is often little left.

Calling this realism is ludicrous; calling it creativity is an affront both to the public's intelligence and to literary artists' creative abilities. Any hack can borrow a thirty-year-old cops and robbers plot, make a few minor alterations (change the robbers to urban terrorists, members of a drug cartel, or a serial killer), sprinkle in some gratuitous sex and violence, and call it a bold new drama for our time. The real challenge is to approach minor everyday situations imaginatively and make them resonate with meaning. If the media would give us such stories and offer us genuine heroes instead of the antiheroes who have dominated stage and screen for the past few decades, our young people would be more likely to aspire to moral living. Similarly, if the fictional parents and teachers presented in films and television shows were noble and wise, our young people would be more inclined to accept the counsel of their actual parents and teachers. Is it any wonder that so many children disrespect their parents and teachers when so many films and TV shows portray adult authority figures as ignoramuses? Is it fair or reasonable for the media to fault parents and teachers for their failures when the media make success impossible?*

Another needed change in media is to treat traditional religion with respect instead of thinly veiled contempt and psychology with a heaping measure of benign neglect instead of reverence. Both print and broadcast media seem convinced that psychologists have the solutions to America's social ills; that is why

---

*Not all media representatives deny their own responsibility for the current culture climate. Ted Turner has flatly stated that the violence shown on television is "the single most significant factor contributing to violence in America" and that movie producers, TV executives, and programmers, including himself, bear some responsibility for the rise in the murder rate. He believes that if the industry can't agree on a ratings system, Congress should force one on it. [17]

psychologists dominate the field of self-help literature and are the most frequent nonentertainers on television talk-shows. Admittedly, some offer helpful advice, but more aggravate social problems by perpetuating relativism, selfism, and the exaltation of feelings.

As long as psychology remains nonjudgmental, it cannot provide answers to our social problems; as long as it remains value neutral, it cannot address our crisis in values. More than anything else, we need to make careful distinctions between right and wrong, good and bad, wise and foolish, and decide what we should, indeed what we *must,* do to solve our social problems. But contemporary psychology has renounced such distinctions and rejected all *shoulds* and *musts.* Even the most promising of the new psychological schools, cognitive psychology, seldom gets beyond the impact of one's thought on him*self* or her*self* and ignores the impact on society in general. Traditional philosophy offered guidance in such matters, but modern philosophers have denied the metaphysical and absorbed themselves with language analysis, so they are no help. Only religion is left to guide our problem solving and decision making.

Sadly, religion is *persona non grata* in contemporary American culture. The audacity of those who have made religion taboo in the broadcast and print media is incredible. They proclaim that every form of censorship is abhorrent to them, wrap within the banner of realism sexual perversion and graphic violence that wouldn't occur to most people in their most aberrant dreams, and at the same time limit or proscribe discussion of the belief in God and the religious values central to the overwhelming majority of Americans. And when religious publishers respond to the crying need for sensible guidance to life's problems, the large secular bookstores all too often ignore their books. With few exceptions, the categories of philosophy, psychology, and self-help are virtually closed to any book that mentions God, regardless of the book's primary subject matter and treatment.

A case in point is Peggy Rosenthal's insightful 1984 book, *Words and Values* (Oxford University Press), an examination of how the language we use can shape our thought patterns. It could have been classified under almost any category except religion, but at least one major bookstore chain managed to assign it that label and remand it to the back aisle of its stores. Similarly, though thousands of titles are published by religious publishers every year, only a handful are displayed in secular bookstores. And many of the same magazines and newspapers that routinely review books about serial rapist-killers dismembering their victims and then eating them refuse to review a book about loving God and neighbor.

The net effect of this exclusion of religion has been to give millions of Americans the erroneous impression that religion is not speaking and perhaps cannot speak to the contemporary human condition—or in some ways worse, that the voice of televangelism is the only voice of religion. Simple fairness and honesty, not to mention an interest in creating a saner, more hospitable culture, demand that the media take a more accepting attitude toward religion. Secular publishers and broadcasters need to be more hospitable to authors who treat social issues from a religious perspective, and secular bookstores need to open their categories to all books and not just those written from a secular perspective.

Far and away the most important single reform the broadcast media can make is to put an end to programming practices that prevent young attention spans from maturing (and that shrink older ones). These practices include the multiplication of sub-plots in dramatic shows and the frequent cuts from one to another, the use of newsbreaks as commercials for the subsequent newscast, and the scheduling of commercial breaks at ten-minute intervals within programs. Each of these practices was devised to maintain viewer attention, but their actual effect is to shorten that attention and necessitate the development of new devices that shorten it further. Everyone loses with these programming practices, not least of all the authors of television scripts, who are forced to produce increasingly superficial and trivial material. Television network executives should mandate fewer subplots and fewer cuts among them, limit newsbreaks to announcements of news events too important to be held for the next newscast, and cluster all commercials in a five- or ten-minute block at the end of each hour of programming, a practice that is already standard in some European countries.

These recommendations for change concern questions of

sponsorship, not censorship. Now, as always, in both publishing and broadcasting, choices are made about what is published or aired. Some material is accepted and much is rejected. Formats are introduced and abandoned. I am suggesting that the media be as vigorous in challenging social and intellectual fashion as they are in challenging tradition. I am urging that considerations of conscience be added to those of profit, not merely for ethical reasons but because doing so is in the media's (and everyone else's) long-term self-interest. The "bottom-line" thinking that has come to dominate the movie, broadcasting, and publishing industries* is not only lacking in idealism: it is unrealistic. The more a society cultivates shallowness and baseness, the more it jeopardizes its future. Newspapers, for example, are already suffering from a loss of advertising dollars and readership because of the public's shrinking level of concentration. A 1990 study by the Times Mirror Center for the People and the Press reports that the current generation of readers "knows less, cares less and reads newspapers less" than any generation in the past fifty years.[18] And publishers' experiments with "lite" news (tastes great and is less filling?) and a fast-food style of communication offer little hope of reversing this trend.

THE CHALLENGE TO BUSINESS LEADERS

No social agency has a more important role to play in overcoming America's social and educational problems than the business community. Because they finance television programming and both commercials and print advertisements, they have the power to change popular culture virtually overnight. Moreover, it is in the interests of their companies to make that change. They now spend $115 billion dollars annually on programming and advertising that indisposes young people to learning and creates negative attitudes toward work. In addition, they spend in excess of $35 billion annually to develop the basic reading, writing, and thinking skills whose development

*Interestingly, toy designers point to a similar change in their industry; management's emphasis, they claim, has shifted from design to marketing and is no longer sensitive to what parents and children want, but only to what will bring the greatest financial gain.

they blocked. They lose tens of billions more to unnecessary time out of work, malingering, pilfering, and other forms of employee disloyalty and dishonesty aggravated by the amorality and materialism of popular culture.* By using their influence to restore traditional values, business leaders will save tens of billions of dollars, increase the productivity of their employees and the quality of their goods and services, and make a singular contribution to America's social health.

Exactly what can business leaders do? First, they can send word to the broadcast media that their sponsorship of programs must meet new, more demanding criteria. In developing their own specific criteria for dramatic shows, companies should consider the following possibilities:

- Conflict, a central element in all good drama, is welcome; immorality needn't always be punished; and happy endings will enjoy no advantage over tragic ones. But immoral actions should not be portrayed in a positive light, nor moral actions as foolish or antiquated. And although protagonists may be presented as complex individuals with both good and bad qualities, they should demonstrate one or more of the values traditionally honored in this country, such as loyalty, courage in the face of hardship, self-discipline, perseverance, love of parents, or faith in God.
- Shows containing sex or violence are generally unacceptable. The only exception to this rule will be when the story line is unique and the author's treatment is of the highest artistic quality. Even then the sex or violence may not be graphically portrayed.
- Stories employing stereotypes of authority figures, such as parents, teachers, and religious leaders, will be unacceptable. Positive stereotypes are no more acceptable than negative ones, but since the latter have been more common in recent

---

*Though it has recently become fashionable to defend the competence and conscientiousness of the American worker, books such as Art Cary's *The United States of Incompetence* and Chuck Colson and Jack Eckerd's *Why America Doesn't Work* document the fact that many Americans have lost the work ethic that contributed to this country's preeminence in the world market.

years and are arguably more harmful to young viewers, proposals containing them will be automatically rejected.

Companies should also consider shifting their support from programming that retards the attention span, feeds the desire for instant gratification, offers an unrelenting diet of scandal and sensationalism, or actively promotes antisocial attitudes and values to programming more supportive of the efforts of home and school. (Most MTV programming would be disqualified on every one of these counts.)

A second initiative business leaders can undertake is reform of television commercials. Over the past thirty years the Federal Communications Commission (FCC) has approved the shrinking of commercial length from sixty seconds to thirty seconds and then to fifteen seconds. Business leaders can appeal to the FCC to return to the original sixty-second standard and thereby reduce the number of attention shifts viewers are subjected to every hour; in addition, they can support the clustering of commercials at the end of the hour so that entire programs can be seen without commercial interruption. Much greater directness may be taken with advertising agencies than with the FCC: business leaders can simply tell the agencies what changes they want in their commercials.* The following possibilities deserve special consideration because of the salutary impact they would have on popular culture:

Fewer shifts of focus within commercials.   In my studies of TV commercials, discussed in an earlier chapter, the average number of shifts of focus—from one scene or camera angle to another—ranged from six to fifty-four for an average of seventeen in a fifteen-second commercial. Shifts within commercials were the most significant single factor in the overall average of *over eight hundred attention shifts per hour of*

*This self-regulation is preferable to the governmental regulation in other countries. For example, a Finnish court ruled that a business cannot use a child's loneliness to promote a product. Thus an ad showing a lonely child losing his depression when he saw McDonald's was banned. In Holland, ads for sweets are required to show a toothbrush in the corner of the screen. In Spain toy commercials must show the product's true size if it costs more than forty-two dollars in United States currency.

television. Little wonder that so many students are so impatient with school lessons and so many employees have difficulty concentrating on their work.

Elimination of appeals to viewers' psychological needs. It is unfair, insulting, and manipulative to link the purchase of a product with social approval, financial success, protection, love, belongingness, or other needs. In the case of children, doing so borders on the criminal.

Elimination of slogans and celebrity testimonials. The skies United Airlines flies are no friendlier than any other airline's; nor is Delta's love of flying more evident than, say, Continental's. The emphasis on slogans adds more irrationality to a culture already steeped in it. And paying athletes and entertainers millions of dollars to express an ad-copy writer's enthusiasm for products they probably don't use is not only blatantly dishonest but reinforces the cult of celebrity that thwarts parents' and teachers' efforts to inspire young people to excellence.

Elimination of shallow value and base appeals. Messages that stimulate lust and envy and that glamorize materialism, hedonism, and amorality often produce effects their creators do not intend. They make people bored with their careers, dissatisfied with their relationships, insensitive toward the needs of others, and neglectful of obligations. They may even lead to criminal behavior.

If business leaders make the kinds of reforms suggested here, what advertising options are left for them? The most obvious one is honest and direct communication about their products and services. If independent testing agencies testify to the quality of the product, cite them; if genuine testimonials are received without solicitation or compensation, detail them; if there are real elements of uniqueness about the product or the process that creates it, demonstrate them. All this can be done in a lively, factual way without contriving artificial dramas with actors feigning rapture over the product. Another option is to publicize the company's commitment to public service and say, directly or indirectly, "We care about our community. We hope you'll consider giving us your business." That is the unspoken message in an ad run annually by Burdine's, a Florida department store chain. The ad announced the winners in Burdine's Teacher of the Year Award, which carries a $10,000 first price, a $5,000 second prize, and other prizes, seventy in all, for a total of $100,000.

THE CHALLENGE TO EDUCATORS

"What shall it profit a whole civilization, or culture, if it gains knowledge and power over the material world, but loses any adequate idea of the conscious mind, the human self, at the center of all that power?" asks philosopher William Barrett.[19] Education that merely stuffs minds with facts threatens that idea and impoverishes us all. Mind-stuffing, however, is not the fault of today's teachers. For the most part, they are only teaching as they were taught, as did their teachers before them, back to the earliest decades of this century when pessimism infected education. Nevertheless, the principal challenge facing today's teachers is to break the cycle and replace mind-stuffing with mind-building. As explained in the previous chapter, that will entail changes in teaching method but not subject matter. Science classes will still teach science; social studies classes, social studies, and so on. But learning will be active instead of passive, with emphasis on *applying* knowledge to solve problems and resolve issues, including moral issues, that typically arise in the subject.

Unfortunately, it is not enough for individual teachers to eliminate pessimism from their classrooms or, in concert with others, to revise the larger curriculum. Pessimism must be eliminated from the entire educational system and its support agencies. Teachers must therefore write to publishers and articulate the need for textbooks filled with engaging problems and issues rather than information to be memorized. They must write to the manufacturers of educational tests, including the Scholastic Aptitude Test and other instruments used for college admission, and persuade them to change their focus from testing memory to testing higher-order thinking skills. (College and graduate-school professors must also persuade the makers of professional examinations, such as the nursing, medical, and law "boards," to make similar changes.) And they must persuade legislators to revise funding formulas to reduce class size so that students can receive the individual attention and opportunity for sharing ideas necessary for the development of thinking and communication skills.

Administrators should play an important role in all these initiatives. Since they typically have more frequent contacts with state education department officials than teachers do, they enjoy more opportunities to make the case for mind-building. Similarly, since they regularly meet with school board members and often belong to community service organizations such as Kiwanis and Rotary Club, they have many opportunities to explain teachers' efforts to refocus education on the development of the mental habits and skills necessary for citizenship, responsible personal lives, and success in the workplace. Equally important, they can raise influential people's consciousness about the negative influence of popular culture on young people's lives and garner support for the reforms outlined in this chapter.

THE CHALLENGE TO GOVERNMENT

Since the provision of high-quality education to all our young people is our best assurance of a safe and orderly society, an economy strong enough to meet increasing competition for world markets, and the election of able political leaders, and since we are not providing that education, government officials should allocate the necessary resources. The all-too-common response that the budget deficit is too great to increase aid to education is hollow. When white-collar scum destroyed the savings and loan industry, no one in Washington said, "We'd love to take care of this problem, but we can't afford it." No, the money was found, and the amount exceeded $500 *BILLION!* When Saddam Hussein invaded Kuwait, there was a vigorous debate over whether military action was appropriate, but not over whether we could afford the billions of dollars it would cost. When the need is perceived to be urgent, funding can be found, the necessary economies can be made. In education the need is urgent, and elected officials should have the wisdom, the foresight, and the courage to champion this cause.

In addition to supporting educational reform, legislators (and jurists) can contribute to the reform of popular culture by purging laws and juridical decisions of relativism and selfism. This can be accomplished by supporting four principles.* The first of these principles is that *people have free will and though in certain circumstances their actions may be coerced, in most cases they choose their behavior and are therefore responsible for it.* In recent years this principle has been eroded, even in law. As Thomas Szasz notes, a number of influential legal scholars have denounced the concept, embracing the psychoanalytical idea that unconscious drives are responsible for behavior. This is the reason, he explains, for the tendency to excuse the criminal and blame society or even, adding insult to injury, the victim.[20] Because the freedoms we cherish, including the constitutionally guaranteed freedoms of religion, speech, the press, assembly, and petition, depend for their meaning on freedom of the will, the reinforcement of this principle must be understood as a social imperative.

The second principle is that *not every form of verbal or physical activity is speech and not every form of entertainment is art.* This may seem obvious enough when stated directly, but since relativism abjures distinctions, some find the principle fascistic when applied to timely issues. It has become fashionable to reason, "If no one's opinion is better than anyone else's, then who can say what constitutes speech? Whatever I say is speech *is* speech for me. Likewise, whatever I say is art is *truly* art." If I trample my neighbor's flower garden I am certainly sending a message, but I am not engaging in protected speech; and if I trample in the manner of Nureyev I am not engaged in an exercise of art. The proper term for my action is vandalism, and it applies with equal accuracy to the trampling of society's values.

The third principle is that *no one has a right to act in a way that injures others.* As Judge Learned Hand expressed it, "Your

*Though these principles are not specifically mentioned in the Constitution or our legal system, they are logical extensions of both and reflect the intellectual presuppositions both are based upon.

right to swing your arm stops at the tip of my nose." Selfism and the exaltation of feelings imply a very different view, the absolute freedom of the individual to do whatever he or she wishes. The confusion that this view has created is nowhere more evident than in the issue of the regulation of television programming. The cry of "censorship" greets even the most modest request for greater programming responsibility and is often accompanied by vivid images of book burning and the stifling of cinematic creativity.* The analogy is bogus. Television is very different from book publishing and cinema in two important respects: it is beamed into people's homes via airwaves that the U.S. Supreme Court has affirmed belong to the citizens of this country; and the public is forced to pay for both programs and commercials, *whether they watch them or not*, every time they buy the sponsors' products. To charge people for beaming unasked-for, objectionable material into their homes and then crying "Foul" when they protest enlarges the meaning of *chutzpah*.

In recent years more and more people are acknowledging that no one has a right to befoul the physical environment. Companies that pollute the air and water are held legally accountable and face heavy financial penalties. Smokers are being required to honor the rights of nonsmokers to breathe clean air. These developments were a result of the public's awareness that factory smoke destroys the environment, polluted water causes illness and death to innocent people, and secondhand cigarette smoke contributes to heart and lung disease. But we also have abundant knowledge that a hazardous social environment can do grave emotional and spiritual harm to people and that conditioning shapes both attitudes and actions. It is therefore time we acknowledged that no one has a right to befoul the social environment. If a religious cultist who brainwashes a few hundred followers to act against their own interests commits a serious offense, what does logic require us to say of popcultists who invade living rooms and brainwash millions?

The Supreme Court dictum that the test of obscenity is

---

*The American Civil Liberties Union, the meaning of its name notwithstanding, opposes the public's right to boycott publishers, record companies, and other businesses whose practices they disapprove of.[21]

whether the work in question has *any* redeeming social, artistic, or educational merit offers citizens too little protection against social pollution, particularly in our time, when relativism and selfism have made the concept of rights sacrosanct, and liberty is considered synonymous with license. We need a more reasonable test of obscenity (I use the word in its broadest reference, not merely a narrow sexual reference) that offers more protection. The test should be whether the social, artistic, or educational value *outweighs* the probable harm.

The fourth and final principle legislators should support is that *the right to life is a higher value than the right to bear arms.* It is ironic that more than two hundred years after the Revolutionary War, the winning side is still loudly proclaiming the right of every citizen to bear arms, whereas the losers don't even allow their policemen to carry pistols.* A twenty-seven year veteran officer of one of the toughest jurisdictions in England told me recently he has never had a gun; in fact, he doesn't even carry his nightstick because he hasn't felt the need to do so. When I asked him, only half-jokingly, whether England had a better class of criminals, he answered, "No, just tighter gun control." Today, with the possession of guns in this country posing a gigantic problem obvious to virtually everyone except the National Rifle Association (NRA), with accidental as well as intentional deaths and serious injuries reaching monstrous proportions, common sense demands strong gun control laws.

The often-cited constitutional prohibition against such a law is a myth. The Second Amendment reads, "A well-regulated militia, being necessary to the security of a Free State, the right of the people to keep and bear arms, shall not be infringed." Since the second half of that sentence is qualified by the first half, the right referred to is not absolute. Today state and national security are guaranteed by a standing army, the National Guard, and various police agencies. Moreover, in the eighteenth century "bearing arms" meant carrying a muzzle-loaded single-shot musket, not modern pistols and submachine guns. As men of wisdom, the Founding Fathers, were they alive today, would surely

*The British use specialized teams like our SWAT teams for situations involving terrorists.

take a more responsible view of gun control than the view taken by the NRA. Legislators should do likewise, even if they incur the wrath of that organization.

THE CHALLENGE TO THE FAMILY

If the artists and scholars, media executives, business leaders, educators, and elected officials discussed in the foregoing pages are people of goodwill who care about the future of America, they will take seriously the challenge to reform popular culture. But it would be naive to expect them to take significant action without the encouragement and support of the general public. The problem is that, with a myriad of social, political, and economic issues shouting for attention and relativism and selfism eroding resolve, that support is difficult to generate and sustain. Leadership is needed; and the most likely agency to provide it is that often maligned and denigrated, politically abandoned, yet fundamental unit of society, the family. The family is the primary agency of love and nurture, and reform of popular culture is essentially an issue of love and nurture—love of fellow human beings and country, nurture of America's children.

Before they can provide effective leadership, families must recognize and reject several misconceptions that paralyze reform initiatives. One misconception is that turning off the TV set will shut out the effects of popular culture. Efforts such as Minnesota teacher Pat Marker's "TV Busters" campaign, which encourages children to turn off TV and do more constructive things, are praiseworthy. But children are influenced by media other than TV, and they suffer from popular culture's influence on other people, particularly their peers. Another misconception is that the task of reforming the culture is best left to philosophers and psychologists. As we have seen, though some of these professionals have genuine insights about the causes and cures of our social problems, most do not because their fields are mired in the same errors that are causing the problems. In the case of philosophy, the errors include denying the objective nature of reality and truth and rejecting the spiritual nature of mankind. In the case of psychology, they include selfism and the exaltation of feelings. Through no real fault of their own, practitioners of these disciplines are more likely to have wrong answers than right ones.

A third misconception is that religious beliefs are strictly personal and have no place in the discussion of public issues. After a thirty-year barrage of antireligious propaganda, it is understandable that many religious people accept this idea and politely keep their beliefs to themselves. This is a mistake that must be corrected for the good of the country. Religion is not merely a personal matter: throughout the ages it has had historical significance unparalleled by any other dimension of life. This country's development, from the day the first Pilgrim landed through the first half of this century, is largely a reflection of its religious convictions. And eminent historians conclude that changes in a civilization's religious views are a reliable measure of its rise and fall. Someone once observed, and we all do well to remember, that the great civilizations have proceeded through the identical stages: from bondage to spiritual faith, from spiritual faith to great courage, from courage to liberty, from liberty to abundance, from abundance to selfishness, from selfishness to complacency, from complacency to apathy, from apathy to dependence, and from dependence to bondage.

Finally, families must reject the misconception that it is unfair and vaguely un-American to protest television's content or format, particularly in an organized way such as boycotting sponsors' products. This reasoning is specious, and media spokespeople know it. First, the public *does* pay for what is shown on television and radio broadcasts. Every cent of the more than $115 billion dollars annually spent on programming and advertising, including the lavish sums given to celebrities for their testimonials, is passed on to the public in the form of higher prices. The cost of every bottle of soft drink or beer, every box of soap or aspirin, every roll of toilet tissue, like that of every other product or service, is marked up to cover this expense. (Given the intermarriage of corporations, the cost of a salted cracker may well reflect advertising expense for a hemorrhoid remedy.) Moreover, as the legislation that created and refined the Federal Communications Commission and the courts have made clear, the airwaves belong not to corporate sponsors or to the networks, but to the people; that is why radio and television stations are required to be licensed.

A related misconception is that it is unfair and un-American to protest the use of tax dollars to support artists who mock Judeo-Christian beliefs and values. Moviemaker Todd Haynes received $25,000 from the National Endowment for the Arts (NEA) for his controversial film *Poison*, which tells the stories of a boy who murdered his father, a sex-potion-drinking fiend, and a homosexually obsessed prisoner. Appearing on a talk show, Haynes quoted the head of the NEA as saying the agency exists for the arts community and not for the taxpayers and added, "Democracy is based on supporting diversity of expression."[22] Though it may be arguable that democracy is based on protecting diversity,* it is ludicrous to hold that democracy requires the public to *support* diversity. If anything is undemocratic, it is the notion that the NEA or any other government agency is unaccountable to the taxpayers.

Having overcome these misconceptions, families can take a number of specific actions to reform popular culture. The basic challenge, and thus the main emphasis in the recommendations that follow, is to enlighten others about the harm done by popular culture and to encourage them to seize their own special opportunities to reform it. In communicating this message, families should remind themselves that many decent, well-meaning, intelligent people have been influenced by relativism, selfism, and the exaltation of feelings. How could it be otherwise when they have grown up in a society permeated with these values! Accordingly, these people will have erroneous views about the media, morality, religion, and education, views that may have hardened into firm convictions. The task of persuading them to set aside these convictions will require understanding, patience, and perseverance. Here are some specific recommendations for action:

---

*It would be more accurate, however, to say that democracy is based on the individual's freedom to embrace divergent views and that the public is required to respect, but not support, that choice.

Write to elected officials and business leaders and share this book's message. Skim the book to find the passages you believe are most important and most relevant to your readers. Express those passages in your own words. Mention the specific actions appropriate for the readers to take* and stress those that you believe are most urgent. Send your letter to your senators and representatives in congress and to the chief executive officers of companies whose products and services you use. If necessary, consult *Million Dollar Directory*, available in most libraries, for the executives' names and addresses. (If the company you do business with is a subsidiary of a larger parent corporation, consult *Who Owns Whom: North America* or the *Directory of Corporate Affiliations*.) If you do not have the time to write letters to all these people, have your children help you with this task, and involve them in carrying out the following recommendations as well.

Share your day-to-day reactions to popular culture with people who have the power to change it. It is tempting to content ourselves with complaining to family and friends about the offensive magazine cover in the supermarket or the offensive program or advertisement on television. That may relieve our anger and frustration, but it doesn't help solve the problem. Whenever you react strongly to something you see or hear, consider who has the authority to effect change and communicate your reaction to that person. In the case of super-market tabloids, the appropriate person might be the store manager or a corporate official, such as the Consumer Affairs representative or the Chief Executive Officer (CEO). In the case of a television show, it would be the sponsoring companies (the commercials run during the show will indicate the sponsors) and perhaps the manager of your local station and/or a network executive. Network addresses are available in your local library and from your cable company. In the case of an offensive commercial, write the CEO of the company involved. Be sure to say exactly what you find offensive and why, and

---

*See the sections "The Challenge to Media," "The Challenge to Business Leaders," and "The Challenge to Government" earlier in this chapter.

specify what you believe should be done about it. Remember that if you are reasonable and balanced in what you say, your criticism is likely to be taken more seriously. So if you object to the commercial but like the sponsor's product or service, say so.

Encourage and support your local schools. The last thing teachers need is another attack from the public. For years they have been blamed by the media for the problems created by popular culture. Many are so accustomed to having people object to what they do that they assume any parent who approaches them will find fault with their efforts. Express your understanding that popular culture has created obstacles for them as well as for you and that they are not responsible for the tradition of mind-stuffing that hinders them from developing students' intellectual skills. Urge them to transform mind-stuffing into mind-buliding, and let the principal and other school administrators know that you expect them to support teachers' efforts for constructive change.

One way to encourage meaningful school reform is to oppose the censorship of books. The reason is not that books can do no harm; they definitely can. It is rather that, historically, the urge to censor has lacked the spirit of moderation demanded by common sense and common decency alike. Examine any list of banned books from the Vatican's *Index of Forbidden Books* to a local vigilante group's more modest selections, and you will likely find some filled with intellectually and spiritually damaging ideas, others whose only fault is dullness, and still others that deserve to be *recommended* reading for children as well as adults. Examples of the last variety are J. D. Salinger's *Catcher in the Rye*, Mark Twain's *The Adventures of Huckleberry Finn*, George Orwell's *Animal Farm* and *1984*, *The Diary of Anne Frank*, Nathaniel Hawthorne's *The Scarlet Letter*, and Shakespeare's *The Merchant of Venice*. The children's classic *My Friend Flicka* was pulled from an optional reading list for fifth and sixth graders in a Florida community because it contained the words *damn* and *bitch*, the latter in reference to a dog. Another book, *Abel's Island*, was removed because of references to drinking wine. Even *Snow White* has been attacked because of its allegedly graphic violence.

People who worry about the damage that books may do to children generally overlook several important facts. First, there is truth in the truism "One picture is worth a thousand words." Books have a threshold of accessibility that is lacking in films and television. If children read something beyond their years, their lack of verbal sophistication will usually prevent them from forming a troubling or harmful image; if they see the same scene in visual form, their immaturity cannot spare them its impact. That is why one MTV video can do more harm than a hundred books. Second, reading is an active, directed mental process involving concentration and interpretation. Though it is possible to read mindlessly, reading tends to promote careful thought and judgment, the very habits necessary to resist the nonsense of popular culture. Third, many books that contain objectionable passages have positive, sometimes highly moral, themes.

The measure of a book is the author's overall treatment of the subject, not the subject itself or particular words used to develop it. *It is as wrong to judge a book by a selected passage as it is to judge it by its cover.* The wisest position for parents to take is to trust teachers' judgment about the books they use,* but to be strong in advocating that students be encouraged to probe, question, weigh, and evaluate everything that they read and not just absorb the authors' ideas. The purpose of reading, Francis Bacon argued, should be neither to accept or reject, but to "weigh and consider" the ideas presented.

Teach your children to evaluate the messages they receive from popular culture. The best protection children can be given against the influence of popular culture is the ability to see through its shallowness and the emptiness of its values. This ability is not developed by listening to lectures from parents or teachers, but from guided practice in observing, analyzing, and discussing what they see and hear. Ideally, this practice will begin in early childhood when children are too young to participate themselves but can only listen to their parents' talking and thereby learn the informal rules of discussion. As

---

*Unless, of course, they have read the books themselves and have good reason to judge them inappropriate.

children become older, they should be encouraged to share their observations and express their interpretations and conclusions. They should never be punished for honestly disagreeing with their elders, even if their ideas are flawed.

Discussions of television, popular music, and the other media should focus on understanding what is said or dramatized; deciding what it means, whether it is reasonable or unreasonable, worthy or unworthy; and speculating about its effects on people's attitudes and actions. Discussions of commercials and print advertisements should address these questions, among others: Does the ad appeal to thought or to emotion? How do the music, background scenes, and action contribute to this appeal? Does the ad exploit hopes, fears, desires? What attitudes and values does it promote—for example, attitudes about success, love, or happiness? Does the ad use any propaganda techniques, such as slogans or testimonials? Is the attempt to persuade fair or unfair?

Encourage other people to speak out about popular culture. The more people who join the effort, the greater its chance of success. Most families have a wide range of associations with other people. They belong to business and professional organizations; churches and religious organizations; and community service and social clubs such as Kiwanis, Rotary, Lions, and Business and Professional Women. Many of these organizations have speaking programs and forums to explore ideas and develop a consensus. At the national level some even sponsor public-service messages and other forms of mass communication. By discussing your commitment to the reform of popular culture with your friends and associates, sharing the letters you have written, and encouraging them to add their voices to yours, you can multiply your individual effort a hundredfold.

America has produced some magnificent achievements in the course of its brief history: life-saving medicines and surgical procedures, tools to unlock the secrets of tiny microbes and vast, distant galaxies, machines to share our thoughts and feelings with other people, transport us quickly from place to place, deepen our understanding, and enrich our lives; and most laudably, a wisely balanced and humane system of government without parallel in the history of humanity. But we must not permit our fitting sense of accomplishment to blind us to the somber reality that a civilization can fall into a downward spiral from which it never recovers. "Evolution," as Alfred North Whitehead sagely warned, "can go backwards." This civilization, I submit, has already begun its downward spiral, and the reform of popular culture is the only way to recover.

That this reform is *possible* there is no doubt. Whether it will be accomplished is at best uncertain. We must first affirm what the Japanese have long known, that a nation's children are its greatest national resource, and their emotional and physical health is the only "bottom line" that really matters. We must shift our emphasis from rights to responsibilities, pleasant illusions to harsh realities, self to neighbor, feeling to thought. The sense of stewardship we are beginning to feel toward our physical environment must be expanded to embrace our moral and intellectual environment. We must purge education of its pessimistic view of human potential and replace mind-stuffing with mind-building. We must forge a partnership among home, school, church, government, business, and the entertainment and communications media, a partnership in which all cooperate in nurturing the social, intellectual, and moral values upon which America was founded: the pursuit of truth through study and reflection; self-knowledge, self-discipline, and self-improvement; a demanding standard of personal conduct; and a life of service to others.

It is a challenge admirably suited to a great nation. And unless this generation proves equal to it, no economic growth, political achievement, or military might can save us from destruction.

NOTES

Chapter 1

1. This is not to suggest that the abuse of children is a recent phenomenon; it has been all too evident in most ages dating to antiquity. It is rather to suggest that it is undergoing a resurgence today. An excellent, if disturbing, historical examination of child abuse is *The History of Childhood: The Untold Story of Child Abuse*, ed. Lloyd de Mause (New York: Peter Bedrick Books, 1974).
2. "PrimeTime Live," ABC-TV, 20 June 1991.
3. Millicent Lawton, "More Than a Third of Teens Surveyed Say They Have Contemplated Suicide," cited in *Education Week*, 10 April 1991, 5.
4. "19% of High School Students Have Had at Least 4 Sex Partners, Study Finds," Reported in *Education Week*, 15 April 1992, 4.
5. "The Montel Williams Show," NBC-TV, 29 June 1992.
6. "The Maury Povich Show," 18 November 1991.
7. "The Oprah Winfrey Show," CBS-TV, 3 June 1991.
8. A Rhode Island Rape Crisis Center Study, cited in James Dobson and Gary L. Bauer, *Children at Risk* (Dallas: Word, 1990), 258.
9. "Harper's Index," a monthly set of statistics compiled by *Harper's Magazine*, cited in *St. Petersburg Times*, 7 January 1991, 13A.
10. "Blackboard Jungle," *U.S. News & World Report*, 13 February 1989, 84.
11. "20/20," ABC-TV, 17 September 1991.
12. Quoted in *The Business of Heaven*, ed. W. Hooper (New York: Harvest, 1984), 54.
13. Quoted in the Association for Supervision and Curriculum Development's *Conference Report Update*, May 1991, 5.
14. Edward Klein, "The Best and Worst of Everything," *Parade*, 30 December 1990, 5.
15. Peter Berger, *A Rumor of Angels* (Garden City: Anchor Books, 1990), 38–39.
16. According to *The New York Times*, the average time per hour devoted to commercials on the major networks in 1991 was as follows: ABC, 10 minutes, 16 seconds; CBS, 11 minutes, 6 seconds; NBC, 11 minutes. Reported in the *St. Petersburg Times*, 6 October 1991, 7A.

Chapter 2

1. Jack Underhill, "New Age Quiz," *Life Times Magazine*, no. 3, 6.
2. Maxine Hairston, "Required Writing Courses Should Not Focus on Politically Charged Social Issues," *Chronicle of Higher Education*, 23 January 1991, B3f.
3. For a scholarly analysis of relativism and related errors, see Mortimer Adler's *Ten Philosophical Mistakes* (New York: Macmillan, 1985), especially chapter 4; also William Barrett's horribly titled but admirably lucid *Death of the Soul: from Descartes to the Computer* (Garden City, N.Y.: Doubleday, 1986).
4. Fulton Sheen, *God and Intelligence in Modern Philosophy* (New York: Doubleday, 1958 edition), 140.
5. John Noble Wilford, "Doctor Challenges Theory on Drowning," *The New York Times*, 7 August 1977, 20.
6. Jeffrey Moussalieff Masson, *The Assault on Truth: Freud's Suppression of the Seduction Theory* (New York: Farrar, Straus, & Giroux, 1984).
7. Donald Naftulin and others, "The Doctor Fox Lecture: A Paradigm of Educational Seduction," *Journal of Medical Education*, 48 (July 1973), 630–635.
8. Jenny J. Vogt, "Condom Club Hopes to Serve a Need," *St. Petersburg Times*, 24 August 1991, 1D.
9. "Texas Schoolbook Massacre: 5200 Errors Are Found in 10 History Books," Reported in *Publishers Weekly*, 2 March 1992, 11.
10. Mortimer J. Adler, *Truth in Religion* (New York: Macmillan, 1990), 36.
11. *The American Heritage Dictionary of the English Language*, 1969, 469.
12. Thomas Szasz, *Insanity: the Idea and Its Consequences* (New York: John Wiley & Sons, 1990), 12–13, 108, 205, 173, 204.
13. Robert H. Bork, *The Tempting of America: The Political Seduction of the Law* (New York: Touchstone, 1990), 8–9.
14. "One Must Not Forget," an interview with Elie Wiesel, *U.S. News & World Report*, 27 October 1986, 68.
15. Jacob Neusner, quoted in *St. Petersburg Times*, 3 November 1990, 4E.
16. Chris Thurman, *The Lies We Believe* (Nashville: Thomas Nelson, 1989), 22.
17. Two books by Viktor Frankl are especially recommended: *Man's Search for Meaning* (New York: Washington Square Press, 1963) and *The Unheard Cry for Meaning* (New York: Simon & Schuster, 1978). Later chapters will explore more of this author's ideas.
18. Charles S. Peirce, originally written in 1878. See *Essays in the Philosophy of Science*, ed. Vincent Tomas, The American Heritage Series, no. 17 (Indianapolis: Bobbs-Merrill, 1957), 54.
19. Barrett, *Death of the Soul*, 139.

20. George Santayana, quoted in Mortimer Adler, *Intellect: Mind Over Matter* (New York: Macmillan, 1990), 102.
21. Gregory S. Jay, "The First Round of the Culture Wars," *Chronicle of Higher Education*, 26 February 1992, B3.
22. Diane Ravitch, "The Precarious State of History," *American Educator* (Spring 1985), 13.
23. Israel Scheffler, *Science and Subjectivity* (Indianapolis: Bobbs-Merrill, 1967), 11, 13.
24. Karl Popper, *The Logic of Scientific Discovery* (London: Hutchinson, 1968), 46.
25. Richard P. Feynman, *"Surely You're Joking, Mr. Feynman"* (New York: Bantam, 1986), 313.

Chapter 3

1. Sheen, *God and Intelligence in Modern Philosophy*, 247.
2. Carl Rogers, *On Becoming a Person* (Boston: Houghton Mifflin, 1961), 119, 176.
3. Shirley MacLaine, *Out on a Limb*, ABC miniseries, 18–19 January 1987.
4. "Larry King Live," CNN, 15 October 1987.
5. Swami Muktananda, quoted in Russell Chandler, *Understanding the New Age* (Dallas: Word, 1988), 64.
6. Ray Bradbury, quoted in ibid., 319.
7. M. Scott Peck, *The Road Less Traveled* (New York: Simon & Schuster, 1978), 281, 283.
8. Robert Schuller, *Self-Esteem: The New Reformation* (Dallas: Word, 1982), 15, 33, 67, 98.
9. Reported in "Hey, I'm Terrific!" *Newsweek*, 17 February 1992, 47.
10. Will Schutz, *Profound Simplicity* (New York: Bantam, 1979), 9.
11. Thomas Howard, "Is Christianity Credible?" in *The Intellectuals Speak Out About God*, ed. Roy Abraham Varghese (Dallas: Lewis and Stanley, 1984), 231–242.
12. John Stossel report, "Good Morning America," ABC-TV, November 1982.
13. *Bottom Line Personal*, 30 June 1991, 9.
14. "The Oprah Winfrey Show," CBS-TV, 4 March 1991.
15. Quoted in Robert McGarvey, "Talk Yourself Up," *US Air Magazine*, Mar. 1990, 88–94.
16. David Shannahoff-Khalsa, cited in Jonathan Weisman, "Though Still a Target of Attacks, Self-Esteem Movement Advances," *Education Week*, 6 March 1991, 1f.
17. Patricia McCormack, "Good News for the Underdog," *Santa Barbara News Press*, 8 November 1981, 10D.
18. David Meyers, *The Inflated Self* (New York: Seabury, 1980), 24.

19. Yochelon and Samenow, cited in Jay Adams, *The Biblical View of Self-Esteem, Self-Love, Self-Image* (Eugene, Oregon: Harvest House, 1986), 99.

20. Arnold Toynbee, *A Study of History*, rev. ed. (New York: Portland House, 1988), 171.

21. Barbara Lerner, "Self-Esteem and Excellence: The Choice and the Paradox," *American Educator*, Winter 1985, 10–16.

22. "Geraldo," ABC-TV, 22 February 1991.

23. David Schuman, *The Chronicle of Higher Education*, 1 April 1992, B1–2.

24. Peggy Rosenthal, *Words and Values* (New York: Oxford University Press, 1984), 98.

25. "The Oprah Winfrey Show," 14 December 1990.

26. G. Hofstede, "Motivation, Leadership, and Organizations: Do American Theories Apply Abroad?" *Organizational Dynamics*, Summer 1980, 42–63. See also William C. Howell and Robert L. Dipboye, *Essentials of Industrial and Organizational Psychology* (Homewood, Ill.: Dorsey), chapter 10.

27. Frankl, *The Unheard Cry for Meaning*, 35, 67, 83.

28. Frankl, *Man's Search for Meaning*, 122–123.

29. Frankl, *The Unheard Cry for Meaning*, 39, 90, 95.

Chapter 4

1. Page Smith, *Killing the Spirit* (New York: Penguin, 1990), 35.

2. Barrett, *Death of the Soul*, 61.

3. Szasz, *Insanity*, 141, 364.

4. Richard Restak, "Is Free Will a Fraud?" *Science Digest*, Oct. 1983, 50–53.

5. David D. Burns, *Feeling Good: The New Mood Therapy* (New York: New American Library, 1980), 40.

6. Ibid., 71.

7. Albert Ellis, "The Impossibility of Achieving Consistently Good Mental Health," *American Psychologist*, April 1987, 364–375.

8. John Dewey, *Experience and Education*, first published in 1938 (New York: Collier Books, 1968), 65.

9. "Miracle Drugs or Media Drugs?" *Consumer Reports*, March 1992, 142–146.

10. "Scared Silent," simultaneously telecast on all major television networks, September 4, 1992.

11. Carol Tavris, *The Mismeasure of Woman* (New York: Simon and Schuster, 1992), 43.

12. Ibid., 332.

13. Ibid., 83, 63, 64, respectively.

14. Ibid., 293.

15. Ibid., 333.
16. Evan F. Nappen, "101 Reasons Why You Need an Assault Firearm," *The Guardian* (Coalition of New Jersey Sportsmen), April 1991. Reprinted in *St. Petersburg Times*, 16 July 1991, 7A.
17. Shelby Steele, "The New Segregation," *Imprimis* (Hillsdale College Bulletin), August 1992, 1–3.
18. Richard J. Perry, "Why Do Multiculturalists Ignore Anthropologists?" *Chronicle of Higher Education*, 4 March 1992, A52.
19. The studies were reported in *Chronicle of Higher Education*, 12 December 1991, A33, and *St. Petersburg Times*, 6 February 1992, 7A.
20. "The Today Show," NBC-TV, 7 September 1992.
21. Gordon Allport, *The Nature of Prejudice* (Cambridge, Mass.: Addison-Wesley, 1954), 355–356.
22. Merry White, *Redbook*, May 1991, 10.
23. For a comprehensive bibliography, as well as an explanation of the strategies used in teaching creative, critical, and metacognitive thinking, see my *Teaching Thinking Across the Curriculum* (New York: Harper and Row, 1988).
24. Jerre Levy, *Educational Leadership*, Jan. 1983, 66–71.
25. "Jim Brown's Rebellion," *USA Weekend*, July 31-August 2, 1992.

Chapter 5

1. Joe Bob Briggs, quoted in *U.S. News & World Report*, 1 October 1990, 17.
2. "Surgeon General Goes Too Far in Attacking Beer Ads," *St. Petersburg Times*, 9 November 1991, 19A.
3. Robert Brustein, quoted in Leslie Bennetts, "Do the Arts Inspire Violence in Real Life?" *The New York Times*, 26 April 1981, section 2, 1f.
4. Diane Mason, "A New Radicalism in NOW," *St. Petersburg Times*, 8 July 1991, 1D.
5. Frankl, *The Unheard Cry for Meaning*, 90–91.
6. Joseph Strayhorn, M.D., "Strategies for Reducing Exposure to Violent Movies: Questions Answered and Unanswered," *NCTV News* (National Coalition on Television Violence), June-August 1991, 4–6.
7. Michael Medved, "Popular Culture and the War Against Standards," *Imprimis* (Hillsdale College Bulletin), February 1991, 1–3.
8. Sut Jhally, *Dreamworlds: Desire/Sex/Power in Rock Video*, Department of Communication, University of Massachusetts, Amherst, 1990.
9. N. E. Gagliardi, "The Sexual Fantasies of a Married Woman," *Cosmopolitan*, June 1991, 186f.
10. "Teen Girls More Sexually Active," *St. Petersburg Times*, 8 November 1990, 1A.
11. Judith Kuriansky, speaking on "A Current Affair," NBC-TV, 13 May 1992.

12. Frankl, *Man's Search for Meaning*, 50–68.
13. Thomas Radecki, *NCTV News*, June-August 1991, 7.
14. Martin Scorsese, quoted in *Newsweek*, 1 April 1991, 48.
15. George Gerbner, quoted in Leslie Bennetts, "Do the Arts Inspire Violence in Real Life?"
16. Ibid.
17. Harry N. Hollis, Jr., *Christian Standard*, 13 July 1975, 7.
18. All the studies referred to here are discussed in *The Early Window: Effects of Television on Children and Youth*, third edition, by Robert M. Liebert and Joyce Sprafkin (New York: Pergamon Press, 1988). This excellent, comprehensive examination details the history and significant research in the field. The exhaustive bibliography contains approximately 450 citations. Page references to the studies cited are, respectively, 10, 71, 231, 94, 154–155, 151, 152–153.
19. Liebert and Sprafkin, quoted in *Newsweek*, 1 April 1991, 51.
20. Liebert and Sprafkin, *The Early Window*, 155–156.
21. Leonard Berkowitz, quoted in Bennetts, "Do the Arts Inspire Violence in Real Life?"
22. Anthea Disney, "Let's Make TV Violence Unpopular," *St. Petersburg Times*, 11 September 1992, 15A.
23. Deborah Prothrow-Stith, cited by Anthea Disney, ibid.
24. Seymour Feshbach, quoted in Bennetts, "Do the Arts Inspire Violence in Real Life?"
25. George Will, "America's Slide into the Sewer," *Newsweek*, 30 July 1990, 64.
26. "Washington Whispers," edited by Charles Fenyvesi, *U.S. News & World Report*, 20 July 1992, 20.
27. Robert Kubey and Mihalyi Csikszentmihalyi, *Television and the Quality of Life: How Viewing Shapes Everyday Experience* (Hillsdale, N.J.: Lawrence Erlbaum, 1990).
28. Reported in the *Chronicle of Higher Education*, 20 November 1991, A39.
29. Robert Rothman, "20-Nation Study Shows U.S. Lags in Math, Science" *Education Week*, 12 February 1992, 1.
30. Mark McGinnis, "An Overdose of Television Has Deadened the Visual Imagination of Our Students," *Chronicle of High Education*, 20 February 1991, B1f.
31. Jane M. Healy, *Endangered Minds: Why Our Children Don't Think* (New York: Simon & Schuster, 1990), 218–34.
32. Joy Davidson, *The Soap Opera Syndrome* (New York: Berkley, 1991).
33. Naomi Wolf, *The Beauty Myth* (New York: Doubleday, 1991).
34. *Parade*, 2 February 1992.
35. E. F. Schumacher, *Small Is Beautiful: Economics As If People Mattered*, originally published in 1973 (New York: Harper Perennial, 1989), 203–4.
36. *Newsweek*, 29 June 1992.

37. *Newsweek*, 20 July 1992, 12.
38. "Hollywood and Politics," CNN, 23 August 1992.
39. Peter Plagens, "Censorship," *Newsweek*, 31 December 1990, 38–39.
40. John Leo, "A Pox on Dan and Murphy," *U.S. News & World Report*, 1 June 1992, 19.
41. C. S. Lewis, *Mere Christianity* (New York: Macmillan, 1972), 92.
42. John O'Toole, *The Trouble with Advertising: A View from the Inside* (New York: Times Books, 1985), 15, 110–14, 224.
43. "Who's Got the Right One?" *Consumer Reports*, Aug. 1991, 520.
44. The Guess ad appeared in *U.S. News & World Report*, 28 September 1992, 16.
45. Carol Bergman, "Tobacco's Cloudy Image on the Silver Screen," *The Christian Science Monitor*, 28 July 1989, 19.
46. "Selling to Children," *Consumer Reports*, Aug. 1990, 518–521.
47. Kenneth Curtis, quoted in *Eternity*, Nov. 1976, 15.
48. "Crossfire," CNN, 24 June 1991.
49. Reported in the *Chronicle of Higher Education*, 2 October 1991, A37.
50. David Stutz and Bernard Feder, *The Savvy Patient* (Yonkers, N.Y.: Consumer Reports Books).
51. Arthur Whimbey, "The Key to Higher Order Thinking Is Precise Processing," *Educational Leadership*, Sept. 1984, 68.
52. Richard Weaver, *Ideas Have Consequences* (Chicago: University Press, 1984), 105.
53. "The Lowdown on Hip-Hop; Kids Talk About the Music," *Newsweek*, 29 June 1992, 50–51.
54. S. Robert Lichter, Stanley Rothman, and Linda S. Lichter, *The Media Elite* (Bethesda, MD: Adler & Adler, 1986).

Chapter 6

1. "Larry King Live," CNN, 25 August 1992.
2. "The Oprah Winfrey Show," CBS-TV, 9 May 1991.
3. Susan Dodge, "Poorer Preparation for College Found in 25-Year Study of Freshmen," *Chronicle of Higher Education*, 20 November 1991, A38.
4. Associated Press release, *St. Petersburg Times*, 9 November 1991, 13A.
5. *St. Petersburg Times*, 6 November 1990, 8B.
6. Leo Alexander, "Medical Science Under Dictatorship," *New England Journal of Medicine* 241 (14 July 1989), 39–47.
7. Quoted in the *New York Daily News*, 26 December 1982, 11.
8. Cited in Bork, *The Tempting of America*, 243.
9. Judith A. Reisman and others, *Kinsey, Sex and Fraud: The Indoctrination of a People* (Lafayette, La.: Huntington House, 1990), chapter 1.
10. Ibid., chapter 2 and page 182.
11. Ibid., chapter 2.

12. Judith A. Reisman, *"Soft Porn" Plays Hardball* (Lafayette, La.: Huntington House, 1991), 60.
13. Ibid., 118–119.
14. Ibid., 126–128.
15. Ibid., 70.
16. Ibid., 172.
17. "Scared Silent," hosted by Oprah Winfrey, all major networks, 7 September 1992.
18. Berger, *A Rumor of Angels*, 74.
19. Barbara Bisantz Raymond, "The Woman Who Stole 5,000 Babies," *Good Housekeeping*, March 1991, 140f.
20. Szasz, *Insanity*, 110–111, 142–144, 147, 336–337, 15, 17, 241, 244–245, 269.
21. Frankl, *Man's Search for Meaning*, 158.
22. Michael Schulman and Eva Mekler, *Bringing Up a Moral Child* (Reading, Mass.: Addison-Wesley, 1985), 13–18, 214.
23. Ibid., 51.
24. Jacob Bronowski, *The Ascent of Man*, quoted in Page Smith, *Killing the Spirit*, 256.
25. *Leviathan*, chapter 5.
26. Harvard professor and author Jerome Kagan, quoted in Katrine Ames, "It's a Small World, After All," *Newsweek*, 14 October 1991, 65.
27. Schulman and Mekler, *Bringing Up a Moral Child*, 86.
28. *Bulletin of the Thomas Jefferson Center*, March-April 1992, 1.
29. Errol E. Harris, "Respect for Persons," *Daedalus*, Spring 1969, 113.
30. "20/20," ABC-TV, 12 April 1991.

Chapter 7

1. "Larry King Live," CNN, 10 June 1991.
2. Tom Mathews, "Fine Art or Foul?" *Newsweek*, 2 July 1990, 46–52.
3. Michael Medved, "Hollywood Vs. Religion," *Imprimis* (Hillsdale College Bulletin), December 1989, 1–3.
4. Barrett, *Death of the Soul*, 157.
5. Smith, *Killing the Spirit*, 5–6, 20, 272–273, 102, 107.
6. Thomas Szasz, *The Myth of Psychotherapy* (Garden City, N.Y.: Anchor Books, 1978), 27–28.
7. Carl Sagan and Ann Druyan, "What Makes Us Different?" *Parade*, 20 September 1992, 4–6.
8. Eric Snider, "Prince of Darkness," *St. Petersburg Times*, 21 April 1991, F1.
9. Carl Raschke, quoted in the *Chronicle of Higher Education*, 9 January 1991, A3.
10. "Tony Brown's Journal," PBS (WUSF, Florida), 26 November 1989.

11. "Controversial Art Work Splits Students, Faculty," *Chronicle of Higher Education*, 2 September 1992, A4.
12. Robert Morey, *Death and the Afterlife* (Minneapolis: Bethany, 1985), 37.
13. Ari Goldman, *The Search for God at Harvard* (New York: Random House, 1991).
14. Christopher Dawson, *Progress and Religion* (Garden City, N.Y.: Doubleday, 1960), 138–139.
15. Ibid., 145–146.
16. *God and Intelligence in Modern Philosophy*, 216.
17. G. K. Chesterton, *Orthodoxy* (New York: John Lane Co., 1908), 266–267.
18. Thomas Jefferson, *Notes on Virginia*, 1784.
19. Alexis de Tocqueville, quoted in Richard Weaver, *Ideas Have Consequences*, 118.
20. Frankl, *The Unheard Cry for Freedom*, 84.
21. Toynbee, *A Study of History*, 224, 229, 249, 254.
22. David Martin, "Modern Sociology and the Turn to Belief in God," *The Intellectuals Speak Out About God*, ed. Roy Abraham Varghese, 87–93.
23. Allen Bergin, Director of Clinical Psychology at Brigham Young University, in "One Scholar's Findings," *St. Petersburg Times*, 5 October 1991, 5E.
24. Paul C. Vitz, "Modern Psychology and the Turn to Belief in God," *The Intellectuals Speak Out About God*, ed. Varghese, 79–86.
25. Robert Jastrow, "The Astronomer and God," *The Intellectuals Speak Out About God*, ed. Varghese, 15–22.
26. Chandra Wickrahasinghe, "Science and the Divine Origin of Life," *The Intellectuals Speak Out About God*, ed. Varghese, 23–37.
27. Stanley L. Jak, "From Scientific Cosmology to a Created Universe," *The Intellectuals Speak Out About God*, ed. Varghese, 61–78.
28. Mortimer Adler, *Truth in Religion* (New York: Macmillan, 1990), 98.
29. Henry Margeneau, "Modern Physics and the Turn to Belief in God," *The Intellectuals Speak Out About God*, ed. Varghese, 39–50.
30. Arnold Toynbee, letter to the *New York Times Magazine*, 10 May 1964.
31. Robert Coles, *The Spiritual Life of Children*, quoted in *Newsweek*, 10 December 1990, 74.
32. Robert Nisbet, *History of the Idea of Progress* (New York: Basic Books, 1980), 352–356.

Chapter 8

1. Linda Phillips and Stephen Norris, "Reading Well Is Thinking Well (with Written Language)," *Philosophy of Education*, ed. N. R. Burbules (Normal, Ill.: The Philosophy of Education Society, 1986).
2. Barrett, *Death of the Soul*, 53.
3. Charles Francis Adams, Jr., quoted in Smith, *Killing the Spirit*, 42–43.

4. Smith, 58.

5. For a detailed discussion of Yerkes's test, see Stephen Jay Gould, *The Mismeasure of Man* (New York: Norton, 1981), 192–225.

6. "The Computer Fallacy," an interview with Joseph Weizenbaum, *Harper's Magazine*, March 1984, 22–24.

7. See, for example, John Goodlad's comprehensive study of the American secondary school, *A Place Called School* (New York: McGraw-Hill, 1984), and Ernest Boyer, *College: the Undergraduate Experience in America* (New York: HarperCollins, 1988).

8. Concerning the teaching of critical thinking, see Edward Glaser, *Experiment in the Teaching of Critical Thinking* (New York: Columbia University Teachers' College Press, 1941). His bibliography lists over 340 important books and scholarly articles on the subject, including Graham Wallas, *The Art of Thought*, 1926; John Dewey, *How We Think*, 1933; and Victor H. Noll, *The Habit of Scientific Thinking*, 1935. For creative thinking see, for example, Sidney Parnes, *Creative Thinking Guidebook* (New York: Scribner, 1967), 53–60.

9. Harold W. Stevenson and James W. Stigler, *The Learning Gap: Why Our Schools Are Failing and What We Can Learn from Japanese and Chinese Education* (New York: Summit Books, 1992), chapter 9, 174–199.

10. Ilma Brewer, *Learning More and Teaching Less* (Bristol, Pa.: Taylor & Francis, 1985).

11. "Mr. Bush's Speech: A View from the Bar," *Education Week*, 15 May 1991, 28.

12. E. D. Hirsch, Jr., *Cultural Literacy: What Every American Needs to Know* (Boston: Houghton Mifflin, 1987), 2, 60–61, 133.

13. William J. Bennett, *The De-Valuing of America: The Fight for Our Culture and Our Children* (New York: Summit Books, 1992), 61–62.

14. Edward Barnes, "Lost Boys of the Sudan," *Life Magazine*, June 1992, 50–58.

15. Carl Jung, quoted in David Solway, *Education Lost* (Toronto: Ontario Institute for Studies in Education, 1989), 55.

16. Oscar Handlin, "Textbooks that Don't Teach," *Atlantic Monthly*, 200 (6), 1957, 110–113.

17. Gregory Anrig, "'A Very American Way': Everybody's Getting into the Act," *Education Week*, 17 June 1992, S7–S8.

18. Stevenson and Stigler, *The Learning Gap*.

Chapter 9

1. Dawson, *Progress and Religion*, 181.

2. *The New York Times* Mirror Center for the People and the Press study and the People for the American Way study were reported in "Indifference Marks Under-30 Age Group," *St. Petersburg Times*, 28 June 1990, 1A.

3. Rollo Walter Brown, *How the French Boy Learns to Write*, special edition (Champaign, Ill.: National Council of Teachers of English, 1948).

4. Anne Bernays, "I Don't Want to Read a Novel Passed by a Board of Good Taste," *Chronicle of Higher Education*, 6 March 1991, B1.

5. Ellen T. Harris, "It Takes Practice and Serious Thought to Learn How to Dislike Art Properly," *Chronicle of Higher Education*, 19 September 1990, A56.

6. Michael Ryan, quoted in "Here They Can Think Their Highest Thoughts," *Parade*, 17 January 1993, 5.

7. Amitai Etzioni, "The Slings and Errors of a New Publication," *Chronicle of Higher Education*, 11 September 1991, B3–4.

8. Will and Ariel Durant, quoted in Reo M. Christenson, "How to Put Premarital Sex on Hold: A Primer for Parents," *Christianity Today*, 19 February 1982, 17.

9. See, for example, Toynbee, *A Study of History*, 1988 edition, 242–243.

10. George Gerbner, *Eternity*, Nov. 1976, 13.

11. "Book Provides a Bedroom View of Presidential History," *St. Petersburg Times*, 4 April 1991, 9A.

12. Tavris, *The Mismeasure of Woman*, 50–53.

13. Lawrence Wallack and others, *Journal of Studies on Alcohol*, vol. 51, no. 5, 1990.

14. Ken Resnicow, U. S. Senate Committee on Labor and Human Resources, "Healthy Students—Healthy Schools Act" hearing, 19 March 1992, Washington, D. C.

15. Jacques Maritain, quoted in Smith, *Killing the Spirit*, 152.

16. This film, "The Fatal Image," premiered on television on 2 December 1990.

17. "Ted Turner Urges TV Violence Ratings," *St. Petersburg Times*, 26 June 1993, 1f.

18. Joshua Hammer and others, "Pages and Pages of Pain," *Newsweek*, 27 May 1991, 39.

19. Barrett, *Death of the Soul*, 166.

20. Szasz, *Insanity*, 228 and following pages.

21. According to ACLU spokeswoman Ramona Ripston, "Crossfire," CNN, 21 July 1992.

22. "Larry King Live," CNN, 3 April 1991.